# MOTHERS, MILITARY, AND SOCIETY

Edited by Sarah Cote Hampson,
Udi Lebel and Nancy Taber

T0294496

DEMETER

**Mothers, Military, and Society**
Edited by Sarah Cote Hampson,
Udi Lebel and Nancy Taber

Demeter Press
140 Holland Street West
P. O. Box 13022
Bradford, ON L3Z 2Y5
Tel: (905) 775-9089
Email: info@demeterpress.org
Website: www.demeterpress.org

Demeter Press logo based on the sculpture "Demeter" by Maria-Luise Bodirsky
www.keramik-atelier.bodirsky.de

Printed and Bound in Canada

Front cover artwork and typesetting Michelle Pirovich

Library and Archives Canada Cataloguing in Publication
Mothers, military, and society / edited by Sarah Cote Hampson, Udi Lebel
and Nancy Taber.
 Includes bibliographical references.
ISBN 978-1-77258-141-6 (softcover)
1. Women and the military. 2. Motherhood. I. Hampson, Sarah
Cote, editor II. Udi, Lebel, 1973-, editor III. Taber, Nancy, 1971-, editor

MIX
Paper from
responsible sources
FSC® C004071

# Acknowledgments

The editors of this volume would like to thank the staff of Demeter Press for their hard work and support in producing this book. We wish to extend our particular thanks and appreciation to Professor Andrea O'Reilly for approaching us and proposing that we join forces in the compilation of this book. Moreover, this experience has created not only a strong professional collaboration between the three of us but an intellectual friendship for which we are grateful. We would also like to thank the four anonymous reviewers of this book, who provided excellent in-depth feedback, which has made this a stronger piece of scholarship. Our special thanks also go to the contributors to this volume—first, for taking the time to write chapters especially for this book and second, for their collaboration expressed in their willingness to revise and improve their work. Finally, we would each like to add our own acknowledgements:

**Sarah Cote Hampson:** I thank my husband, Christopher, for his support throughout the years of working on this volume. I dedicate my work on this volume to him and to our daughters, Anna and Elisabeth.

**Udi Lebel:** I thank Neomi Lebel, my mother, who raised us during and between wars, always extending your boundless warmth, security, and love. Mom—it is your love and encouragement that empowered and enabled me to become who I am. This book about motherhood, wars, military, and care is actually a book about the challenges of your, or maybe our, life story. It is you and dad's picture on my desk as in my heart.

**Nancy Taber:** I thank the mothers in my life for their inspiration over the years. They have each affected me in differing and important ways, helping me learn about and value multiple forms of mothering. In particular, I thank my mother, aunts, and grandmother for their support and love.

# Contents

# Introduction: Mothers, Military, and Society in Conversation

Sarah Cote Hampson, Udi Lebel, and Nancy Taber[1]

We would be hard pressed to find two concepts that are typically perceived to be dichotomous in so many ways as motherhood and the military. Many societies often place the two at odds with each other or refuse to acknowledge any connection between them. However, as this book explores, these two concepts are in fact interrelated in multiple, complex ways. As societies vary from one another, constructed concepts of "motherhood" and "military" may at times be in direct conflict with each other, at other times in alignment (or both at the same time), and as the contributions to this volume attest, these concepts are almost always intersecting or in conversation with each other. Our choice of cover demonstrates this complex interaction. Although love and peace are often considered to be motherly feminine and camouflage as military masculine, the cover camouflage combines these concepts. It could be seen as overly militaristic: femininity (and therefore motherhood, often perceived as a key element of femininity) is co-opted. It could also be seen in the reverse, as overly feminine and co-opting the military. We think that the cover represents both these things and neither of them. We hope that it leads our readers to question the ways in which mothers, military, and society intersect. Additionally, camouflage has become a fashion statement. It is often worn by girls, boys, women, men, or by those who do not fit into this binary, and possibly by people who feel that they have no direct connection to the military. The image of camouflage reveals the ways in which the military is not a closed institution separate from society, but one that permeates daily life (i.e., popular culture, news media, video games) through the valuing, mirroring, and contesting of militaristic ideals. In this volume, we interrogate these connections.

In this introduction to the volume, we first offer a discussion of some ways in which the concepts of "motherhood" and "military" have been defined and contested in academic scholarship that spans multiple disciplines. In doing so, we situate this book within existing literature on feminist studies of militaries and militarism. In introducing the contributions to this volume, we also highlight the unique ways in which this volume expands and advances this conversation.

## "Motherhood" in Context

"Motherhood" as a concept has been defined and invested with meaning from various perspectives across academic disciplines. In the essentialist context, motherhood is often framed as giving life. It is identifiable with reproduction, giving birth to, raising, and nurturing children. Though not an essentialist, Mechthild Hart terms motherhood as subsistence production, in that mothers' "labour and production is directly oriented towards life–its creation, sustenance and improvement" (Hart 95). In the institutionalist context, motherhood is a "soft" type of support (O'Reilly, *From Motherhood to Mothering* 125-36). The child's character is formed by guidance, training, and gentle touches, which aspire to make an impression on one who will eventually have to find his or her own way in life (Ruddick; Noddings). Andrea O'Reilly, for instance, explores how "motherhood, as an institution, is a male-defined site of oppression, [but] women's own experiences of mothering can nonetheless be a source of power" (*Rocking the Cradle* 11). In the psychosocial context, motherhood is warmth, security, peace, and relaxation (Hollway), and an envelope of protection, routine, and domesticity (Owusu-Bempah).

Motherhood has also been marked as an oppressive institution in many social contexts, though not all. Some Western scholars have noted motherhood can work to have a limiting and reductive effect on women (Hart). The identification of women with motherhood has been perceived as a meaningful component in the imposition of patriarchy, which by definition gives preference to men, masculinity, and the marketplace (Gouthro). In Western patriarchal ideology, motherhood is cast as the leading institution, which often serves to ensure that women remain in the private, domestic sphere, and hinders their ability to achieve goals or overcome challenges in the public sphere (O'Reilly, *From Motherhood to Mothering*; Douglas and Michaels). As feminist political theorists have noted, it is this relegation to the private sphere that has often left many mothers unable to fully participate as equal citizens in democratic society as well as to benefit from the economic rewards stemming from such participation. As Susan Moller Okin notes, "The substantial inequalities that continue to exist between the sexes in our society have serious effects on the lives of almost all women.... Underlying all these inequalities is the unequal distribution of the unpaid labor of the family" (25). In patriarchal Western society, motherhood and mothering, therefore, sometimes lead to disempowering experiences for women.

However, as Nancy Taber reminds us in "Connecting the Past and Future through Contemporary Discourses of Motherhood and Militarism in Canada: *Bomb Girls* and *Continuum*" (chapter four of this volume), maternal studies scholars have also long acknowledged that this perspective on motherhood is not the only way that motherhood may be experienced or practised. In her chapter, Taber quotes Andrea O'Reilly as saying: "The concept of 'mother' [and mothering] is not a singular practice but is always context bound" (*From Motherhood to Mothering* 15). O'Reilly argues that motherhood is not essentially disempowering. Rather, it is the "gender essentialism of modern motherhood" that O'Reilly believes to be the root cause of the symptoms of disempowerment as experienced by mothers in Western patriarchal society. The solution, O'Reilly argues, is to dislodge gender (and racial) essentialism from the concept of motherhood. O'Reilly's edited volume *Mother Outlaws*, for instance, highlights the ways in which feminist mothering, lesbian mothering, and African American mothering can all be sites of resistance to the patriarchal model. Through contextualizing the meaning of motherhood and mothering, such empowerment of mothering becomes visible.

Contextualizing motherhood–and different experiences and perspectives on the meaning of that term–is an important part of the work this volume does in furthering the literature on maternal studies. This volume examines the ways in which constructions of motherhood are shaped by–but can also challenge–their cultural and societal contexts. Authors explore the various ways in which mothers are part of meaning-making around both motherhood and military as well as part of challenging the dominant cultural uses of those concepts. Anwar Shaheen and Abeerah Ali's "Mothers, Martyrs and Messages of Eternity in the Popular Cultured of Pakistan" (chapter two of this volume), for instance, explores mothers' relationship with meaning-making around the concept of martyrdom in Pakistan. Moreover, Patricia Sotirin's "Trope of the U.S. Military Mother: A Feminist Analysis" (chapter one of this volume) questions and challenges notions of "good" and "natural" motherhood within Western military social constructions. The chapters in this volume take up the call to look into the complex dynamics between conceptions of motherhood and the societies within which those conceptions are at work.

## "Military" in Context

To the important analysis of locating how motherhood is defined and works within certain social contexts, we add another dimension–the social construction of militaries and militarism. Like motherhood, the concept of "military" is infused with socially contextual meanings. In reviewing critical military studies, it can seem, at least at first glance, that most social constructions of "military" are in stark contrast to some of the conceptions of motherhood discussed earlier. The military is, by definition, an institution that sends its members to war. Some of them will not return. Although the military argues it provides security to civilians, that very security is achieved by soldiers losing their lives while they experience chaos, destruction, and horror (Goldstein). This conception of the military appears to stand in contrast to the image of motherhood as "naturally" life bringing and reproductive. Interestingly, Barbara Ehrenreich, a critical military scholar, explores how "warrior elites" also reproduce themselves, but patriarchally and without the need for a mother through the military indoctrination, training, and socialization of new warriors.

Since motherhood may be viewed as essentially feminine, the military might be, therefore, viewed as essentially masculine. Indeed, many scholars of militaries and militarism have defined the cultural context of militaries in this way. From an institutional perspective, militaries are masculine, hierarchical, and total institutions, whose members are expected to forsake their previous identities, to perceive their commanders as exclusive epistemic authorities, and to be willing to die in conflict (Goffman; Lebel, "Second Class Loss"). From a psychosocial context, the military is unknown, chaotic, dangerous, brutal, and capricious (Kgosana and Van Dyk). From these perspectives, motherhood and the military are set up dichotomously as life versus sacrificial death (Lebel "Militarism versus Security"). However, masculinities literature and feminist literature demonstrates that even in a hegemonically masculine institution such as the military, masculinity is performed, accepted, and contested in multiple ways (Higate; Taber, "The Canadian Armed Forces") as is femininity (Taber, "You Better Not Get Pregnant").

Additionally, particularly in Western contexts, militaries have become central and prestigious institutions that give their members, both living and dead–and most of them men–the highest possible social prestige (Feinman). It is an institution in which the symbolic capital granted to its senior officers holds the highest conversion value in terms of gaining political capital, especially within cultures identified with militarism, republicanism, and nationalism (Lebel, "Second Class Loss"). While motherhood is the leading institution that often serves to ensure that women remain in the private, domestic sphere, and that hinders their ability to achieve success in the public sphere, the military is the leading institution that invites men into the public sphere. It is where men may realize their masculinity while providing them justification for neglecting the domestic sphere. Cynthia Enloe traces the ideological connection between masculinity and militarism in *Bananas, Beaches and Bases*:

> *When it is a patriarchal world that is "dangerous," masculine*
> *men and feminine women are expected to react in opposite but*
> *complementary ways. A "real man" will become the protector in*
> *such a world. He will suppress his own fears, brace himself and*
> *step forward to defend the weak, women and children. In the*
> *same "dangerous world" women will turn gratefully and*
> *expectantly to their fathers and husbands, real or surrogate.*
> *If a woman is a mother, then she will think first of her children,*
> *protecting them not in a manly way, but as a self-sacrificing*
> *mother. In this fashion, the "dangerous world" [ethos] ...*
> *is upheld by unspoken notions about masculinity. (13)*

This dichotomous understanding of motherhood and military, however, reflects a particular Western and patriarchal understanding of how these two concepts intersect. In recent years, exceptional work by feminist critical military scholars has begun to break down these received truisms around motherhood and military and their relationships with society. Most notably, this scholarship comes from feminist scholars of militarism and colonialism across multiple disciplines. Some scholars, such as Sarah Ruddick, for instance, suggest that maternal thinking may offer the ideal framework for praxis of nonviolence in international relations. Others, such as Ann Stoler, Amy Kaplan, or Nancy Scheper-Hughes, however, point to the ways in which mothers "especially under conditions of scarcity, famine, oppression, and political disruption–can both instruct and allow women to readily surrender their sons" (Scheper-Hughes 1). Other feminist postcolonial scholars such as Anne McClintock, for instance, critique Western women's role in the ideological work of colonialism. McClintock writes that the Western "cult of domesticity was a crucial, if concealed, dimension of male as well as female identities ... and an indispensable element both of the industrial market and the imperial enterprise" (5). Additionally, some feminist postcolonial scholars, such as Nancy Hunt, trace the physical and psychological impacts of the traumas associated with colonialism's sexual violence on Indigenous women and their ability to become mothers. Postcolonial feminist scholars are paying particular attention to the social and historical contexts for discussing the ways in which motherhood and military are entwined. These scholars show us that attention to race, class, ideology, and power dynamics are essential in any rigorous exploration of the relationships between motherhood, military, and society.

## Mother and the Military in Conversation

This volume enters into the conversation on motherhood and military and their relationship to society from multiple perspectives. The chapters deal with the ways in which motherhood and the military are connected to both each other and the societies in which they exist. Moreover, we have sought contributions from authors that would speak to non-Western, nonessentialized conceptions of motherhood and military. We have asked each contributor to think carefully about the ways in which their scholarship or experiences can and should be contextualized, and the ways in which "motherhood" and "military" are embedded with contested meanings. We have wished to seek out compelling developments, both empirical and theoretical, that may challenge the existing knowledge and expand the work in this field to reach beyond its preexisting arenas and include gender, culture, and sociology. The chapters in this book, therefore, span multiple disciplinary approaches, and reflect varied social and cultural contexts where the concepts of "motherhood" and "military" are in conversation with each other.

This volume is necessarily and usefully interdisciplinary. Just as conceptions of motherhood and military are socially constructed, so too must the scholarly perspectives on these terms and their interrelatedness be diverse. Education scholarship, for instance, shows how individuals learn about such social institutions as the military, whereas sociology helps to understand how those institutions work toward that meaning-making. Furthermore, the discipline of cultural studies is well equipped to investigate the connections between meaning-making and popular representations. Together in one volume, these diverse perspectives can inform each other.

The different ways in which "military mother" is conceptualized throughout the book points to the multiple ways in which mothers engage with and are connected to the military–as members, mothers of serving members, bereaved mothers, as critics and supporters of the military, as peace advocates and as images in popular culture. These connections are problematized through a gendered lens, but not all authors use the term "feminist" and not all authors agree on how the term is used. Although some may take the position that all women in the military are feminists (as argued by Mercer in chapter eight) because of the very nature of their non-traditional roles, others argue from different theoretical traditions such as Patricia Sotirin's (chapter one) feminist poststructural stance (Weedon) and Taber's (chapter four) feminist antimilitarist one (Enloe). The power in the multiplicities of feminist theories is that depending on the stance that one takes, a different picture of the world emerges.

Moreover, this volume also contains a feature that is unusual in most scholarly volumes, but which we believe to be valuable in furthering the scholarly conversation on motherhood and military–personal narratives. In these personal narratives- from either scholars and/or military members–these individuals reflect on their own experiences with the contested meanings around motherhood and military. The inclusion of these narratives in this volume reflects a commitment to feminist epistemologies regarding the significance of voice and perspective in research (see, for example, Presser). Feminist methodology has long included the use of narrative as a form of inquiry into larger cultural phenomena related to intersecting issues of gender, race, class, and sexuality, among other issues. The narratives contained in this volume are not meant to be representative of the many diverse experiences that people have with the interactions between motherhood and military. Rather, these narratives invite readers–both academic and non-academic alike–to engage with the larger scholarly questions raised in the first section of the book in a deeper, more critical way.

## Imagining Motherhood and the Military: Images, Cultural Representations, and Communities

The chapters of this book have been grouped into two main sections that we believe express the book's main contributions. The first section of the book is titled "Imagining Motherhood and the Military: Images, Cultural Representations, and Communities," and it aims to examine the relationships between motherhood and the military as they are fixated, formed, and distributed by cultural agents and other ideological apparatuses (Althusser).

In "Tropes of the U.S. Military Mother: A Feminist Analysis," Patricia Sotirin examines several dominant cultural images of the "military mother" (defined as a woman with children in the military), which support and contest war, and explores their role in the social imagination. Her chapter demonstrates the variety of ways in which mothers are conceptualized in relation to the American military. Anwar Shabeen and Abeerah Ali then provide an analysis outside North America; they apply the subject of imagery and cultural representation to militarism and views of martyrdom in Pakistan. They examine many forms of popular culture in Pakistan, including war songs and Sufi folk literature, in order to demonstrate the power of popular culture to shape feelings of patriotism and identity as they contribute to militarism. Sarah Cote Hampson next takes up the topic of media representations of mothers in the U.S. military context in her chapter "Military Moms in the Spotlight: What Media Attention on Mothers in the U.S. Military Means for Public Policy." Hampson notes that negative public discourse in the media serves to reinforce existing informal norms around pregnancy and breastfeeding that stigmatize mothers serving in the U.S. military. Her use of the term "military mother" refers to serving military members who are also mothers, which complements Sotirin, who uses it to refer to mothers with a child in the military.

Then, Nancy Taber takes a pedagogical perspective, and explores popular culture representations of mothers in militaristic institutional contexts (WWII bomb making and futuristic police services) in Canadian television. In her chapter "Connecting the Past and Future through Contemporary Discourses of Motherhood and Militarism in Canada: *Bomb Girls* and *Continuum*," Taber finds that these programs challenge gendered stereotypes while simultaneously supporting militaristic norms. Udi Lebel and Gal Hermoni close out this section with their chapter, "Public Grief Is Maternal: The Gendered Discourse of Military Bereavement." Lebel and Hermoni take a psychosocial, psychocultural, and sociopolitical approach to explore how bereaved mothers of Israeli soldiers have formed communities and undertaken social activism. The authors ask why in Israel public grief is specifically maternal, and explore the development and social role of these bereavement communities. This section as a whole demonstrates how the concepts of motherhood and the military intersect in diverse national contexts–such as Canada, Israel, Pakistan, and the United States–and highlights similarities and differences in the ways in which each of these countries conceives of, engages with, and practices in motherhood and militarism.

## Me-Mother-Military: Personal Experiences

The second section of the book, "Me-Mother-Military: Personal Experiences," introduces the reader to military mothers' subjective narratives, which have resulted from their own unique journeys and experiences, and are written in a form that integrates personal stories with theory and methodology. It begins with an autoethnography, a type of qualitative method bridging research and narrative. In "Mom Wore Combat Boots: An Autoethnography of a Military Sociologist," Morten Ender critically reflects on the ways in which being the son of a female military member shaped his life and career. The next chapter in this section, "Choosing Motherhood in the U.S, Air Force," by Elle Kowal, connects personal experience to American military statistics and policies as well as to research about the experiences of military women, in order to give readers a close look into how military policies and practices play out in everyday life. In "'You Can't Have a Baby in the Army!' and Other Myths of Moms in Military Service," Naomi Mercer describes the challenges she faced as a mother serving as an officer in the U.S. military. These authors call attention to some of the ways in which combining a military career with a family is still difficult for many mothers in the U.S. armed forces, and offer some suggestions for policy changes. Their stories are important in that they demonstate the ways in which personal experience intersects with research. The volume concludes with a short creative nonfiction piece by Beth Osnes, which reflects on the interconnectedness of the experiences of motherhood and militarism and their place in society. It highlights the need for, as Osnes states, "shifts in perception."

Throughout the book, we provide direct connections between chapters and themes, so readers can clearly see how the personal intersects with the theoretical and the methodological, and how one author's argument links to the others. We hope that this book precipitates shifts in perceptions for its readers, and with those with whom our readers interact.

## Endnote

1 The editors of this volume are equal contributors, and the order of names is alphabetical.

## Works Cited

Althusser, Louis, "Ideology and Ideological State Apparatuses", In: Althusser, Louis (Ed.), *Lenin and Philosophy and other Essays*, New York: Monthly Review Press, 1971.

Chamallas, Martha. *Introduction to Feminist Legal Theory*. Wolters Kluwer Law & Business, 2013.

Douglas, Susan J., and Michaels, Meredith W. *The Mommy Myth: The Idealization of Motherhood and How It Has Undermined Women*. Free Press, 2004.

Ehrenreich, Barbara. *Blood Rites: Origins and History of the Passions of War*. Metropolitan Books, 1997.

Enloe, Cynthia H. *Bananas, Beaches and Bases: Making Feminist Sense of International Politics.* 2nd ed.,University of California Press, 2014.

Feinman, Ilene Rose. *Citizenship Rites: Feminist Soldiers and Feminist Antimilitarists.* New York University Press, 2000.

Goffman, Erving. *Asylums: Essays on the Social Situation of Mental Patients and Other Inmates.* Aldine Transaction, 2007.

Goldstein, Joshua S. *War and Gender: How Gender Shapes the War System and Vice Versa.* Cambridge University Press, 2001.

Gouthro, P. "Globalization, Civil Society and the Homeplace." *Convergence,* vol. 33, no. 4, 2000, p. 57-77.

Hart, Mechthild U. *The Poverty of Life-Affirming Work: Motherwork, Education, and Social Change.* Greenwood Press, 2002.

Higate, Paul. *Military Masculinities: Identity and the State.* Praeger, 2003.

Hollway, Wendy. "Conflict in the Transitions to Becoming a Mother: A Psycho-Social Approach." *Psychoanalysis, Culture, and Society,* vol. 15, no. 2, 2010, pp. 136-55.

Hunt, Nancy Rose. "An Acoustic Register: Rape and Repetition in Congo." *Imperial Debris: On Ruins and Ruination,* edited by Ann Laura Stoler, Duke University Press, 2013, pp. 39-65.

Kaplan, Amy. "Manifest Domesticity." *Background Readings for Teachers of American Literature,* edited by Venetria Patton, Bedford/St. Martin's, 2006, pp. 292-311.

Kgosana, Charles Makatipe, and Gideon Van Dyk. "Psychosocial Effects of Conditions of Military Deployment." *Journal of Psychology in Africa,* vol. 21, no. 2, 2011, pp. 323-26.

Lebel, Udi. "Militarism versus Security? The Double-Bind of Israel's Culture of Bereavement and Hierarchy of Sensitivity to Loss." *Mediterranean Politics,* vol. 16, no. 3, 2011, pp. 365-84.

Lebel, Udi. "'Second Class Loss': Political Culture as a Recovery Barrier-The Families of Terrorist Casualties' Struggle for National Honors, Recognition, and Belonging." *Death Studies,* vol. 38, no. 1, 2013, pp. 9-19.

McClintock, Anne. *Imperial Leather: Race, Gender, and Sexuality in the Colonial Contest.* Routledge, 1995.

Noddings, Nel. Starting at Home : Caring and Social Policy. University of California Press, 2002.

Okin, Susan Moller M. *Women in Western Political Thought.* Princeton University Press, 2013.

O'Reilly, Andrea. *From Motherhood to Mothering: the Legacy of Adrienne Rich's Of Woman Born*. State University of New York Press, 2004.

O'Reilly, Andrea. *Mother Outlaws: Theories and Practices of Empowered Mothering*. Women's Press, 2004.

O'Reilly, Andrea. *Rocking the Cradle: Thoughts on Motherhood, Feminism and the Possibility of Empowered Mothering*. Demeter Press, 2006.

Owusu-Bempah, Kwame. *Children and Separation: Socio-Genealogical Connectedness Perspective*. Psychology Press, 2007.

Presser, L. "Negotiating Power and Narrative in Research: Implications for Feminist Methodology." *Signs*, vol. 30, no. 4, 2005, pp. 2067-90.

Ruddick, Sara. *Maternal Thinking: Toward a Politics of Peace*. Beacon Press, 1995.

Scheper-Hughes, Nancy. "Maternal Thinking and the Politics of War." *The Women and War Reader*, edited by Lois Ann Lorentzen and Jennifer E. Turpin, New York University,1998, pp. 227-33.

Stoler, Ann Laura. *Carnal Knowledge and Imperial Power: Race and the Intimate in Colonial Rule*. University of California Press, 2010.

Taber, Nancy. "The Canadian Armed Forces: Battling between Operation Honour and Operation Hop on Her." *Critical Military Studies*, doi: https://doi.org/10.1080/23337486.2017.1411117. Accessed 15 Jan. 2018.

Taber, Nancy. "'You Better Not Get Pregnant While You're Here': Tensions between Masculinities and Femininities in Military Communities of Practice." *International Journal of Lifelong Education*, vol. 30, no. 3, 2011, pp. 331-48.

Weedon, Chris. *Feminist Practice and Poststructuralist Theory*. 2nd ed., Oxford, Blackwell, 1997.

# I.

# Imagining Motherhood and the Military: Images, Cultural Representations, and Communities

Chapter One

# Tropes of the U.S. Military Mother: A Feminist Analysis

Patricia Sotirin

*Few women who have borne sons and raised them to the age of
potential military service have been able to escape the pressures
that are generated by ... militarized expectations of
motherhood.... It is the confluence of militarized family
dynamics, a militarized popular culture, and a militarized state
that makes the myths of militarized motherhood so potent*
(Cynthia Enloe, *Manuevers* 254)

For feminist scholars, the "potent myths" of the military mother offer a critical focus of study at the intersections of militarism, maternalism, nationalism, and feminism. In her discussion of military mothers, Cynthia Enloe cautions that not every mother is similarly bound to the military. Material-economic circumstances, the lived politics of intersectionalities, and historical moments make a difference in lived complicities, oppressions, and resistances. Thus, the military mother offers a fecund site for feminist analysis, yet there is a limited body of work on this topic. Accordingly, this chapter parses the trope of the military mother as a site of feminist analysis. I reread existing feminist research through the lens of feminist poststructuralism (Weedon) to examine the associations, contradictions, and contexts characterizing the ideological work of this figure.

The chapter begins with an explanation of methodology and proceeds by identifying several figures of the military mother drawn on existing research in order to highlight ideological constructions and paradoxes. In addition, I point to two figures currently emerging out of contemporary conditions of marketization, notably stratified social and eco-nomic insecurities, and intensified militarization. In the end, I argue that together these figures of the military mother alert us to complex ideological relations that normalize maternal quietude, patriotic sacrifice, and the homogenization of disparities, and they reconcile us to the militarization of motherhood and social life.

## Reading Feminist Research on U.S. Military Mothers

I begin by clarifying my referent because the label "military mother" is often applied to a woman in the military who is also a mother. The military mothers Americans hear about in the news are leaving their children behind while on deployment or they are breastfeeding in uniform (Basu; Roche-Paull). Women in the military are fighting not only those who put American national interests at risk but also the prejudices and obstacles entrenched in the institution itself (Prividera and Howard; Thompson). They deserve our concern and attention chapter (see chapter three in this volume for Sarah Hampson's dis-cussion of this type of mother, and chapter four, for Nancy Taber's discussion of mothers in militaristic institutional contexts). However, their expanding role in the military has overshadowed the more traditional referent of the military mother as a mother of a military serviceperson. This is the figure considered in this chapter.

My discussion is limited to U.S. military mothers in the twentieth and twenty-first centuries in order to contextualize mothers within specific historical experiences and cultural discourses. In her varying guises, the military mother has been both central to and refigured within relationships among state, military, civil, and domestic entities and forces. As I will show, the figures of the military mother are both ideologically powerful and ambiguous: they have been variously mobilized in the service of recruitment and morale through gendered exhortations of duty, obligation, nurture, and love, yet those very qualities have been complicated by stratifications of class, race, ethnicity, loss, and precarity.

I conducted a database search for feminist scholarship on military mothers, following citations and links to related research on such databases as Google Scholar, Project Muse, Taylor & Francis Online, and

Sage Fulltext. My search parameters included keywords such as "military mother and femin* (ism, ist, inity)," "mother of soldier," and "U.S. military recruitment and mothers." I selected texts that took the military mother as the primary focus and were explicitly feminist or relevant to military mothers. My reading of the resulting texts focused on the following questions: "what is the figure of the military mother implicit (or explicit) in this text?"; "what ideological associations and oppositions articulate a figure of the military mother?"; and "what are the contexts framing these ideological constructions?" Although the military mother figure at the heart of some texts was quite explicit, I assembled textual cues in other cases to identify this figure. In other words, I extrapolated the ideological features of these figures from the texts, many of which used differing methodological approaches and methods of analysis. Thus, the military mother figures I advance are not typifications of experience or research but sites of analysis focusing on the juncture of feminism, militarism, and motherhood.

My discussion is informed by Enloe's conception of "militarization." According to Enloe,

> *Militarization is a step-by-step process by which a person or a thing gradually comes to be controlled by the military or comes to depend for its well-being on militaristic ideas. The more militarization transforms an individual or a society, the more that individual or society comes to imagine military needs and militaristic presumptions to be not only valuable but also normal. (Maneuvers 3)*

This conception has been the basis for her insightful analyses of the ways that women are necessary to the ongoing centring of militarism and militaristic ideas and relations in societies around the world. Militarization entails a myriad of women's mundane roles–for example, wives, sex workers, or mothers–and decisions–for example, reproductive policies or consumer choices. Among the implications of militarization are the normalization of the juncture between the mother and the military and the taken-for-granted sensibleness of a mother's support for military service as a solution to such issues as gendered violence, poverty, race discrimination, educational deficits, social segregation, anti-immigrant policies, and more.

My framework for reading feminist work on the military mother is informed by Chris Weedon's approach to feminist poststructuralist critique, which entails challenging the constitutive force of such dominant ideologies as militarism, masculinism, and maternalism. Dominant ideologies advance definitions of reality, gendered subject positions, and moral orders that are taken as natural, politically neutral, ahistorical, and commonsensical–this is the "work" of ideology. However, under scrutiny, such taken-for-grantedness is revealed as partial, partisan, historically situated, and damaging for some while privileging for others, which is the reason dominant meanings and identities may be sites of struggle. Ideologies operate, according to Stuart Hall, as chains of connotative associations in discursive clusters, semantic fields, and discursive formations ("Ideology" 137). Tropes of the military mother connote or articulate other representations creating a complex interplay among ideological meanings and discourses. I use the term "articulation" to refer to connotative associations that constitute identities and configurations of meaning enabling or disenabling possibilities (Slack).

One strategy of critique that Weedon suggests is to disarticulate chains of association by challenging the relations of equivalence and opposition that constitute them along with the implicit valuation of these meaning-making relations. For example, some feminist scholars question the chain of associations "mother/home/nation" (Cohn). Another strategy is to reveal the normative force in gendered binaries such as the coupling of military service and hegemonic masculinity with patriotic motherhood and militarized mothering (Enloe, *Manuevers*) and the inequities such binaries insinuate into everyday life (Hall, "The Work of Representation"). The goal is to question the implications of these constructions and to thereby disrupt the unreflective reproduction of the particular versions of meaning, reality, and possibility they offer. By reading available feminist scholarship on the military mother through a feminist poststructuralist lens, I show how feminist research opens up a "discursive space" against the closures affected by dominant ideologies, which enables alternative questions and constructions of the military mother. Exploring and expanding such discursive spaces is the work of critical feminist analysis; hence, I offer the figures below as invitations to such development.

Finally, I acknowledge that my interpretations only make sense in the context of my experiences and identities. Thus, it is critical to note my own situated identities as a white, heteronormative, academic military mother. In this regard, writing this chapter has involved what Kathy Ferguson calls a "doubleness of perspective" (xi, 30)–that is, my ongoing awareness of the tensions between my own insinuation within these figures as a military mother and my critical sensibility as a feminist scholar (see Morten Ender, chapter six this volume, Elle Kowal, chapter seven, and Naomi Mercer, chapter eight, for contributions that focus on personal experiences as related to motherhood and the military).

## Tropes of the Military Mother

I begin by considering the mother's reproductive power and her associated value for the nation and the military. The cultural figure of the mother is centrally bound to a Western cultural image of the healthy and civilized nation (Bernstein; Davin). More pointedly, Raka Shome observes, "to produce modern subjects is to ensure that the home as the basic unit of the nation is civilized, for home is the site for the production of the nation's future" (397). Hence, the binary becomes clear: home is civilized, war is hell. Furthermore, this cultural conflation casts mother/home/nation as what must be fought for and protected. As Spike Peterson observes, the spatial and temporal associations of woman and nation compel national defense:

> Nation as woman expresses a spatial, embodied femaleness:
> the land's fecundity, upon which the people depend, must be
> protected by defending the body/nation's boundaries against
> invasion and violation. But nation as woman is also a temporal
> metaphor: the rape of the body/nation not only violates frontiers
> but disrupts–by planting alien seed or destroying reproductive
> viability–the maintenance of the community through time. (44)

The conflation of nation and woman militarizes the mother's reproductive value; this militarization then justifies not only military defense of the nation but violence and even rape as military strategies. Carol Cohn observes that the gendered dichotomy of "the protector and the protected" motivates war and militarism under the slogan that troops are "fighting to protect mother and nation" (144). Thus, the conflation of mother with nation and the gendered dichotomy of protector(male)-protected(female) militarizes the cultural figure of the mother.

When the mother has birthed and/or raised the nation's fighting forces, she gains additional ideological associations. The military mother is not only the ideological justification for military defense but a necessary complement to military service and action: the military mother stands for homefront support and homelife before and beyond military life and war. In addition, maternal and military ideologies converge in binding the military mother to patriotic duty and sacrifice: just as the mother is called to sacrifice her own needs, interests, indeed, her own life, in care of her children, she is also called to sacrifice her sons and daughters to the service of her country. I explore these entangled ideological commitments in the celebration of maternal sacrifice as patriotic citizenship as well as the militarization of maternal anxiety.

## The Patriotic Citizen Mother

The patriotic citizen mother willing to sacrifice her children for the nation (Scheper-Hughes) is, in Enloe's view, the ideal militarized mother: "The profile of the fully militarized mother might look something like this…. She is a woman who imagines that, by being a good mother in the eyes of the state, she is helping to confirm her own status as a citizen of the nation. She is a woman who accepts unquestioningly the phrase 'patriotic mother'" (*Maneuvers* 253). As an ideal, this figure models stoic and unquestioning support for military service and the equation of maternal self-sacrifice with patriotic duty. Rather than protecting her child from harm, the patriotic mother is expected to willingly give her child up to military service and to knowingly put her child in harm's way for the good of the nation (Garner and Slattery "World War II" 7).

During the First World War, iconic images of the patriotic mother were featured in recruitment posters and newspaper articles supporting U.S. conscription (Garner and Slattery, "Mobilizing Mother") as part of an intense campaign to build public support for military service and the war effort, given that the country had taken a neutral stance for the first few years of the war in Europe. This iconic mother figure invoked appeals to higher values: duty, sacrifice, and love of country. These higher values could be even more important than maternal care for and protection of her son. One poster at the time depicts a mother (elderly, white, wearing an old-fashioned dress and bonnet) and a tall young man in uniform next to her under the caption "America, Here's My Boy." Sending a son to war was a sign of patriotic citizenship, especially given that women did not yet have the right to vote. Newspaper articles and government propaganda in both the First and Second World Wars contrasted this patriotic citizen mother to a "bad" mother– a mother too selfish to send her son to war or too permissive to prepare him for military discipline (Garner and Slattery "Mobilizing Mother"; "World War II"). These mothers were cast implicitly but sometimes very explicitly as threats to the nation's security ("Mobilizing Mother").

As Malathi De Alwis points out, this maternal figure invokes at times of war a gendered binary of "moral mothers and stalwart sons," in which mothers have a moral obligation to put the good of the nation ahead of their maternal duties, whereas their sons are called to be resolute, heroic, and aggressive. Even as it is celebrated, this dichotomy enacts a mortal bargain: both mother and son are positioned to justify the son's battlefield death in exchange for national honour and gratitude. As Ana Garner and Karen Slattery show, upholding this moral-mortal bargain requires the mother's complicity with the press, the military, and the dominant culture ("Mobilizing"). Gina Peréz contends that the patriotic mother thus advances a militarized notion of citizenship contingent upon unquestioned loyalty and obedience rather than democratic participation (Peréz 58). For Enloe, elevating women as mothers-of-soldiering-sons values women as citizens chiefly for their maternal sacrifices for the nation. Consequently, pro-natalist policies can be understood to espouse a militarized nationalism (Enloe, "All" 54).

The hegemonic work of the patriotic-mother ideal promotes a dehistoricized and naturalized claim on motherhood, but it is countered in the situations and experiences of nonwhite mothers and youth. Obscuring these race and class differences is central to the cultural power of this figure. Yet deeply engrained cultural biases and structural inequities make this ideal impossible for some military mothers. For example, Wendy Christensen notes that single black mothers may be suspicious of recruitment appeals to support their child's recruitment as a patriotic duty, given that pernicious stereotypes undermine their status as citizens. Whether they are demeaned as welfare dependents or promoted as "superstrong" black women, they "fail" as citizens and as mothers because their parenting cannot protect their children from profiling, discrimination, and struggle. A child's active military status can redeem a claim to citizenship for these mothers (Christensen, "Black Citizen-Subject" 2518).

The moral duty of patriotic sacrifice for minority mothers is further undermined by controversies over the percentage of combat deaths among African American and Hispanic personnel from the Vietnam War to the wars in Iraq and the continuing war in Afghanistan.[1] Although army combat deaths among black soldiers in the early years of the Vietnam War were higher than their representation in the force, this has not been the case in subsequent wars (Segal and Segal 19). However, Hispanics were overrepresented in combat casualties between 2003 and 2009; hence, the suspicion that they served as a "brown shield" (Burk and Espinoza; Rivera). A primary factor in military enlistment is low family income. Those with less education and socioeconomic status are more likely to fill lower-level military positions, especially combat roles, leading to a charge that "the poor serve as 'cannon fodder'" (Lutz 184). Finally, both legal and illegal immigrants are required to register with the Selective Service–the agency responsible for the required registration of all male U.S. citizens aged eighteen to twenty-five in case of a military draft. Those who volunteer for active duty can expedite the citizenship process; between 2001 and 2008, 37,250 immigrants in the military were granted U.S. citizenship (Lutz 174). David Segal and Mady Wechsler Segal point out that this route toward citizenship has been important for Hispanic assimilation and acculturation. Yet in the current climate of heightened national security, immigrants are criminalized and deported, and profiling, segregation, discrimination, and state violence against racial/ ethnic groups and individuals proceeds with renewed vigor. These controversies problematize the ideological work of the patriotic citizen mother by questioning the requisite, even morally sanctioned, militarization of patriotism and duty, given disparities of race, ethnicity, class, and immigrant status.

I turn now to the figure behind the mortal bargain of the patriotic citizen mother and the stalwart son: the Gold Star mother. "Gold Star Mother" designates a mother whose child has been killed during active military service (see Udi Lebel and Gal Hermoni, chapter five, for a discussion of bereavement in the Israeli context). In the U.S., the last day of September is congressionally dedicated to Gold Star mothers and families. The gold star designation is a First World War legacy modelled on the blue star banners that families with active service members were allowed to hang in their windows. As the First World War began to take a toll, federal officials became concerned that the public would become too focused on wartime deaths if the customary sign of mourning–black crepe in the windows–became too common in the windows of military families (Graham). So families that lost a service member were encouraged to display a banner with a gold star. The gold star became a sign of honour rather than a display of mourning that disciplined mothers to a suitable dignity, quelling both despair and anger and helping to pacify antiwar sentiments among women. For example, Canadian mothers of First World War soldiers were expected to accept their wartime losses in silence "so as not to damage the morale of others" (Evans 8).

Between 1930 and 1933, the United States government took 6,654 Gold Star mothers and widows–average age sixty-five–on all-expense paid and apparently quite lavish "Gold Star pilgrimages" to their loved ones' graves in Belgium, England, and France (Graham; Wood). Though broadly celebrated, these pilgrimages incorporated the race and class problems of their time. First, they were racially segregated: African American mothers were taken on separate trips with second-class accommodations. The NAACP encouraged these women to boycott the government's invitation, and 55 of the 219 eligible mothers declined the trip. Those who went found a stark contrast between their second-class status in America and their relative acceptance in European cities like Paris (Graham). Racial discrimination remained a policy in the Gold Star Mothers Association, which for seventy-seven years refused to accept membership applications from any noncitizen mothers, even though their citizen sons died in combat. In 2005, the Association rescinded the policy (Zraick), and membership rules now grant nonvoting associate membership to non-U.S. mothers (Gold Star Mothers, Inc.).

Class also troubles the legacy of the Gold Star pilgrimages. During the final trips, the U.S. was suffering through the Great Depression. In the summer of 1932, the "Bonus Army"–an assemblage of seventeen thousand impoverished veterans–marched on and occupied the Washington Mall to protest the delay in their promised bonus pay. In contrast to the lavish outlay for Gold Star mothers, these vets were forcibly removed from the Mall and their demands dismissed (Wood). The incident attests to the cultural status granted Gold Star mothers and their political value as seemingly depoliticized figures in contrast to the veterans.

The Gold Star mothers embody maternal sacrifice, patriotic duty, and cultural constructions of honourable death and acceptable loss.[2] This significance of these associations was recently demonstrated in a widespread public response to then presidential candidate Donald Trump's criticism of Ghazala Khan, a Muslim American Gold Star mother, for remaining silent during her husband's speech at the Democratic National Convention and his claim in a subsequent interview that like her, he had also sacrificed for the country through hard work as a real estate developer. Khan responded in a *Washington Post* op-ed titled, "Ghazala Khan: Trump Criticized My Silence. He Knows Nothing about True Sacrifice." Not only veterans' groups but groups on both sides of the presidential campaign demanded reverence for Khan's Gold Star status. Illustrative is the statement by Paul Rieckhoff, the founder of Iraq and Afghanistan Veterans of America: "In the military and veterans community, Gold Star families are sacred. They're a group of people who uniquely understand the price of freedom and the cost of war" (qtd. in Zraick). The incident quite clearly demonstrates the veneration of maternal sacrifice to war and the iconic patriotic status of the Gold Star mother.

## The Anxious Military Mother

The contemporary ideological figure of the "good mother" is constructed through a set of cultural-historical ideals. Since the 1970s, these ideals have framed what Sharon Hays terms "intensive mothering," which requires mothers to invest unlimited time, energy, and resources into enriching the lives of their children. Yet as Andrea O'Reilly points out, "Given that no one can achieve intensive mothering all mothers see themselves as failures" (10), especially given that mothers are assigned ultimate responsibility for their children yet can neither change the rules nor escape from the scrutiny of the social gaze and its internalization. Thus, intensive mothering in the twenty-first century is marked by "powerless responsibility" (O'Reilly 11) and anxiety (Warner).

Unsurprisingly, studies of recruitment campaigns suggest that enlistment appeals essentialize maternal anxiety and seek to reassure mothers in order to win their support for their child's enlistment (Christensen "Recruiting"; "Black Citizen-Subject"). Since the U.S. military became a volunteer force in 1973, recruitment has been critical to maintaining military strength, and contemporary recruitment campaigns like "Army Strong" are professional and targeted. Gender-essentialized strategies target parents. Mothers are reassured that recruit training and lifestyle are safe, comfortable, and an extension of parental care aimed at instilling the qualities of ideal (hetero-normative, class privileged) manhood ("Recruiting"). In contrast, fathers are assumed to feel pride more than anxiety and to relate more readily to the military as a masculinized institution ("Recruiting"). This is a double-edged gendered strategy: the appeal of "warrior masculinity" is contrasted to maternal anxiety. At the same time, this appeal co-opts the father's concerns and assuages the mother's, derailing her potential disapproval. Thus, intensive mothering and militarization of maternal anxieties are mobilized in the service of military recruitment; note the tagline to the Army Strong campaign targeted at mothers: "You made them strong. We'll make them Army Strong."

## Mobilizing Race, Ethnicity, and Class

These gendered strategies targeting mothers are specific to race, ethnicity, and class as well. For example, white middle-class parents may worry that their children might have better choices than joining the military after high school like college; hence, recruiters reassure them that the military is a good career choice. In contrast, for lower-class parents, the military promises job training and employment in the face of limited options (Segal and Segal). Military service affords a child room and board, full-time paid employment, job training, educational and medical benefits, and career counselling ("Step 2"). Furthermore, the military's policies on racial integration, job training, and benefits have been perceived as more attractive than many other employment possibilities by minority groups–especially black men and Hispanic men and women who are represented in military service in greater percentages than their percentage of the total U.S. population (Burk and Espinoza; Segal and Segal). Echoing charges made against military recruitment strategies since the beginning of the all-volunteer force in 1973, Michelle Rivera cautions that targeting economically vulnerable youth constitutes a "poverty draft" (223).

In a study of recruitment materials, Christensen finds that middle-class white mothers were assured that military service would give their slacker sons discipline and direction, getting them off the couch and away from video games and "guyland" ("Recruiting" 196). She argues that such appeals address the extended adolescence typical of white middle- and upper-class youth. However, for African American mothers, overrepresented in recruitment ads as single parents, the message is that army discipline, authority, and masculinity will provide a co-parenting influence to counter a deficit (fatherless) family structure and the presumption that black single mothers "are especially worried about their child's continued adolescence, irresponsibility, potential criminality, and contribution to society" ("Black Citizen-Subject" 2517). Barbara Omolade poignantly poses the dilemma of the African American mother as follows: "'Which war zone does she protect her son from: The military or the street?'" (149).

In these recruitment strategies, black military mothers are doubly co-opted into surrendering maternal concern and responsibility. First, worries over war and the risk of death are overshadowed by assurances that military service will translate into enhanced employment and life opportunities. Second, the father missing from the black single mother's family is replaced by a masculinist military ethos that promises to make a man of her son. Both of these strategies exploit a dominant stereotype of female-headed black family life as deficit and dysfunctional that neglects the various configurations of bloodmothering, other-mothering, women-centered childcare networks, and extended family stability (as opposed to marital stability) that contrast with the norm-ative nuclear family model (Bush). As Peréz observes, recruiters may "deploy the language of security and protection to advance the idea that military service protects 'at risk' youth from danger and instills critical values allegedly absent in poor families, namely discipline, honor, and the value of hard work" (69). Mitigating the maternal anxiety of black single military mothers, thus, plays on essentialist assumptions, racial stereotypes, and the stigma of poverty.

Studies of recruitment campaigns directed to mothers and families of Hispanic youth point to not only the use of stereotypes based in poverty and ethnic culture but also the anxieties in the post-9/11 security state. Hispanic enlistment–substantially higher over the past two decades (Parker et al.)–involves complicated considerations for

Hispanic youth such as everyday race-based surveillance and suspicion occurring at both national and local levels; the need to contribute to gendered household economies; the lack of labour market opportunities besides the military; and the negotiation of restrictive sexual norms and expectations (Peréz; Garza; Segal and Segal). Based on her observational study among Puerto Rican American families in Chicago, Peréz argues that these young people are drawn to military service in part to contend with the racialized hypervigilance of the larger culture: "Wearing a uniform is one way of negotiating the racialized systems of surveillance and trends to a culture of law and order" (58). For Hispanic youth, the uniform garners respect and cultural capital for navigating both the gendered relations of status and loyalty in local youth cultures and for deflecting the threats of the larger culture. She found that for young Puerto Rican women, the uniform also mediates cultural norms that women should be "*en la casa*" both as productive contributors to the family economy and to enforce premarital chastity. In Garza's analysis of an army recruitment campaign—"*Yo Soy el Army* ["I Am the Army"]—she points to a presumed equation between Hispanic family values (honour, respect, loyalty, love of family, and country) and military values and how this link has crafted a story of Hispanic military service and combat valour. Several ads in this campaign feature an enlisted son and his mother using images that advance "masculinist, patriarchal sensibilities" by casting the mother as proud and affirming and the son as a role model and protector of mother-nation (256).

My point here is that an essentialized maternal anxiety is mobilized in the service of military recruitment across class, race, and ethnic groups. This strategy is mediated by particular ideological constructions and lived vulnerabilities that differentiate the appeals and opportunities targeted to differently situated groups. Nonetheless, the militarization of the anxious mother is critical to military recruitment of voluntary enlistees. Maternal anxiety is also the basis for exhorting unquestioning homefront support for military service.

## Active Duty Anxiety

Active duty confronts the military mother with a paradox: despite the injunction to safeguard her children, she must cede control and responsibility to the military establishment, even though she knows that her child may be ordered into dangerous, even deadly situations.

Thus, this paradox reinforces the central affective force of intensive mothering: maternal guilt (Warner). Unsurprisingly, mothers' public confessions of their anxieties are commonplace in public media coverage of war and the military (Cappuccio; Slattery and Garner "Mother as Mother"; "Mothers of Soldiers"). The military establishment channels maternal anxiety into expressions of care and support for active service personnel; in essence, the military mother is enlisted along with her child into military service. Christensen observes that "'The GoArmyParents website explains: 'Your Soldier has chosen this profession. While it's natural for you to worry, your Soldier still deserves your full support because your nation's security is now in your Soldier's well-trained hands'" ("Recruiting," 205). A mother's anxiety is rightly channelled into support rather than criticism or protest for the good of her soldier, the military forces, and the nation's security.

Likewise, a genre of military mom advice texts confirms maternal anxiety and offers support and community for mothers of active duty and reintegrating service personnel. There are blogs, websites, and Facebook pages in use by military moms. A few recent book titles suffice to characterize the nature of these venues: *Be Safe, Love Mom: A Military Mom's Stories of Courage, Comfort, and Surviving Life on the Homefront* (Brye); *Love You More Than You Know: Mothers' Stories about Sending Their Sons and Daughters to War* (Reinart and Mayer); *Mom's Field Guide: What You Need to Know to Make It Through Your Loved One's Military Deployment* (Doell); and *Stay Strong Stay Safe, My Son* (Callies). Christensen's study of online groups for military mothers documents the self-disciplining among group members to quell criticisms of the military, to dissuade mothers from political commentary, and to reinforce the responsibility of mothers to give their active duty children unqualified support ("Technological Boundaries"). The military also addresses the anxious mother directly in letters to families, a page on the unit or fort's website, and events such as on-base "family days."

Why encourage public displays of maternal anxiety over active duty service? First, the military establishment encourages mothers to express their anxiety by sending care packages and communications to their active duty child as well as by suppressing criticism and protest of the military and military actions. Thus, anxiety is constructively channelled and disciplined to self-enforced acquiescence. Second, although the thrust of all of these venues is to acknowledge mothers' anxieties, indeed, to encourage public confession of fears and anxieties, at the same time, the mother is positioned as the steadfast embodiment of and responsible for maintaining "home" as valued, comforting, and supportive. Thus, maternal anxiety and steadfastness offer affective markers of the significance of and support for military defense. In the following section, I describe a critical portrait of anxiety, class, and the military mother.

## Homogenizing Differences: Anxiety, Motherlove, and Homefront Support

In statistical analyses of military demographics in relation to general population demographics, Amy Lutz has found that low family income was the only key predictor of military enlistment (184). Similarly, Meredith Kleykamp shows that both lower socioeconomic status and high institutional presence of the military in the neighbourhood were predictive of military enlistment directly out of high school. The gendered politics of economic status are race and locale based. Yet in the cultural figure of the military mother, these exclusionary subject positions are not supposed to matter. Instead, motherlove and the promise of home are assumed to cross class and race lines. This hegemonic incorporation of the military mother as an anchor against historically embedded systemic disadvantages is fleshed out with affective intensity in a documentary filmed in the Keweenaw Peninsula, the northern rural area of Michigan where I live. In *Where Soldiers Come From*, filmmaker Heather Courtney follows five young men from their decision to enlist together after high school through four years of army service, including their deployment to Afghanistan and the difficulties of their return to civilian life. Although the focus of the film is on the soldiers themselves before, during, and after their military service, two of their families are featured as well. These are low-income families with minimal prospects. Economic struggle, rural conservatism, and limited education frame these mothers, families, and soldiers.

One of the mothers becomes quietly central to the scenes of home and family. She is proud of and anxious for her son. In one scene, while celebrations over Obama's 2008 election flicker on a television, she says, "Now we'll see what he'll do for the boys." In this rural, lower-class conservative area, her hope is palpable and poignant. When her son returns, damaged and lost, her fears seem realized, and she recedes into the background of the film–she is a silent but caring presence, still a militarized mother. The boys struggle: one succumbing to depression and anger despite his efforts to get help from an unresponsive Veterans Administration (VA) office, another with community college demands that he clearly finds irrelevant except for an art class.

Despite the lack of opportunities and the day-to-day struggles of these young men, their families, and their communities, the film clearly depicts the cultural condensation of mother/home/nation. The anxious mother figure contributes to a political quietude by homogenizing class, race, and gender differences into a seemingly universal faith in motherlove and the mother as the anchor of the soldier's family.[3]

## The Activist Military Mother

Whereas most of the figures I have considered thus far have been accommodative, the dissenting military mother is engaged in political confrontation. As Cohn and Jacobson put it, "the relation of women to war is, in a sense, *always already political*" (emphasis in original, 104). The dissenting military mother seemingly counters the hegemonic sociocultural forces rendering other mother figures complicit with militarism and nationalism. Yet this figure offers her own sociocultural ambivalences. The association of mothers with peace and with a maternal ethos opposed to violence and war is a cultural mainstay (Elshtain; Enloe, *Maneuvers*; Ruddick; Sheehan). Indeed, Mother's Day began as a feminist pacifist antiwar protest. In 1870, pacifist Julia Ward Howe wrote the "Mother's Day Proclamation," calling on women to unify for international disarmament and peace, spurred by protective love for all children and life in general. I distinguish between the antiwar mother and the peace activist mother because although they may overlap, the cultural associations, political histories, and relationship to feminism of these figures are distinct as are their complex relations with their sons and daughters in uniform.

## Antiwar Protests and the "Bad" Military Mother

I turn first to the antiwar mother, a figure whose presence on the public stage has been prominent throughout the twentieth century. Prior to the First World War, women suffragists were adamantly antiwar; mothers protested the potential sacrifice of their sons to a war that was not in American interests (Graham). The Women's Congress of 1915 and the Women's International League for Peace and Freedom prom-oted not only women's suffrage, but motherhood and motherly caregiving as a basis for uniting women across borders to protest foreign policy and war and to promote permanent peace (Wilmers). Despite the public visibility of these groups, antiwar and pacifist protests became increasingly contrary to dominant understandings of patriotism and citizenship.

Although activist military mothers may claim moral high ground on the basis of maternal values for preserving life and caring for others (Mullen), at the same time, they risk shaming a son or daughter in uniform who pledged allegiance and loyalty to the military. Hence, a dichotomy between "good" mother-citizens and "bad" unpatriotic mothers who put their care as mothers above their patriotic duty haunts the figure of the antiwar activist mother. This dichotomy was unsettled during the Vietnam War, as military mothers began to voice their opposition to American military strategies and political policies (Slattery and Garner, "News Coverage"). The widespread unpopularity of the war allowed mothers to express antiwar sentiments and concerns that their child may die in a war that did not serve national interests. More recently, Slattery and Garner contend that during the past twenty years, the press has given more space to mothers' concerns over the legitimacy and worthiness of American wars ("Mothers of Soldiers"). They note that fully two-thirds of the news stories they studied depicting mothers of soldiers during the first Iraq War included "some expression of anti-war sentiment" by the mother (439). They conclude that although all mothers were depicted as supporting their child in combat, they were not all shown to be supportive of the war–a strategic discursive distinction that successfully avoids shaming their children in uniform.

The social acceptability of a mother's protest against a war in which her child is fighting marks a shift from the strict patriotism demanded of First and Second World War citizen mothers. However, in her study of stories about the Iraq War on the network morning television news programs between 2003 and 2005, Sondra Cappuccio has found that in the main, military mothers on these shows served in two roles: "supporter/caregiver" and "representative/proud mother." Few mothers expressed any dissent and when they did so, "this dissent was nothing more than a straw man" (6). Christensen notes a similar sanctioning among military mothers' support groups ("Technological Boundaries"). Cappuccio's study shows the tenacious ideological associations between the "good mother," patriotism, and nationalism and the media's role in sustaining these associations.

Despite the possibility that a military mother may voice criticisms of war without being condemned as unpatriotic, the suspicion that anti-war mothers are guilty of bad mothering by putting their public protests above their role as good mothers remains a sanctioning force. This is well illustrated in the public defamation of Cindy Sheehan, a "Gold Star" mother. Sheehan mounted a protest campaign against the Bush administration's Iraq war decisions motivated by her grief over her son's needless combat death. As a mother, her grief and anger over her son's death commanded public attention and sympathy. But her claim to moral authority on the basis of motherhood became a point of vulnerability; critics cast her as a bad mother, one whose desire for publicity took precedence over the day-to-day care of her own children (Knudson). Moreover, Sheehan's antiwar activism against the Obama administration's Middle East drone warfare expanded her public persona as an anti-war Gold Star mother. Francis Shor argues that the reverence and empathy elicited by a Gold Star mother are insufficient in the current moment to counter American militarism and exceptionalism and to morally engage the American public with those in other countries whose lives have been devastated by American military action. She calls for "inclusive and anti-imperial empathy" (248), which is more than the gold star can elicit.

## Mothers and Peace

Mothers protesting for peace have long premised their efforts on the expansive empathetic capacities of maternal care and responsibility for life. However, the familiar association between mothers and peace is framed by an essentialist dichotomy–women by nature are peace loving and life nurturing, whereas men are combative and prone to violence. Contemporary feminist debates seek not only to build a counter-essentialist case for women and peace but to articulate a more sophisticated understanding of feminist nonviolence, pacifism, and peacebuilding. Although the figures of military mothers I highlight here do not incorporate the nuances of these debates, they are useful in drawing attention to the popular assumptions that remain potent sources of both inspiration and derailment for women working for peace.

Sara Ruddick, a key feminist maternalist and peace advocate, identifies three prominent figures of the mother and peace. First, the *mater dolorosa*, the mother of sorrows, who mourns war's destruction and collective suffering; she works to hold "lives together despite pain, bitterness and deprivation" (215). This figure was explicitly invoked by *Las Madres de la Playa de Mayo* or Mothers of the Disappeared in Argentina, a now four-decades-long protest action by mothers publicizing the political kidnappings and deaths of their children by a repressive regime. Las Madres has become an iconic symbol of the power of maternal grief and moral resistance (Bosco; Foss and Domenici; Taylor). Another example is the Committee of Soldiers' Mothers in Soviet Russia, which enacts public displays of maternal care and grief to bring public attention to *dedovshchina*–the brutal disciplinary tactics used by the army on conscripts–and to protest their sons' deaths in unnecessary military conflicts (Elkner).

The second figure Ruddick identifies is the outsider, the feminist separatist, who speaks as an estranged voice of suspicion against a patriarchal culture given over to the "collective terror, enthusiasm, and patriotic exhortation" of masculinist violence and war (219). An example is the Greenham Common Peace Encampment in Berkshire, England–a decades-long women-only protest initiative against the use of nuclear weapons, which is premised on maternal protection of children's safety and the safety of future generations. Criticisms of these peace activists unsurprisingly invoke the "bad mother," and charge the activists with neglecting their own children, maintaining a lesbian witches' coven, and threatening values of home and family (Shepherd).

Ruddick's third figure is the peacemaker devoted to nonviolence, mutual safety, and reciprocal respect, yet whose own life may be governed by norms of femininity that ultimately reproduce her own subordination through "harmful habits of compliance and self-denial" (221). This dynamic can also be found in the work of peacebuilding organizations that have mobilized women in postconflict social reconstruction through creative initiatives responsive to local relations, practices, and circumstances (Cole and Norander; De Alwis et al.; Jacobson). Certainly, dismissing mothers' peacework as "natural" "erases the extensive, hard, political work" involved in the protests, initiatives, and alliances undertaken and sustained by women (De Alwis et al. 182). Yet this work can inadvertently reproduce the assumption that the space and practice of formal peace negotiations is masculine, whereas informal, local peacebuilding is feminine. Furthermore, Mary Moran warns that peacebuilding is complicated, particularly when it involves neoliberal reforms, external NGOs, or alliances across entrenched antagonisms. These are fragile, contrary processes that risk provoking conservative social and economic discriminations, which disproportionately disadvantage women. There may also be gendered backlash and even violence in domestic and institutional relations.

Still, there is much to commend in the work I have cited as examples of the three figures of mothers working for peace. De Alwis rightly argues that maternal activism is more complicated and contingent than ideological characterizations admit, and as a political force, it has been resilient and malleable. Yet persistent ideological associations attend the work of mothers for peace, associations that Micaela di Leonardo identifies as a pernicious trope: the Moral Mother who is "nurturant, compassionate, and politically correct–the sovereign, instinctive spokeswoman for all that is living and vulnerable. The Moral Mother represents the vision of women as innately pacifist, and men as innately warmongering" (602). Di Leonardo argues that this image inherently promotes a sentimentalized, heteronormative, and homogenizing ideology of motherhood. In contrast, feminist analyses of militarization (Enloe, *Maneuvers*, "All") and the struggle of peacebuilding undertaken by mothers' groups worldwide issue hope that the conservative pull of the Moral Mother can be countered in the close analyses, political strategies, and lived complexities of women working for peace. In the context of this chapter, di Leonardo's critique reminds us of the need to recognize the Moral Mother's entrenched ideological associations as they appear in prevalent military mother figures and to champion more complex, nuanced images of military mothers.

## Precarity and the Military Mother

The military mother figures I have reviewed to this point have been developed in feminist analyses of militarization, war, and motherhood. However, I want to call attention to two figures that have not been studied in order to encourage critical feminist analysis of their ideological work and implications. Both of these figures emerge out of contemporary conditions of neoliberal precarity. As Julie Wilson puts it, neoliberal market competition has become integral to everyday life in all aspects as has the autonomous and self-responsible individual. With the increasing privatization of social safety nets, risk and insecurity pervade the sensibilities and material resources of everyday life (45). Julie Wilson and Emily Yochim argue that under these conditions of neoliberal precarity, U.S. mothers have become "resilient" subjects "who must cultivate capacities to cope with the shriveling resources and broken promises that neoliberalism brings to social life" (14). Intensive mothering is morphing into "responsibilized" mothering:

> *Mothers are the ones who ultimately come to compensate for lost jobs, underfunded public schools, decimated state budgets, and the volatilities all these bring to family life, as mothers constantly retool and expand their women's work–taking on more and more social responsibility with less and less social support–in hopes of bringing some measure of stability to their shaky family scenes. (22)*

As risk, threat, and insecurity become commonplace features of everyday life, the traditional responsibilities of mothers for family, children, and domestic life are intensified and expanded as women fill in the gaps in social and material resources and opportunities.

## Responsibilized Caregiving

Neoliberal precarity and the responsibilized mother are evident in the care gap experienced by severely wounded military veterans. In the U.S., the privatization of caregiving services and the social and psychotherapeutic emphasis on self-sufficient families have significantly undermined state welfare services and shifted the political terrain for the politics of care to individuals and families (Rose). The responsibilized mother of the wounded veteran is the caregiver who fills in the gaps in medical and military support after her child returns from military service as a "wounded warrior." These women are known as "Silver Star Mothers" (Newton and Newton). An idealistic image of maternal resilience is evident in the title of a book profiling ten Silver Star mothers whose sons returned from the Iraq and/or Afghanistan wars with grievous injuries: *Unbreakable Bonds: The Mighty Moms and Wounded Warriors of Walter Reed* (Guerin and Ferris). As the title suggests, these mothers have redevoted their own lives to caring for a severely injured military son or daughter. In press comments, Senator Elizabeth Dole applauded the "selfless devotion, duty, and strength" of the Silver Star mothers; Speaker Nancy Pelosi noted their "courage, and enduring love"; David S. Ferriero, Archivist of the U.S., described the mothers' attributes as "compassion, persistence, fierce advocacy, and courage"; Colonel Paul McHale (U.S. Marine Corps, ret.) extolled their stories as "an amazing fusion of moral courage and limitless love ... the story of motherhood, tested and unbroken ... [that] radiates wisdom, tenacity, compassion, and resolve" (ii). Such praise is cultural compensation for the impossible responsibilities expected of and assumed by this military mother figure. This figure joins an entrenched ideal of maternal self-sacrifice, the neoliberal individual's responsibility for privatized care services in the face of inadequate resources (Clarke), and a feminized model of caring labour that has been historically marginalized, depoliticized, and economically devalued as "bonds of love" (Folbre).

The accolades for the responsibilized military mother obscure the burden of care taken on by families and friends, especially since the stakes become more devastating in the face of the inefficiencies and deadly inadequacies at government medical care facilities serving severely wounded active duty and veteran military personnel. "Caregiving in the U.S. 2015," reports that 5.5 million wives, husbands, siblings, parents, children, and friends are caring for wounded veterans, and of these, 68 percent consider their situation stressful. Another 60 percent are performing medical or nursing tasks for which they have little or no training (National Alliance for Caregiving and AARP). The uneven distribution of resources addressing caregivers is evident in the shortcomings of the Caregivers and Veterans Omnibus Health Services Act of 2010, which authorized a broad range of VA services for caregivers, yet only 22,000 of the 1.1 million families caring for a post 9/11 veteran or military member receive extensive assistance, given the strict eligibility criteria. And marginalized populations are most likely to be left out. James Burk and Evelyn Espinoza report that access to the VA health care system is skewed by institutional racism so that minorities with health issues incurred during military service are "less likely than whites to have injuries classified as service connected" and thus are screened out of VA services (414).

The precarity of care for post-9/11 wounded veterans is evident in the 2014 RAND study "Hidden Heroes: America's Military Caregivers," which documents both veterans' reliance on aging parents, largely mothers, and the waning public support for services beyond VA benefits (Ramchand, et al). The study identifies three factors making the future of caregiving support uncertain, particularly for the younger post-9/11 service members and veterans: 25 percent rely on aging "baby boomer" parents for care, largely mothers; 33 percent rely on spouses in marriages that are increasingly fragile; and 80 percent of available support programs beyond VA benefits are from recently formed nonprofit organizations, which are "vulnerable to waning public interest, lowered philanthropic support, and shortfalls in capacity to deliver services effectively" (Ramchand et al.). In other words, these veterans and their mothers are living out the insecurities and impossibilities of neoliberal privatization and precarity. The Silver Star mother figure, thus, highlights the following: the privatization of caregiving labour in the face of inadequate medical and military response to the long-term needs of wounded military personnel; the invisibility of caregivers' needs and suffering; and the ready cultural accolades that discipline caregivers to stoicism, self-sacrifice, quiet despair, and ever more maternal responsibility.

## Precarity and Grief

Combat deaths occasion cultural rituals affirming the value of the ultimate sacrifice, but there are military deaths that cannot be readily articulated to patriotism and militarism. Yet these deaths now exceed those incurred during the performance of military duties. I speak here of active duty and veteran suicides. Whereas the Gold Star mother is honoured for a loss that is deemed a worthy sacrifice, a mother's grief from a military suicide cannot be normalized as worthy in the same way. Judith Butler argues that such distinctions implicate a moral-political failure to acknowledge the grievability of human life grounded in our shared vulnerabilities. The two grieving mother figures, thus, draw attention to the ethical fissures that riddle cultural relations of honour, shame, celebration, and marginalization attending military mothers and their children's deaths. The mother of a military suicide is subject to a loss that cannot be categorized as honorable and a grief that cannot be socially normalized. It is a loss that implicitly undermines the promises of service and sacrifice.

I draw this figure of the grieving military mother from recent statistics about suicide in the military. Although suicide has always been an issue, government statistics over the past decade suggest an alarming increase in suicide rates among American veterans. In 2014, a Department of Veteran's Affairs report documented a 44 percent increase in suicides among veterans under thirty years of age between 2009 and 2011 (Shane III). In 2013, veteran suicides were 22.2 percent of all U.S. suicides according to the American Foundation for Suicide Prevention. Congress unanimously passed the Clay Hunt Suicide Prevention Act of 2015, and the military has taken aggressive steps to identify and support those with a propensity for suicide (Hauser). Still, in a 2016 report, the department estimated that about twenty veterans a day committed suicide in 2014, and veteran suicides were 22 percent greater than for civilians of the same age. Suicide rates were highest among veterans twenty-nine years old or younger, and the risk for women veterans was 2.5 times greater than for U.S. civilian women. Military suicide stands as the ultimate failure, whether of individual hope, family care, community support, or government resources.

In both official and popular media reports, mothers appear as indexical signs of a loss that could have or should have been prevented. They testify to the conditions of vulnerability, insecurity, and precariousness that frame contemporary social life. Yet collective grievability for military suicides sits uneasily with the rhetoric of a nation grateful for a veteran's service. Veteran suicide bespeaks a failure to adequately attend to the wounds of war and to resolve the nation's debt of gratitude. There are implicit suspicions: the mother (and the nation) let the service member down; the military (and the mother) did not respond adequately to signs of trauma, hopelessness, and anger; and the nation, the military, and the mother should have been able to save this veteran. The grieving mother is a sign of debt and failure both intimate and national. She is an object of pity and suspicion–an unresolvable complication in the ideological framing of acceptable military death and maternal grief as a special citizenship status.

Butler urges feminists to challenge the differential distribution of violence and vulnerability with questions that are relevant to a critical inquiry into the mother of a military suicide. She asks, "How does a collective deal, finally, with its vulnerability to violence? At what price, and at whose expense, does it gain a purchase on 'security' ... Can we provide a knowledgeable explanation of events that is not confused with a moral exoneration of violence?" (42). Butler's questions set the mother of a military suicide in the context of contemporary precarity, a military ethos of violence and honourable death, and the politics of grievability.

## Conclusion

My reading of feminist work on the military mother has identified paradoxical injunctions, cultural associations, social sanctions, material conditions, and historical contexts that render these figures heuristics for further feminist study. The "good" military mother is a figment of ideological imagination but also a powerful incentive for resisting the militarization of social life and the hegemonic subjugation of differences in the interests of nationalistic defense and protectionism.

Motherhood, motherlove, nationhood, militarism, war, honour, citizenship, grief, and duty are intertwined in the prevailing images that shape how to be a military mother. Furthermore, the meaning and role of the military mother is confounded by contradictions, ambivalences, and negotiations. She is and is not the (white and privileged) patriotic citizen; the anxious mother anchoring the family/home/nation; the honoured grieving mother; the antiwar protestor trading on maternal empathy or the peace activist framed by an essentialized maternalism; the responsibilized caregiver; or the ambiguous mother of a suicide. As Hall points out, though at times, any one of these figures may "hail" us, none exhaust our possibilities or experiences ("Ideology"). At the same time, each of these figures draws us into dense signifying chains that have compounded resonances and complex implications. The articulation of mother, care, and family through militarization and the nation is deeply entrenched in reproductive and accommodative relations, yet the ideological stability of the mother's militarization may shift given differing social formations and historical moments (Lebel). Finally, though the power of dominant articulations cannot be denied, what I have found most compelling is the ongoing rearticulation of the trope of the military mother in all her guises to projects of social history and cultural life. She is a nodal point in our cultural hegemonies, hopes, and struggles.

## Endnotes

1 Despite the impact of death and grief on families of military service members, it is only recently that the grieving processes of surviving family members have been addressed in a large-scale federally funded study. The National Military Bereavement Study details differences in survivors' grief experiences in order "to inform policies effecting survivor care" and "how available resources impact resilience or vulnerability in surviving families" (Cozza et al.). Called the first large scientific study of the impact of bereavement, the study seems long overdue in its focus on the impact of grief on the emotional and material wellbeing of military family members.

2 The label "Hispanic" does not designate a monolithic group. As Irene Garza notes, many groups are included under this umbrella term, including Cuban American, Puerto Rican, Mexican American, Latina/o, South American, Chicana/o, and others. Further hetero-geneities arise from "racial identification, class status, national origin, patterns of migration, generational longevity in the US, regional diversity, language preference and so on" (Garza 249).

3 Although my focus is on U.S. military mother figures, I want to acknowledge the gravity of women's welfare needs in war-shattered economies in other parts of the world. Ruth Jacobson points out that in postconflict societies, women-headed households are often characterized by poverty and psychosocial distress; without male kin, mothers, widows, and abandoned women often cannot gain access to reconstruction resources offered by both the state and NGOs. This is exacerbated under the "market fundamentalism" requirements imposed by the World Bank and the International Monetary Fund, which entail cutbacks in state-funded welfare programs and privatization of public goods and services. These cutbacks often disproportionately disadvantage women-headed households and mothers who have lost their sons, land, and livelihood in war.

## Works Cited

American Foundation for Suicide Prevention. "Suicide: 2015 Facts & Figures." *American Foundation for Suicide Prevention,*15 Oct. 2015, www.nationalcouncildocs.net/wp-content/uploads/2015/10/2015-National-Facts-and-Figures.pdf. Accessed 10 Mar. 2016.

Basu, Tanya. "Photo of Soldiers Breastfeeding in Uniform Goes Viral." *Time*, 13 Sep. 2015, http://time.com/4032913/female-soldiers-breastfeeding/. Accessed March 15, 2016.

Bernstein, Lisa, editor. *(M)Othering the Nation: Constructing and Resisting National Allegories through the Maternal Body*. Cambridge Scholars Publishing, 2008.

Bosco, Fernando J. "The Madres de Plazo de Mayo and Three Decades of Human Rights' Activism: Embeddedness, Emotions and Social Movements." *Annals of the Association of American Geographers* vol. 96, no. 2, 2006, pp. 342-65.

Brye, Elaine Lowry. *Be Safe, Love Mom: A Military Mom's Stories of Courage, Comfort, and Surviving Life on the Home Front*. Public Affairs, Perseus Books Group. 2015.

Burk, James, and Evelyn Espinoza. "Race Relations within the US Military." *The Annual Review of Sociology*, vol. 38, 2012, pp. 401-22.

Bush, Lawson. "Black Mothers/Black Sons: A Critical Examination of the Social Science Literature." *The Western Journal of Black Studies*, vol. 24, no. 3, 2000, pp. 145-53.

Butler, Judith. *Frames of War: When Is Life Grievable?* Verso, 2009.

Callies, Debi. *Stay Strong Stay Safe, My Son*. Very Proud Marine Mom (VPMM), 2004.

Cappuccio, Sondra Nicole. "Mothers of Soldiers and the Iraq War: Justification through Breakfast Shows on ABC, CBS, and NBC." *Women & Language*, vol. 29, no. 1, 2006, pp. 3-9.

Christensen, Wendy M. "Recruiting through Mothers: You Made Them Strong, We'll Make Them Army Strong." *Critical Military Studies*, vol. 2, no.3, 2016, pp. 193-209.

Christensen, Wendy M. "The Black Citizen-Subject: Black Single Mothers in US Military Recruitment Material." *Ethnic and Racial Studies*, vol. 39, no. 14, 2016, pp. 2508-26.

Christensen, Wendy M. "Technological Boundaries: Defining the Personal and the Political in Military Mothers' Online Support Forms." *WSQ: Women's Studies Quarterly*, vol. 37, nos. 1 & 2, 2009, pp. 146-66.

Clarke, John. "New Labour's Citizens: Activated, Empowered, Responsibilized, Abandoned?" *Critical Social Policy Ltd*, vol. 25, no. 4, 2005, pp. 447-63.

Cohn, Carol. "Women and Wars: Toward a Conceptual Framework." *Women and Wars*, edited by Carol Cohn, Polity Press. 2013, pp. 1-35.

Cohn, Carol, and Ruth Jacobson. "Women and Political Activism in the Face of War and Militarization." *Women and Wars*, edited by Carol Cohn, Polity Press, 2013, pp. 102-23.

Cole, Cynthia, and Stephanie Norander. "From Sierra Leone to Kosovo: Exploring Possibilities for Gendered Peacebuilding." *Women & Language*, vol. 34, no. 1, 2011, pp. 29-49.

Courtney, Heather, director. *Where Soldiers Come From.* Quincy Hill Films, LLC, 2012.

Cozza, Stephen J., et al. "National Military Family Bereavement Study." Uniformed Services University of the Health Sciences Center for the Study of Traumatic Stress, Bethseda, MD, 2015, www.military survivorstudy.org/. Accessed 15 Jan. 2018.

Davin, Anna. "Imperialism and Motherhood." *Tensions of Empire: Colonial Cultures in a Bourgeois World*, edited by Frederick Cooper and Ann Laura Stoler, University of California Press, 1997, pp. 87-151.

De Alwis, Malathi. "Moral Mothers and Stalwart Sons: Reading Binaries in a Time of War." *The Women and War Reader*, edited by Lois Ann Lorentzen and Jennifer Turpin, New York University Press, 1998, pp. 254-71.

De Alwis, Malathi, et al. "Women and Peace Processes." *Women and Wars*, edited by Carol Cohn, Polity Press, 2013, pp. 169-93.

Di Leonardo, Micaela. "Morals, Mothers, and Militarism: Anti-militarism and Feminist Theory." *Feminist Studies*, vol. 11, no. 3, 1985, pp. 599-617.

Doell, Sandy. *Mom's Field Guide: What You Need to Know to Make It Through Your Loved One's Military Deployment.* Warrior Angel Press, 2006.

Elkner, Julie. "*Dedovshchina* and the Committee of Soldiers' Mothers under Gorbachev." *The Journal of Power Institutions in Post-Soviet Societies*, vol. 1, no. 1, 2004, pipss.revues.org/243. Accessed 10 Mar. 2016.

Elshtain, Jean B. *Women and War.* University of Chicago Press, 1995.

Enloe, Cynthia. *Maneuvers: The International Politics of Militarizing Women's Lives.* University of California Press, 2000.

Enloe, Cynthia "All the Men are in the Militias, All the Women Are Victims: The Politics of Masculinity and Femininity." *The Women & War Reader*, edited by Lois Ann Lorentzen and Jennifer Turpin, New York University Press. 1998, pp. 50-62.

Evans, Suzanne. *Mothers of Heroes, Mothers of Martyrs: World War I and the Politics of Grief*. McGill-Queen's University Press. 2007.

Ferguson, Kathy E. *The Man Question: Visions of Subjectivity in Feminist Theory*. University of California Press, 1993.

Folbre, Nancy. *The Invisible Heart: Economics and Family Values*. New Press. 2001.

Foss, Karen A., and Kathy L. Domenici. "Haunting Argentina: Synecdoche in the Protests of the Mothers of the Plaza de Mayo." *Quarterly Journal of Speech* vol. 87, no. 3, 2001, pp. 237-58.

Garner, Ana C., and Karen L. Slattery. "Mobilizing Mother: From Good Mother to Patriotic Mother in World War I." *Journalism & Communication Monographs*, vol. 14, no. 1, 2014, pp. 5-77.

Garner, Ana C., and Karen L. Slattery. "The World War II Patriotic Mother." *Journalism Studies*, vol. 11, no. 2, 2010, pp. 143-57.

Garza, Irene. "Advertising Patriotism: The 'Yo Soy El Army' Campaign and the Politics of Visibility for Latina/o Youth." *Latino Studies*, vol.13, 2015, pp. 245-68.

Giles, Wenona, and Jennifer Hyndman, editors. "Introduction: Gender and Conflict in a Global Context." *Sites of Violence: Gender and Conflict Zones*. University of California Press, 2004.

Graham, John W. *The Gold Star Mother Pilgrimmages of the 1930s: Overseas Grave Visitations by Mothers and Widows of Fallen U.S. World War I Soldiers*. McFarland and Co, 2005.

Guerin, Dava, and Kevin Ferris. *Unbreakable Bonds: The Mighty Moms and Wounded Warriors of Walter Reed*. Skyhorse Publishing, 2014.

Hall, Stuart. "Ideology and Ideological Struggle." *Cultural Studies 1983: A Theoretical History*, edited by Jennifer Daryl Slack and Lawrence Grossberg, Duke University Press, 2016, pp. 127-54.

Hall, Stuart. "The Work of Representation." *Representation: Cultural Representations and Signifying Practices*, edited by Stuart Hall. Sage Pubs Ltd. 1997, pp. 13-64.

Hauser, Christine. "'Buddy Check on 22!' Veterans Use Social Media to Fight Suicide." *The New York Times*, 24 Apr. 2016, p. A19.

Hays, Sharon. *The Cultural Contradictions of Motherhood*. Yale University Press, 1998.

Jacobson, Ruth. "Women 'After' Wars." *Women and Wars*, edited by Carol Cohn, Polity Press, 2013, pp. 215-41.

Khan, Ghazala. "Ghazala Khan: Trump Criticized My Silence. He Knows Nothing About True Sacrifice." *Washington Post*, 31 July 2016, www.washingtonpost.com. Accessed 23 Aug. 2017.

Kelly, Liz. "Wars against Women: Sexual Violence, Sexual Politics and the Militarised State." *States of Conflict: Gender, Violence and Resistance*, edited by Susie Jacobs and Ruth Jacobson, Zed Books. 2000, pp. 45-65.

Kleykamp, Meredith A. "College, Jobs, or the Military? Enlistment During a Time of War." *Social Science Quarterly*, vol. 87, no. 2, 2006, pp. 272-90.

Knudson, Laura. "Cindy Sheehan and the Rhetoric of Motherhood: A Textual Analysis." *Peace & Change*, vol. 34, no. 2, 2009, pp. 164-83.

Lebel, Udi. "War Opponents and Proponents: Israeli Military Mothers from Rivka Guber to Four Mothers." *Motherhood and War: International Perspectives*, edited by Dana Cooper and Claire Phelan, Palgrave McMillan, 2014, pp. 159-79.

Lutz, Amy. "Who Joins the Military?: A Look at Race, Class and Immigration Status." *Journal of Political and Military Sociology*, vol. 36, no. 2, 2008, pp. 167-88.

Moran, Mary H. "Gender, Militarism, and Peace-Building: Projects of the Postconflict Moment." *The Annual Review of Anthropology*, vol. 39, 2010, pp. 261-74.

Mullen, Peg. *Unfriendly Fire: A Mother's Memoir*. University of Iowa Press, 1995.

National Alliance for Caregiving and AARP. "Caregiving in the U.S. 2015." *NAC and AARP*, June 2015, www.aarp.org/content/dam/aarp/ ppi/2015/caregiving-in-the-united-states-2015-report-revised.pdf. Accessed 20 Mar. 2016.

Newton, Steven, and Diana Newton. *The Silver Star Families of America*. 2015, www.silverstarfamilies.org/. Accessed 2 May 2016.

Omolade, Barbara. "We Speak for the Planet." *Rocking the Ship of State: Toward a Feminist Peace Politics*, edited by Adrienne Harris and Ynestra Kings, Westview Press, 1989, pp. 171-90.

O'Reilly, Andrea. "Introduction." *Mother Outlaws: Theories and*

*Practices of Empowered Mothering*, edited by Andrea O'Reilly, Women's Press, 2004, pp. 1-28.

Parker, Kim, et al. "6 Facts about the U.S. Military and Its Changing Demographics." Pew Research, 13 Apr. 2017, www.pewresearch.org/fact-tank/2017/04/13/6-facts-about-the-u-s-military-and-its-changing-demographics/. Accessed 3 Jan. 2018.

Pérez, Gina M. "How a Scholarship Girl Becomes a Soldier: The Militarization of Latina/o Youth in Chicago Public Schools." *Identities: Global Studies in Culture and Power*, vol. 13, 2006, pp. 53-72.

Peterson, V. Spike. "Gendered Nationalism: Reproducing 'Us' Versus 'Them.'" *The Women & War Reader*, edited by Lois Ann Lorentzen and Jennifer Turpin, New York University Press. 1998, pp. 41-49.

Prividera, Laura C. and John W. Howard. "Repealing the Direct Combat Exclusion Rule: Examining the Ongoing 'Invisible War' Against Women Soldiers." *Women & Language*, vol. 37, no. 1, 2014, pp. 115-20.

Ramchand, Rajeev, et al. *Hidden Heroes: America's Military Caregivers.* The Rand Corporation, 2014. www.rand.org/content/dam/rand/pubs/research_reports/RR400/RR499/RAND_RR499.pdf. Accessed 10 Mar. 2016.

Reinart, Janie, and Mary Anne Mayer, editors. *Love You More Than You Know: Mothers' Stories About Sending Their Sons and Daughters to War.* Gray & Company, Publishers. 2009.

Rivera, Michelle M. *Hate It or Love It: Global Crossover of Reggaetón Music in the Digital Age.* Unpublished Doctoral Dissertation, University of Illinois, Urbana. 2014.

Roche-Paull, Robyn. *Breastfeeding in Combat Boots: A Survival Guide to Breastfeeding Successfully While Serving in the Military.* Hale Publishing, 2016.

Rose, Nikolas. *Governing the Soul: The Shaping of the Private Self.* Taylor & Frances/Routledge, 1990.

Ruddick, Sara. "'Woman of Peace': A Feminist Construction." *The Women & War Reader*, edited by Lois Ann Lorentzen and Jennifer Turpin, New York University Press, 1998, pp. 213-26.

Scheper-Hughes, Nancy. "Maternal Thinking and the Politics of War." *Peace Review: A Journal of Social Justice*, vol. 8, no. 3, 1996, pp. 353-58.

Segal, David R., and Mady Wechsler Segal. "America's Military Population." *Population Bulletin*, vol. 59, no. 4, 2004.

Shane III, Leo. "Suicide Rate Spikes among Young Veterans." *Stars and Stripes*, 9 Jan. 2014, www.stripes.com/report. Accessed 10 Mar., 2016.

Sheehan, Cindy. *Peace Mom: A Mother's Journey through Heartache to Activism*. Simon & Schuster. 2006.

Shepherd, Laura J. "Sex or Gender? Bodies in World Politics and Why Gender Matters." *Gender Matters in Global Politics: A Feminist Introduction to International Relations*, edited by Laura J. Shepherd, Routledge, 2010, pp. 3-16.

Shome, Raka. "Global Motherhood: The Transnational Intimacies of White Femininity." *Critical Studies in Media Communication*, vol. 28, no. 5, 2011, pp. 388-406.

Shor, Francis. "Grieving US Mothers and the Political Representations of Protest During the Iraq War and Beyond." *Motherhood and War: International Perspectives*, edited by Dana Cooper and Claire Phelen, Palgrave Macmillan, 2014, pp. 241-52.

Slack, Jennifer Daryl. "The Theory and Method of Articulation in Cultural Studies." *Stuart Hall: Critical Dialogues in Cultural Studies*, edited by David Morley and Kuan-Hsing Chen, Routledge, 1996, pp. 112-27.

Slattery, Karen, and Ana C. Garner. "Mother as Mother and Mother as Citizen: Mothers of Combat Soldiers on National Network News." *Journalism*, vol. 13, no. 1, 2012, pp. 87-102.

Slattery, Karen, and Garner, Ana C. "Mothers of Soldiers in Wartime: A National News Narrative." *Critical Studies in Media Communication*, vol. 24, no. 5, 2007, pp. 429-45.

Slattery, Karen and Ana C. Garner. "News Coverage of U.S. Mothers of Soldiers During the Vietnam War: Shedding the Image of Spartan Motherhood." *Journalism Practice*, vol. 9, no. 2, 2015, pp. 265-78.

"Step 2: Decide If You're Ready." *Ten Steps to Joining the Military*. Military Advantage, Monster Worldwide, Inc, www.military.com/recruiting. Accessed 15 Mar. 2016.

Stoler, Ann Laura. "Intimidations of Empire: Predicaments of the Tactile and Unseen." *Haunted by Empire: Geographies of Intimacy in North American History*, edited by Ann Laura Stoler, Duke Univeristy Press, 2007, pp. 1-22.

Taylor, Diana. "Making a Spectacle: The Mothers of the Plaza de Mayo." *Journal of the Motherhood Initiative for Research and Community Involvement*, vol. 3, no. 2, 2001, pp. 97-109.

Thompson, Marie. "Military Sexual Trauma: Bridging the Chasm Between Trauma and Support." *Women & Language*, vol. 37, no. 1, 2014, pp. 131-38.

Turpin, Jennifer. "Many Faces: Women Confronting War." *The Women & War Reader*, edited by Lois Ann Lorentzen and Jennifer Turpin, New York University Press. 1998, pp. 3-18.

U.S. Army. *Army OneSource*. U.S. Department of Defense, www. myarmyonesource.com. Accessed 5 May 2016.

U.S. Department of Veterans Affairs. *Suicide Prevention: Veterans Crisis Hotline*. U.S. Department of Health and Human Services, www. veteranscrisisline.net. Accessed 15 Mar. 2016.

Warner, Judith. *Perfect Madness: Motherhood in the Age of Anxiety*. Riverhead Books, 2005.

Weedon, Chris. *Feminist Practice and Poststructuralist Theory*. 2nd ed. Blackwell Publishing, 1997.

Wilmers, Annika. "Feminist Pacifism." *1914-1918-Online. International Encyclopedia of the First World War*, edited by Ute Daniel et al., Freie Universitat Berlin, Berlin, 2015, https://encyclopedia.1914-1918-online.net/pdf/1914-1918-Online-feminist_pacifism-2015-11-10.pdf. Accessed 19 Apr. 2016.

Wilson, Julie A. *Neoliberalism*. New York and London: Routledge, 2018.

Wilson, Julie A. and Emily Chivers Yochim. *Mothering through Precarity: Women's Work and Digital Media*. Duke University Press, 2017.

Wood, Alison Davis. *Gold Star Mothers: Pilgrimage of Remembrance*. University of Illinois, 2003.

Zraick, K. "Ghazala Khan is a Gold Star Mother. Here's What that Means." *New York Times* 1 Aug. 2016, www.nytimes.com/2016/08/02/us/ghazala-khan-is-a-gold-star-mother-heres-what-that-means.html. Accessed 12 Sept. 2016.

# Chapter Two

# Mothers, Martyrs, and Messages of Eternity in the Popular Culture of Pakistan

Anwar Shaheen and Abeerah Ali

## Introduction

This chapter has a special focus upon popular culture, conceived as "a form of culture that today carries the connotations of ... ordinariness rather than eliteness, [and] of standardization rather than individuality" (Oswell 74). It deals with the popular conception of martyrdom contrasted with the high ideal of martyrdom in Pakistan, and analyses cultural notions preserved in the form of folklore, war poetry, and in print and electronic media. Moreover, the popular perceptions about martyrdom are elicited through interviews with mothers of persons engaged in security services. This chapter asserts that (a) people's concepts of martyrdom and patriotism have evolved undoubtedly from religious (mostly revealed but interpreted by humans), historical (ancient to modern), and cultural (high to popular) factors; and (b) the role of mothers has been very strong in consolidating such concepts through socialization. Mothers procreate and are upset when their children are hurt, but ideally and paradoxically, the same mothers are expected to infuse in the youngsters the spirit of martyrdom for a noble cause–seemingly a sort of selfishness by the collectivity. This muddling around selfless and selfish motherhood increases because of the challenges posed by the global phenomena of suicide bombers, terrorists, and the self-acclaimed "*jehadis*," who have mushroomed in

Pakistan in recent decades,[1] and whom the state has now shown its commitment to crush.

At the outset, this chapter outlines the perspectives commonly used to understand martyrdom and motherhood. It discusses the religious and popular concept of motherland, motherhood, and martyrdom, and then delves into the Sufi and folk literature to provide a background to the contents of modern media now overwhelmingly shaping the conceptions of the masses. Analysis of war songs by the authors[2] is presented to show their power in cultivating feelings of patriotism, heroism, and pride in one's own identity (tribal, ethnic, or national). Finally, the chapter explains the manner in which the common mothers of today think of martyrdom of their children, based on interviews with mothers (see Nancy Taber, chapter four, for a discussion of mothers and the military in Canadian popular culture, and Udi Lebel and Gal Hermoni, chapter five, for a discussion of maternal public grief and bereavement).

## The Context: Pakistan

Pakistan has a complex ideological fabric based on a multitude of cultures, ethnicities, religions, and sects of the dominant religion– Islam. It has a broad range of ideologies defining norms governing gender relations, and has made a variety of political experiments in the country. In such a complex organic whole, one has to assess any concept and its application carefully. There is a range of liberal, progressive, and conservative frameworks as well as societal, communal, and familial values in Pakistan that guide people in making their life-course decisions. The liberal discourse criticizes state control, calling the state in Pakistan as an "oversized state," which has encroached upon the civic space. The nationalistic-patriotic ideas prevail among a large section of society, and these get reinforced in time of any national crisis. Mothers and families have suffered across the country from the innumerable terrorist attacks in the post-9/11 years. In crisis, young men rush to hospitals to donate blood and collect material donations, if needed. Attacks on one sect are not appreciated by people of other sects, although each sect takes its own convictions as the ultimate truth. The whole nation mourned the ruthless killing of 236 school children on 16 December 2014, and they were declared "young martyrs" Amid these factors, an antihegemonic discourse exists, largely projected by civil society, the media, and feminist circles. Human rights groups, which are the first to point out such violations, have been victimized boldly and shamelessly by both state and nonstate actors, especially since 2005. Since the nation has been through a prolonged war against religious extremism and terrorism, there have emerged pockets of people who accept violation of human rights as a normal occurrence. Given the fact that the overall population of the country is 208 million persons, even a small proportion of those who are insensitive to extremism and terrorism should be quite alarming (Abbas, *Pakistan's* 233). A critical discourse about the political policies that dragged Pakistan into such a conflagration also exists, which makes people question the legitimacy of sacrificing the lives of over fifty thousand civilians and security personnel. The society is also divided on the government policies to stop terrorism and urban violence.

Thanks to media freedom and information revolution, all those actors–Mujahidin, Taliban or their facilitators– have been vehemently criticised in Pakistan as they had brought the Afghanistan's war inside Pakistani territory, or were involved actively in combating the Soviet Union's control on Afghanistan, or had supported terrorism and ongoing conflict across borders. Regarding military operation against these actors, many mothers and members of the general public also question the concept of fighting a war against fellow countrymen and using humans as cannon fodder. Such mothers' viewpoints are not investigated or publicized as such. Yet since women have now entered the armed forces and are now guarding the national monuments in the public eye, the idea that defenders and martyrs can only be men is vanishing. Terrorists are rarely supported by common people. Yet they can understand how losing friends and family to drone attacks, for example, may transform peaceful citizens into terrorists. Moreover, this is no longer a domestic affair. Embedded in global politics, economy and culture, Pakistanis and the global community influence each other. Global outreach of media has created a global community, which can collectively witness *jihadis*'s activities; thus, "knowledge and responsibility result from the global community that is created by the spectacle of martyrdom in mass media" (Devji 99). So in a democratic country, the people are held responsible for installing a government, and are expected to overthrow it if it becomes oppressive. Hence, the concepts about militarism and nationalism and the appeal to humane and motherly emotions are in no way unique to Pakistan. Moreover, such appeals may not be based on religious grounds, as is explained in the following pages.

## Perspectives on Motherhood and Martyrdom

### a. Religious perspective

Dying for some noble cause is the way to martyrdom–the most splendid form of death from a religious point of view. The religions of Islam and Christianity emphasize that mothers who sacrifice their children for the sake of their religious community and divine love would be glorified. Praise is showered upon the virtuous mothers who live as mothers of martyrs in the community memory. Stories of martyrdom speak of mothers' agony, and such narratives are repeated time and again to infuse same spirit in the society for future challenges. Generally, from the perspectives of their mothers, the deceased children are martyrs, no matter if they were involved in a rightful struggle or otherwise, or even if they were victimized (Oh 65-66).[3] Military persons, even if they die in road accidents are called martyrs. In Pakistan, Islamic scholars of the four major schools of jurisprudence have declared the kind of terrorism and insurgency carried out by *jihadi* outfits as against Islam, so those who fight them receive religious legitimacy to purge the land of the people who corrupt it, by calling their act as: "*fasad fil ard*"–creating conflict and trouble on earth (Abid 305-19). This chapter is interested in the description of mothers in Islamic literature that equates them with martyrs because of their rigorous responsibilities of pregnancy and childbirth. The martyrs *(shuhada)* are among the highest categories receiving God's blessings. A woman dying in childbirth is also a martyr, according to saying of the Prophet of Islam (Schleifer 1-2).

### b. Nationalistic-Patriotic Perspective

Dying to safeguard one's country, tribe, or community is regarded from nationalist point of view. According to Suzanne Evans, the image of mothers of martyrs is complex and needs careful assessment. Women join the public celebrations for national martyrs on special occasions, too. Nations respect their founders' ideals and believe that devotion and fidelity to the memory of the founders can keep the homeland safe. Medals are given as recognition of the spirit of patriotism. Recently, after Pakistan's involvement in the U.S.-led "war on terror," the country faced grave challenges to its own existence because of terrorism. The question as to whether it was a U.S. war being fought by Pakistanis or whether it was Pakistan fighting for its own survival, has been answered both ways. Earlier it was more of a U.S. war. Salman Abid, however, sees it as Pakistan's war, and presents an efficient democracy as a solution to problems generated by this involvement. In 2013, there were 1717 terrorist attacks, killing 2,451 people and wounding 5,438, whereas in 2014, there were 1,206 attacks, killing 1723 and injuring 3,143 people. A National Action Plan was, therefore, announced on 24 December 2014. This plan as well as the National Security Policy announced for the years 2014 to 2018 both sought to crush terrorism. This hegemonic regime was, however, contested from within the country.

## c. Ideological Perspective

Ideologies are sets of guiding principles for action. One may find ideologies safeguarding political right and ideals of human equality and dignity. Various ideological trends–imperialism, secularism, fascism, democracy–are seen nurturing spirit of sacrifice for such ideologies. Analyzing the politics of mothers' anguish during the First World War, when the Canadian mothers were appreciated for sacrificing their children for the sake of civilization, justice, freedom, and God, Evans argues that in times of crisis, societies put everything at stake for a higher and greater cause, even sacrificing maternal love. Later, the stories of such mothers are propagated and used by martyrologists to unite the society in order to face the challenges of wars. Evans concludes that in the end, the mothers of martyrs support the choices of their children to face death while fighting for a cherished cause (3).

## d. Antimilitaristic Perspective

Discussing the politicization of motherhood, Alexis Jetters et al. refute the notion that motherhood is a purely apolitical, emotional, and child-centred business. Rather, they argue that motherhood is not an isolating job diverting women from social concerns and struggles. Women have fought the efforts of the state and military to co-opt motherhood for their nationalistic cause. They protest to save their own and others' children. They understand this responsibility not only as a motherly one but as a collective and moral responsibility assumed in a macroscopic perspective. This protest could no doubt happen in cases in which militaristic agenda of the governments was taken with suspicion, but where there was a patriotic cause pursued and convincingly projected by governments, mothers have responded differently. Two broad categories are found relevant for this study: militarist and antimilitarist mothers. The authors describe motherhood beyond being an individual and highly personal experience; rather, they see it as a social institution. Thus, so-called good mothers are those who conform to the popular image, whether it promotes militarism or antimilitarism.

### e. Antinuclear Perspective

Pakistan joined the nuclear club in 1998, which has been celebrated with great pride by a section of state and society. In a survey of posters, lapel pins, medals, badges, paper hats, and buttons, Iftikhar Dadi shows the high-pitch patriotism in Pakistan, against which the antinuclear lobby has also registered its viewpoint. Nuclear weapons became popular with people in an unprecedented manner. However, the euphoria soon vanished when the nation suffered economic pressure from external circles (Dadi 186). It was in fact a show of class-specific nationalism. There are voices resisting nuclear proliferation, and, instead, they demand the same resources to be spent on public development.[4] The creative writings on this issue also favour resistance to the process of proliferation; hence, they uphold the efforts saving humanity from killing and agony of a nuclear holocaust. Saving people from a torturous death is also a motherly attitude that one can find in peace activism. The peace promoters are alerted at the very flicker of a nuclear threat, and it has happened in the past in the growing tensions between India and Pakistan. On the other hand, the prowar lobby asserts: "We have not made atom bomb only to threaten."

### f. Cultural Perspective

Apart from any religious or nationalistic underpinning, heroism is also promoted by literature, folklore, media, and films, which draw upon old and new facts, often mixed with fiction. Heroes and heroines, too, are picked, glorified, and celebrated to reinforce traditional worldviews.[5] Factual stories abound because of prolonged war against terrorism, and are, thus, propagated through social media as well. Strangely, persons upholding noble cause are disputed, whereas the outlaws may become heroes or heroines, depending on the public choice. Apart from the government, now many awards, medals, and new modes of recognition by the society are in vogue to encourage noble causes of saving life and national pride.

## Literary and Cultural Perspective on Mothers and Motherland

In South Asian cultures, both women and land are considered mothers; both give birth to life, and nurture and provide all necessities of life. The rural women extract their livelihood from the beloved earth and adore it more than men do. But portraying the motherland as feminine is problematic because it is then treated as "beloved female" and poets (mostly male) sing its adoration so avidly. As Ehsan Akbar says, "homeland is the place of forgiveness and mercy like a mother; its maternal kindness has been bestowed upon us selflessly, since eons" (qtd. in Yaqoob 127). Another poet Abid Ali Abid calls the soldiers "*suhag*"[6] of the nation–meaning that the nation is feminine, a bride, and is married to soldiers, and both are, thus, bound in precious relationship (qtd. in Yaqoob 153). The feelings of defender of motherland, expressed by a modern Pakhtun poet, refer to him fighting for her honour and name. The soldier, now in shroud, vows to keep her flag high by giving his life. He declares his love to his homeland as "my arms are my *ghairat*,[7] you are Shireen and I am Farhad, O' homeland" (Khattak 250-51). This sentiment is a continuation of what Baba Hotak, a Pakhtun poet of medieval times, once expressed.

The problem emerging here is the predominance of men in the field of poetry, as they have more literacy and are allowed more vocal expression than women. Culturally, the concepts of honour and masculinity are intertwined and synergetic, and are vividly and forcefully delineated. A poet, Shah Sharaf says, "Don't show your back if you are a 'man,' this is against the norm of nobles, and, if '*ghairat*' fills some one's heart, it is as sacred as Toor; ... The '*ghairat*' is moustache of men, without which his face is devoid of glow" (qtd. in Kunjahi, *Punjabi* 64). This poem shows the kernel of the concept of masculinity, which has been popular for centuries. In short, the concepts of honour, masculinity, and gallantry dominate the cultural notions about motherland.

## Concept of Martyrdom in Islam and Pakistan

### a. Religious Concept

The Quran says, "Those who are killed in the path of Allah, do not call them dead; they are alive, and you do not have the understanding of their life" (*Al- Quran,* II: 154). National poet, Muhammad Iqbal holds that "Martyrdom is what a true believer actually wants; no worldly treasure or conquest of land."[8] The great Pakhtun poet, Khushhal Khan Khattak says, "the status of kings is either throne or the gallows; if life is devoid of respect, death is far better than it."[9] And see the reward: an everlasting radiance of life.[10] These three sources delineate how the ideal of martyrdom is understood by the Muslim Pakistanis in general.

### b. Popular Concept

There are stories and eyewitness accounts of the martyrs' bodies found unharmed and fresh after months and years in the graves. Moreover, some other evidence and events reveal the fortune promised for the martyrs in hereafter. A popular magazine *Ubqari*, published the story of Sawar Muhammad Hussain who was awarded *Nishan-e Haider*–Pakistan's highest military award. This martyr laid his life about fifty years ago; his body was found untouched, peaceful and glowing for that long. A dilapidated body of another martyr was found, and its face turned into a perfect, normal face when the mother wanted to see it. Moreover, another martyr's body remained fresh and bleeding for many days, and, miraculously, a piece of brick with *Kalma*[11] written on it was found in his reopened grave (Shahid 264). Such examples, usually not questioned, reinforce the popular belief in the divine promise for martyrs in hereafter.

## The Concept of Martyrdom in Sufi Literature

The celebrated Punjabi Sufi poets have generally preached love for God Almighty, and the message of eternity for those who laid life for Allah flows in their magnificent expressions. Sultan Bahu says the following:

> *One must, hence, shake off the load of ego,*
> *Of life itself, for without dying in love,*
> *The goal of life cannot be attained!*
> *Countless other means have I tried and failed*
> *(qtd. in Javeid and Bhatti 67).*[12]

Shah Latif of Sindh says, "O son of Adam, the dust of the grave is your real dust." Baba Farid says, "My mother was mad as she named me *'jeewan'* [life], when the destined day of death came, there was nothing, no life, no name" (qtd. in Hasrat 126), and "Farid you will get the pillow of brick and bed of dust [grave]; ants will eat up your body; on one side you will lie who knows for how long" (Kunjahi, *Kahey Farid,* 85). In short, one can achieve eternity only by forsaking this world and coalescing with the Beloved, or God.

The Sufi message emphasizes the transitory nature of this world. Thus, it preaches about dying for a lofty cause, and forsaking pleasures. It advises caution against the charms of human love or any luxuries achieved through means other than the love of the Eternal Being. It calls for laying down life for an ultimate good, since the temporal attractions keep man distracted from the path of God, which is "*nijat*" (liberation). Referring to the trying events of revered prophets (Yunus, Abraham, Ayub, Zakariya, Yahya), the martyrs of Karbala, renowned Sufis (Sarmad, Mansoor), and of romantic legendary figures, Ghulam Farid says, "By bearing the pains of love, everyone did his bit, Farid, you also sacrifice your head, as it is your turn now." And then he says, "I sacrificed my head while reciting the name of God, and so accepted the challenge of love" (qtd. in Koreeja 163-65, 192).[13] Thus, by glorifying the sacrifice for the love for the Divine Creator, the creature [human] can transcend its weakness through martyrdom. Farid, in his poem, "*Yar Sipehra,*" meaning a beloved "*mujahid,*" a pride-worthy defender, shows that the defender, the human beloved and the Ultimate Being, all evolve from the same feelings (Koreeja 346-48).

## The Concept in Folk Literature

### a. Epic Literature

Epics relate history, emotions, ideology, and the main events of wars. Many epic stories are available in different regions of Pakistan. A very famous one in Punjab is that of Dulla Bhatti. The Pakhtun region has numerous celebrated epics. Let us first take this region. A survey of epic poetry shows that women are rarely mentioned in it, as in the battle scenes only men fight and get killed. For instance, see renowned fighter Balus Khan of Balochistan (Hamdani 265-6). In such stories a woman is rarely mentioned. However, she may have a minor role in some battle, or she may be called upon by her brave sons, or she may be only addressed at the death of her son or husband, as in this example: "O Beebo, shed your tears on your Nawab's death, if you wish to see him for the last time, come and see him in eternal sleep" (qtd. in Hamdani 285). Another hero, Dilasa Khan, faces a Sikh *sardar*, who says, "I have come to defend my honour," and Dilasa says, "I am not afraid of you; Jehad is my life and my *murshid* [spiritual mentor] is always kind to me. I am always victorious over the infidels ... If I die, I'll go to paradise" (qtd. in Hamdani 300). Strangely, only in Pushto epics, is *"huris"* of the paradise expected and mentioned frequently as a reward of male martyrs, as in these examples: "Palaces, honey, wine, milk and drugs are for Omar Nawab" and "May God bless you; give you *huris* and paradise" (qtd. in Hamdani 191, 209, 301).

In Kohat, a part of Khyber Pakhtunkhwa, a legend about an anti-colonial hero, Ajab Khan of the Afridi tribe, tells that when, in retaliation to his attacks on British cantonment to grab arms and ammunition, the British army dishonoured Pakhtun women after entering his locality. They could not catch Ajab Khan, but he was severely condemned by his mother. She put him to shame, "I wish I had not been your mother. Until you avenge this insult, do not come to me. If you proved impotent, I'll not cry on your corpse nor let you be buried in my land. [Because] Pakhtun mother gives birth only to *ghairatmand* children [those having spirit and courage to defend honour]." Moreover, girls of Ajab's village also pleaded (Hamdani 380), so he set out to revenge, and abducted the British commander's daughter; the British had to compromise (Hamdani 376-84). In Khyber Pakhtunkhwa, there are numerous stories[14] about wars with alien rulers, tribal feuds, *tarboor* (cousin) rivalry, and rebels who used to loot valuables and distribute them among the needy. All such stories show how bravely the Pakhtun tribesmen have embraced martyrdom for various ideals. Even dying for tribal honour is a revered act. So the concept of martyrdom is quite broad.

## b. Var: The Punjabi Epics

The Punjabi people, having historically produced military men and won medals for their gallantry during the colonial era, have suffered a lot of bloodshed in history, mostly because of invaders from the Western routes, the kings of Delhi from the East, or the British. Punjabi literature has a popular form of epics, called *"var"* (plural *varain*), which, although they preserve historical events, are less authentic for having been moulded by different singers. Nonetheless, these epics are a beautiful blend of reality, fiction, romance, and courage that routinely glorify brave death.

*Vars* talk frequently of the love that parents and siblings have for persons who are threatened or even tortured to death. For instance, in the var named Shah Dawood, the vazir pleads with the cruel king to show mercy to young Prince Dawood by saying his mother and sister would be in agony if the king tormented him (Haider 48). In *vars*, mothers also appear on the battlefield to resolve the conflict. Moreover, mothers have dreams about their children; they pray and offer vows when sons go on adventure or wars, and they are saddened when they hear about their children's death. But these mothers do not prevent their sons from embarking on their heroic missions. In the *var* of Jaimal Phatta, the mother of Jaimal and Phatta, two Hindu brothers, asks her sons not to give their sister in marriage to Muslim Emperor Akbar as he had ordered. She asked them to fight till become martyr if they are true sons of her, and had taken her milk (Haider 70). This is a story of martyrdom for honour upheld by Hindus (Haider 65-73).

Dulla Bhatti, a very famous hero of *vars*, was a rebel *dacoit*, who attacks caravans and distributes the booty to the poor. Dulla's mother, Ladhi, though, condemns him for not being able to take revenge for the death of his father and grandfather, who were killed by the Moghul kings. She says, "If you are a son of Rajput, think about your life time. All humans are born and all die, but the men, who are killed, their legend lives on." Dulla, then twisting his moustaches, pats his sword and vows to take revenge. He utters: "No one can face me; I'll erase Mughal houses; kill the white tiger to walk on his hide; no king can dare counter me." His mother dislikes his words and warns him not to be so arrogant, as "many came and death took away their pride, so not to be proud of your body, your youth and friends of fair weather." When the Mughal army attacks Dulla's village, loots it, and abducts many women, Dulla replies to his mother's call and charges at the Mughal troops. The Mughal commander requests Dulla's mother to accept him as a brother. She says, "the lion does not eat a fallen prey," ( Haider 90), so Dulla got his prisoners released, but he was killed deceitfully.

These stories of sacrifice are highly inspiring. The story of Dulla's *var* shows royal atrocities on peasants, their looting and attacking of local women, which hurts their pride as they are Rajput, a great warrior tribe. Famous Sufi poet, Shah Hussain through his poetry and his spiritual guide also gave moral support to the rebel forces (Sheikh 51-52). Dulla dies for a kind of "people's rule," and the oppressed folk still today call out for Dulla to come to rescue them. This, of course, is an eternal reward by the masses, which makes Dulla a legendary icon, although he was a rebel for the Mughals. The encouraging role of his mother is also prominent, who pushed him to death and to martyrdom.

## The Concept of Martyrdom in Folk Poetry

Almost all forms of folk poetry promote values attached to the idea of virtue, bravery, and death for a cause; as a poet Minthar Solangi says, those "who died for the motherland, will live forever" (qtd. in Humayuni 259). The poet Shah Latif Bhittai paints a very positive image of women who prepare men for fighting bravely, instead of stopping them out of their love and motherly feelings. So, if circumstances demand, they must forsake their emotions and motivate their sons to fight courageously until achieving victory or achieving death. He explains a woman's feelings as follows:

*I will not believe if they say he ran away*
*But I must trust the news if you kill him*
*If he has wounds on his back I'll die of shame*
*And if he has wounds on his front*
*I'll dress them and will feel proud of it*
*O' my love! If you die in battle I'll cry for you*
*Life is a game of four days but the taunting stays forever*
*Who wears armour dress in war has still a greed for life*
*Brave is the one who always wants war. (Saleem 23)[15]*

Such notions are expressed in "*sur kedaro*" (war poetry). The poet presents a woman first as distraught. She has no news from the warfront, and she is afraid of their martyrdom. Then the poet portrays a war scene with people with injuries and cries; and the same woman is there, showing boldness and inspiring men to fight courageously until death. She tells them that if they bring shame due to their cowardice, even the vultures would not eat their flesh. If the men died, the woman's head would be high. In the poem, initially, she appears as a distressed woman–a typical mother, sister, or wife. Then she overpowers the typical motherly or sisterly feelings. Fahmida Hussain is right in pointing out that such war, courage, and inspiring women characters can be traced back to the Karbala, a proud chapter of Islamic history (380-83).

In the form of folk poetry "*jindri*" (literally meaning "life"), Shaikh Imamuddin Hakim Hazarvi says, "Be humble in youth, do good till you live, death is inevitable, this world is transitory, poor spirit"; and "Neither you did anything good, nor attended the mosque, nor attained martyrdom, so [you] remained an evil-doer forever; poor spirit, how would it be pardoned" (qtd. in Malik 65, 89). Other examples of *jindri* also carry similar messages (Malik 143-77). In a poem about mother's love, an old woman says, "O' spirit, my child, I sacrifice my life for you, do not go away alone, or I'll not let you go, life is only for two days" (Malik 223).

The poetry form of "*tappay*," especially in Pushto, has preserved great record of female emotions, as mother, wife, and beloved. The mother says, "you cannot do anything else bravery; you have taken a Pakhtun mother's milk." The woman says, "I sacrifice myself at your double-barrel gun; it hangs on your shoulder but I walk with [its] pride." And then a loud declaration: "if men could not safeguard you my dear homeland then we, the virgins, would do this pleasant duty." But men are never hesitant in their duty, as they vow: "I'll let me be cut into hundred pieces but would secure you my homeland against the enemy" (qtd. in Rohila 14, 15, 48, 153).

Historically, the Balochs have been through long vendettas in which thousands of brave men were killed on both sides, with the purpose to grab more pastures and settle tribal conflicts. The poets, who once sang about bravery of their own tribesmen and demeaned the enemies, soon realized the futility of war, so they called for peace. The epic phase of poetry then led to romantic poetry. Jam Durrak, the most popular classic Baloch poet, talking about the Baloch Afghan War, is keen to accept death as destiny, instead of servitude (Naseer; Marri 208).[16]

## Folk Tales and Legends

The popular romances of Heer Ranjha, Sussi Punoon, Sohni Mahinwal, Mirza Sahiban, Umar Marvi, and others have been treated by the poets in order to elevate the feelings of earthly love, among common humans, to divinity, thus turning it into a mystic pursuit. Here, love becomes an article of faith, rather the whole of faith, and the lovers (mostly women) become immortal by sacrificing their life for love. The high ideals are, thus, glorified as worth dying for. The common theme of temporariness of this world echoes in these legends. Even those legends, known mainly for romance, adventure, and magic carry this theme. Mian Muhammad Bakhsh in "*Saiful Malook*" says, "'O' mother, your words are order for me, and sacrificing life under your command for me is *shahadat* [martyrdom]"; and 'it is not wise to be committed to this world; this is like a bride, who has millions of husbands, and has eaten them up" (qtd. in Aqeel, 219, 272). Before the spread of modern media, these tales were effectively used to teach popular and folk wisdom, especially the concepts of honour and righteousness.

## Modern Media

### a. Print Material

A good number of books written by ex-military men explain the feelings of those who put the safety and honour of the country above their own life. Their stories are, as expected, full of nationalistic spirit. Soldiers' families and parents are also mentioned in war accounts or analyses. Misconceptions and misinformation about events of war are also clarified. For instance, the book *Janisaraan-e Watan* tells stories of martyrs and fighters of the 1971 war, who get shocked at the death and martyrdom of their fellow soldiers. The magazines and newspapers also play their role in this regard. Biographies of soldiers express feelings of their family. Their mothers have been their source of inspiration and strength through their tribulation. For instance, Colonel Siddique Salik says, "I, as prisoner of war, spent two painful years in Indian camps, and my mother's face remained my source of strength. When I was released, all came to welcome me, but, by then, she had gone to the heaven" (qtd. in Shahid 397).

### b. Modern Poetry and Prose

Martyrdom has been a highly revered and celebrated concept and status for the poets. Innumerable modern poets have paid tribute to the martyrs and soldiers who give their blood to secure the motherland. A good analysis of this poetry has been presented by Qasim Yaqoob. He quotes renowned Urdu poet Josh Maleehabadi as saying, "I swear on the free minded [soldiers] who defeat death; who rise above while buried under tons of dust; one who is fond of martyrdom cannot die; one who dies for the honour of country cannot perish; martyrdom, when it lifts the veil from the rosy face [of life], timeless life sings all around" (qtd. in Yaqoob 154).

Death is a sorrowful event for every normal human being; thus, Majeed Amjad says, "Mothers whose children were bathed in blood, will live with short breaths and tears for centuries" (as above 189). Yet the faith in fortune gives strength at times. If one finds forceful energizing tone in war songs, there is also an appreciating awe-inspiring tone in verses addressing the martyrs. Both types support the spirit of patriotism.

The regional languages of Pakistan have also produced a good deal of patriotic poetry, which gives the touch of genuineness to the feelings of the poet who can communicate directly with the simple folk. Just take one example of Saleem Ahsan: "Well, in the well of my village there is cold water and there is light in the water; the crops are enjoying a new youth and every plant is pleasant with its growth; the sandy rocks of my village are looking to me like Toor [Sinai] of Moses; it is the honour of my land and is pride of my country" (qtd. in Javeid 107-08). A poem, "The Martyr's Mother" by K.R. Zia goes as follows:

> We find the pleasures of paradise beneath your tender feet;
> you are a cool shade of peace, and comfort filled with love and
> affection; why should I not salute you for thousands time;
> you are the respected mother of pride of the nation, the martyr;
> often has the "Toor" of the heart been burnt; [but] you have never
> fainted like meek Moses; you have sacrificed your son for this
> country; [and] you have accepted the orders of Almighty like
> Prophet. (qtd. in Javeid 56-57).

Many fiction writers have taken up patriotic themes. Tariq Jami, for instance, has written about a *mujahid*'s mother, who waits for her son's letter from the warfront, but in vain. She believes that he must be busy fighting with enemy with full strength, and this idea gives her great pride and strength toward her aging body (Javeid 52).

## c. Drama

Urdu stage drama has shown little contents of bravery, valour, and sacrifice, although it has been a popular theme for the public. The main reason could be the lack of a commercialized approach of the theatre owners or the poor quality of the plays themselves. There were a few dramas with nationalistic, patriotic, and historic themes of good literary quality, but they could not be staged. They were more suitable for reading. Examples include the following: *Shaheed-e Wafa* by Abdul Halim Sharer; *Karbala* by Prem Chand; *Jang-e Roos-o Japan'* by Zafar Ali Khan; *Jhansi ki Rani* by Muhammad Umar Noor Elahi; and *Laila-i Watan aur Saib ka Darakht* by Deen Muhammad Taseer. Although these dramas were not performed, they still acquired a wide readership (Ashraf 233-41).

## d. Films

After partition, amid great ideological and identity confusion that Pakistani society was thrown into, the films were produced that portrayed state-friendly themes and versions of history. Thus, some popular films produced after Partition were less objective and of a more propaganda style–for instance, *Kartar Singh* (1959) and *Khak-o Khoon* (1971) based on partition violence. Even today, films are produced on patriotic themes, war heroes, dacoits, and rebels, including Dulla Bhatti. Many popular Punjabi films have very traditional characters of mothers, appealing to the emotions, as well as threatening their sons in case of their disobedience. The "mother's milk," building a sacred relationship, becomes a blackmailing device, when the mother utters the cliché: "I'll not absolve you of my milk, if you do not do this."[17] Women put their sons to wars, dangerous expeditions, and on missions to avenge any misdeed, especially if someone has threatened or blotted the honour of the family, considered embodied in chastity of women. Amid the bloody scenes of the fight, mothers stand proud if their sons die as victorious. The true story of Dulla Bhatti preserves all such contents dramatically. Such legends carry these messages forcefully, for they were believed to protect the honour of the motherland–the mothers, sisters, daughters, all women, and the whole nation. Women in general, and mothers in particular, have been the perpetrators of such an ideology of honour for centuries. Women feel strong when men show courage, and mothers nurture this boldness while raising their sons. Such ideals still hold validity, but deep inside a mother's heart is fear. She does not want her son to be in pain, as she has devoted her youth to raise her children. Such a paradoxical relationship between her love and dreams for sons and the social demands of bravery prevails in all cultures of Pakistan.

The legendary hero of the super-hit Punjabi film *Maula Jutt* (first released 1979), can be seen as the one which made Sultan Rahi (the actual actor) a type character, who challenges all forms of injustice, cruelty, and dishonouring in the films, which also set sales records. Though not widely known or discussed, the hero and villains portrayed two real political rivals respectively–General Zia, president of Pakistan, and Zulfikar Ali Bhutto, elected prime minister, whom Zia managed to hang through a court decision (Mirza 50-52). Sultan Rahi made a Guinness World Record, for appearing in the largest number of his films, which largely carried the same image of a revengeful fighter, an outlaw and a villain standing tall and furious among enormous bloodshed carrying his *gandasa* (big axe)–a symbol of Punjabi chivalry, bravery, and independence,[18] which he shows against the cruel landlords. His dominance over the powerful exploiters was cathartic for millions of viewers; thus, he became a legend, and a symbol of protection, honour, and bravery for the oppressed masses (Akkasi 73). At times, some of these films were banned for violence, too, yet that could not diminish Sultan Rahi's popularity.

Pakistani films have generally portrayed a distorted version of local cultures, false ideology, violence, much romance, censored sex, and brave superhuman heroes. Some well-known Pakistani titles about patriotic themes include the following: *Shaheed, Zarqa, Yeh Amn*, and *Jago hua Sawera*. Many of them flopped because they showed the harsh realities of poverty; thus, they could not thrill people with fantasy or match their taste for fake adventure and glamour (Mirza 43-61).

### e. TV Plays

Few TV plays have been made on the martyrdom themes, whereas there are innumerable stories available. The plays reenacting the *Nishan-e-Haider* (highest military award in Pakistan) heroes are four in number, and are available online. The role of mothers, however, is not portrayed prominently, especially in these plays. Only in the story of Rashid Minhas, the Air Force martyr, the mother is rather prominent, as the young hero is shown expressing desire to fly high up and go beyond the skies. In fact, such plays' contents are so powerful that even the mother's roles need not to be manipulated to sharpen the impact. The overall production quality sways the viewers. The gloomy patriotic song at the end of Rashid Mihas's story is stunning:

> *O martyrs of the right path, portrayal of loyalty,*
> *When you had set out on the journey of martyrdom*
> *The Holy Prophet would have taken you in his arms*
> *Ali[19] must be feeling proud of your courage'* [20]

The power of electronic media is no doubt at the center of inspirational paradigm of all the so-called good and bad warriors nowadays.

## f. War Songs

These songs have a magical effect in boosting the courage and morale of the armies and people during times of war. During the wars of 1965 and 1971, dozens of invigorating songs were produced; they are still very popular and heartening, and are imbued with the spirit of a war between right and wrong, (i.e., Islam and infidelity), thus evoking a spirit of "*jehad.*" A male chauvinistic song, a hit in 1971, shows severe contempt for the Indian Prime Minister, Mrs. Indra Gandhi:

> *These sons are not "for sale" at the shops*
> *O woman! what are you looking for in the bazar?*
> *Great fortune those mothers have*
> *Mothers who gave birth to these [sons]*
> *Great fortune those sisters have*
> *Who raised such brothers in their laps.*

Then, there are appreciative songs for the soldier, who is lovingly called "a colonel" or "general" and whose wife welcomes him home. Another very famous song is full of prayers for the beloved *sepoy*, who has gone to war. This song was sung by the most popular female singer, Noor Jehan, who in another song sings, "the gaze of wives, mothers and sisters prays silently for you–the gorgeous young men of the land." Another war song with army band and a high note of war, which is powerful in its impact, goes as follows:

> *O Mujahid wake up now, it is time for martyrdom,*
> *The victors have no fear of death,*
> *To give life is the greatest jihad,*
> *The Quran says so ... Allah-o-Akbar.*

Here, *jehad, mujahid,* bravery and martyrdom are all praised as male qualities; women are seen as being weak–a fact highlighted and criticized by Rubina Saigol in her analysis of nationalism, militarism, and gender difference (*Qaumparasti* 133-52). Bravery, in all cases, remains the highest watermark of all such feelings and pursuits, and freedom becomes the ultimate aim. Romantic poet, Akhtar Sherani says, 'Love is my life and freedom my faith ... but for freedom I would even sacrifice my love." The powerful voice of Baloch poet, Mir Gul Khan Naseer, roars the following: "Freedom demands on its holy altar the tribute and great sacrifices from the braves. O' my beloved [freedom] raised in the lap of motherland, I have expensed all my belongings. ... It is the call of love for land; the *ghairat* and honour have called now; where is the dagger, and where is the shroud?" (182, 189).

And now look at the defeated soldiers. About 90,000 Pakistanis became prisoners of war in India in 1971. After about two years they returned. Again patriotic songs were created to welcome them back. For instance, Tabish Siddiqui said, "You have always been dear to us but now are even dearer, as you are our great strength; you are our heart and soul" (qtd. in Yaqoob 198).

A detailed analysis of war songs reveals that they forcefully reincarnate images of masculinity defending the beloved (female) motherland. Any threat to motherland is taken as a threat to a woman's chastity, and an enemy crossing borders is seen as intending to 'rape' the woman or mother who cannot defend herself (Saigol, *Qaumiyat* 47-60). This image is linked to the concept of women as commodity and property–something to be possessed and protected. Such a patriarchal foundation of love for nation or country or homeland reduces mothers to mere producers of defenders, whom they raise as brave honour-conscious persons ready to avenge threats coming to the notions of nation. In case of a defender's death, the mother is also given some appreciation, which might bring her a little solace. The glory of martyr's status and the nation's celebration of such death both are attempts to relieve her grief. National and local electronic and print media give coverage to events of death of security personnel; all martyrs are celebrated forever thereafter.[21] The whole mission is geared to enhancing the bond with the motherland. The preference remains that the ordinary people should sacrifice for high ideals. These ideals do not motivate the commoners, the sons and the mothers, at the beginning to perform the duties expected of them, but when death strikes, the high notions do begin to comfort. Yet the ordinary folk rarely accept the high notions so willingly. This fact is explained in the following section.

## Hearts Speaking of Martyrs

The descriptions available about the feelings of the martyrs' families are very touching: pride and grief intertwine as one sees on edited television pieces made for public consumption. In reality, a defender's mother is very much like any mother. Printed material reveals that the elder family members do know the reality of martyr's death, and they try to reconcile the shock of death, but martyr's children are in confusion. People who have military service as a family profession are seen showing more courage and pride in sacrificing their children for the motherland (Shahid).[22]

The details show that martyrs' stories from regular armed forces are disseminated through the media and their family sources. An interesting case, however, is the antistate guerrilla fighters– the self-acclaimed *mujahids*, the *jehadis*, and the outlaws–who work on clandestine missions are liable to be punished when found. They die for their chosen cause, and are called martyrs by their groups.[23] These *mujahids* leave their homes sometime after taking permission from mothers and fathers to go for *jehad*.[24] One such mother said the following about her son's death: "I am happy that I'll be called as a mother of a martyr on the Day of Judgment" (qtd. in Shahid 377). One father said the following: "I am proud that my son died as a martyr; for the holy land, I can sacrifice Riaz Ali and Amjad Ali [his living sons], too" (qtd. in Shahid 431). Similar expressions can be found among Kashmiri mothers of young martyrs: "Yet only one son have I sacrificed on the honour of motherland; if the rest of my children lay their life for the same cause, even then the debt of the martyrs of held Kashmir would not be paid" (qtd. in Shahid 323). Such events abound in a land perpetually at war within its borders and outside, too.

## Ideals and Reality

Martyrdom may follow an intuition. Captain Azam's mother dreamed about Azam having a bleeding heart and chest, but wearing a crown and riding a horse. In the same dream, on her asking he said: "this is a splendid place, with light all over and around." She then realized she had been informed of her son's martyrdom beforehand. Azam died in Kargil, and was awarded *"Tamgha-e Basalat"* in recognition of his bravery (Shahid 26). That was a high recognition. A Siraiki mother-illiterate, rural, poor, powerless, knowing little about the true spirit of religion and political conditions–accepted her son's death as a martyr's one, and when she was asked if she was sure he had become a martyr, she replied in the affirmative.[25] Here was an ordinary woman being comforted by a vague, high concept. Her son had actually been part of a banned organization, but such facts did not matter for her. Many dead bodies belonging to banned organizations are not sent home, but if they are, their communities celebrate them as real martyrs. It is true that militant outfits have recruited their members, fighters, and suicide bombers from economically impoverished areas. The families have provided this cannon fodder both knowingly and unknowingly. A number of stories of those engaged in activities in Kashmir and Afghanistan, through militant organizations, and embracing death, are recorded. Undoubt-edly, they go on such missions willingly and enthusiastically, at least the stories tell this. They mostly inform their families, especially the parents, and may leave instructions for their children to get education and carry on their fathers' missions (Shahid 376).

For instance, a Pakistani fighter, Younus, on his last trip to Afghanistan, advised his mother not to cry on his death as a martyr because he was going to give his "life for upholding Islam in the face of devil squad' (qtd. in Shahid 379). Younus, a young boy of fifteen years, got twenty-one days training in Kunar, Afghanistan, and fell ill afterward. His mother worried about his long illness and prayed: "O God! I have devoted this son for uplift of your religion, and had hoped that he would become martyr for this cause; I'll be mother of a martyr, and he would welcome me at the door of Paradise" (qtd. in Shahid 376-77). He recovered, got religious and military training for another two years, and finally died in Afghanistan as a commando. Persons engaged in guerrilla or antistate warfare are more motivated, for they have to break a psychological barrier as well, which makes a regular military or security person's career seem more rewarding and honoured. Military/ paramilitary and security training prepares and teaches the discipline needed for the job. It instils patriotism as well, unknown to nonmilitary people. Many young men join these forces thoughtlessly, but later they find them challenging and worthwhile. People closer to such environment are more motivated than those at distance, yet the spirit to serve the nation or religion may spark in anyone anywhere because of an overall environment of gratitude, appreciation, and pride attached to it.

## The New Culture of Martyrdom

Using the notion of an eternal reward after death, terrorist networks have been brainwashing and exploiting enthusiastic young men, who have their own conceptions of *"jehad"* (holy war), *"kafir"* (infidel), and *"shahadat"* (martyrdom). These terrorists have been killing thousands of target people along with their own death. A boy under terrorist training may ask, "When are you going to give me the suicide jacket? Let me become *shaheed* by killing these infidels. I am keen to go to paradise, where the Prophet (peace be upon him) would welcome me, and I'll be awarded by *huris* [the companions in paradise]." This typical dogmatic approach, as a short-cut to paradise, has been projected and instilled in the minds of innocent persons who are prepared to kill themselves for *huris*. A broad range of techniques are used for this purpose. It is interesting to see that the role of mothers, if involved, in infusing this type of martyrdom was seen only in illiterate and poorer areas. These are areas where mothers do not know the true nature of their son's mission, and if they had known, no typical mother would have approved it. However, indoctrination by mothers is common in cases of sectarian and religious conflicts, but research is not available to provide proof of this indoctrination. This aspect needs more investigation. Some literature reveals that those who went for *jehad* in Kashmir and Afghanistan knew their mission, and their families were aware, too, at least partially. The mission was focused against the infidels. The persuasion videos shown to them are marvelous; they can declare anyone infidel, as the label was also given to top religious and political leadership of Pakistan in a video with Dr. Arshad Waheed, depicted as a hero, as well as a successful preacher of *jehad* (Abbas, *Intehapasad* 23-4).

Earlier it was a widely held belief that "poverty, unemployment, madrassah education or brainwashing by local semi-educated clerics and aggressive response to the militant organizations' recruitment drives, all persuaded the young poor males to *jehad*" (Abbas *Intehapasand* 21).This was the case in the early stage of terrorism, which lasted until 1999. But later, a particular interpretation of Islam, more suitable to terrorists, became instrumental to a large extent in recruiting men to join. Reportedly, the chief of banned outfit, Tehrik-e Taliban Pakistan, used to issue "tickets to paradise"; and a certificate of *Shahadat* (martyrdom) was also given after death. The prestige attached to martyrdom also included certain privileges for the deceased's family. They were actively remembered and celebrated as martyrs to encourage others to join (Abbas *Pakistan's* 67-68).

In the second phase of militancy[26] in Pakistan, there was little connection between poverty and terrorism; rather, a multitude of factors (cultural, political, social, and economic) worked together, which made becoming a terrorist a deliberate choice. Terrorists began coming from educated, middle-class backgrounds. They were young professionals or students; this fact makes one think about the supportive role of educated middle-class mothers as well in promoting the terrorist's agenda through socialization and through indirect actions (Abbas *Intehapasand* 22). Women have been suicide bombers, although they are few in number. They were first used of by *Lashkar-e Jhangvi*, a banned sectarian outfit, now active under a new name, who trained women *fida'een* (devotees ready to sacrifice) (Abbas *Pakistan's* 62).[27] There is lot difference between killing oneself for a purpose, and asking one's own son or daughter to sacrifice their life. One should dread the day when mothers intentionally make their children suicide bombers.

## Findings of the Interviews

Interviews with forty-five mothers and family women of persons working in defence/security services were conducted. It was a difficult task, making mothers and relatives of martyrs speak up their feelings about death of their dear ones. Selection and availability of such sample was not easy, as all these cases were not covered in media. Selection was made to ensure variety in sample. Diverse views and aspirations about martyrdom were received. The respondents related to presently in-service persons, expressed the belief that "death is inevitable, so why to be afraid of it, and above all, martyrdom is a big ideal; a unique status." Contrarily, it was revealed that although the martyrs are generally believed to be alive, the "separation and anguish are mind-bending." A daughter of a junior commissioned officer found her father very soft, yet she will not let her own children join the military. A wife of an army officer gave a similar reply: "I pray him to be a *ghazi* [successful living soldier], and do not think of him as a martyr; this is a feeling which cannot be anticipated unless you come to face it as a reality; and when realized, it is only God who consoles us. Anyhow, such thoughts about close relations give us a tremor in the spine." Many mothers aspired for their children to follow their soldier father as a role model. These mothers prepare children for such a laudable role. A mother of a security person serving in the SWAT operation postponed his marriage until he returned safe and sound, for she feared his return was uncertain. A wife of security guard expressed her concern as well as the feeling that "the country is in trouble and needs such services, and *shahadat* is all about your intentions; circumstances can take people anywhere; the destiny has to happen."

During the 1960s and 1970s, in areas known as "the sword arm of country," young men joined the army because of unemployment and poverty. But such men were highly respected as *faujis* (soldiers).[28] A sister of two soldiers and now mother of a soldier recalled the following: "Brothers used to go and our mom and we the siblings used to wait for a letter or news from them for months, especially when the country was at war in 1965 and 1971." Of course, war is not only fought at borders and cantonments; soldiers' families and the whole nation are involved in varying degrees; mothers then become the greatest' emotional contributors to support war. A soldier's wife reported that she had idealized her husband's profession, but as a mother of young children, she is now hesitant to think of sending them to military service. Another mother declined to allow her son to enter a police job. Four mothers were shocked and displeased at the question and the idea that their sons could be killed on the job in the coast guard. This shows how conflicted the mother is. But one participating mother also said: "We are nothing without our country, and at times mothers become selfish." Amid such bewildering ideas, when mothers consider the judgment by their children, their own conscience and the promised incentives in hereafter, they overpower the fear and, then become bold.[29]

The priority and incentives for serving the nation as soldiers have been changing. New occupations have emerged. Now wars are less bloody, more technology driven. Earlier, the mothers and family used to socialize and motivate children for laying life for the nation, but that is less now,[30] despite a wonderful support system for the martyrs. Now the spirit of sacrifice is nurtured through institutions–the media, religious institutions, the educational system, and the unofficial agencies recruiting fighters, regardless of their motives or legitimacy. It, however, cannot be deduced that patriotism has decreased. Women in their various capacities, mothers being the foremost, bestow love and nurture strength among males, who pay it back through selfless struggle to defend them–women, mothers, motherland. This is men's way of appreciating them. The folk literature as well as the modern poetry and prose carry on fortifying this tradition.

## Conclusion

The prevalent notions, feelings, and reactions of the common people and those affected by death of security and defence persons can be analyzed with the help of perspectives outlined in the chapter. The very subjective natures of love (for mother, family, and motherland), sacrifice, grief, and pride hinder scientific explanation for the phenomenon of acceptance of martyrdom. Mothers also have multiple notions in their mind about martyrdom, hence a range of reactions is recorded. On the basis of the literature review, discussions, fieldwork, and personal experiences, we can confidently conclude that martyrdom has been an evolving concept in changing sociopolitical conditions. The old and new generations of mothers, sisters, and wives, as socialized beings and socializing agents, do respond to change. Now, the security related jobs are not merely jobs–sources of livelihood–but a matter of pride and reward, too. As one mother explained, "after all even the prophets had been fighting for the noble cause"; another mother said, "if my son has saved so many lives by giving his life, it is surely a matter of pride." So inevitably martyrdom becomes both a religious obligation, inviting great reward in paradise, and a national duty. For secular minds, there is little motivation in such a death, so only the religious-nationalistic paradigm works. Hence, martyrdom has much incentive-giving away one transitory life and having an eternal return. Thus, the family's grief is mixed with a tint of spiritual elation. The popular culture, media, and folklore all support the religious and nationalistic conceptions of sacrifice. The voices of reason in this matter, at least, have proved faint, and, hence, defeated. Both the martyrs and the mothers of martyrs stand out as the ultimate medal winners.

## Endnotes

1   A good book explaining the phenomenon of *jehadis* in Pakistan is Mir, Amir, *The Fluttering Flag of Jehad*. Mashal, 2008.

2   The authors have analyzed the war songs in Urdu and Punjabi for they knew these as their first language and mother tongue respectively; for the rest of the regional languages, translation was used. Two books were also helpful in it: one by Saigol, and other by Yaqoob, listed in the Works Cited.

3   Irene Oh, "Engendering Martyrs: Muslim Mothers and Martyrdom."

4   For instance, see publications of Mahbub ul Haq Development Centre, Islamabad.

5   One film, *Salute*, was made about Aitezaz Ahsan, a young school boy who died and became a martyr after stopping a terrorist attack at his school gate.

6   "*Suhag*" means the good luck, pride, protection, and happiness of having a husband.

7   The word "*ghairat*" as used in Pakistan cannot be exactly translated. It is sense of honour, very strong spirit to defend it, and a cultural notion and ingredient of social respect instilled through socialization.

8   Actual verse is: *Shahadat hai matloob-o-maqsood-e momin, Na maal-e ghaneemat na kiswerkusha'i.*

9   Khushhal was a warrior poet of a warrior Pakhtun tribe. He has the strongest voice in welcoming martyrdom.

10  "*Sila-e shaheed kiya hai, tub-o taab-e jawidana.*"

11  Statement showing the kernel confession of Islamic belief.

12  "*Tadon faqir shatabi ban'da jad jaan ishq wich haaray Hoooooo.*"

13  Poetry of all known Sufi poets is available online in various formats.

14  Some of the stories are referred to in Raza Hamdani's book.

15  Same ideas are also available in Pushto *Tappay* sung by women. *Tappa* is a form of poetry with one small and one long line; not necessarily having any linked meanings but only the rhymes.

16  "*Kalat kabhi ghulami ki zanjeeron ka aseer nahin raha, nang-o naamus ki hifazat ki khatar hum nay maut ko apna muqaddar thehra liya hai*" (208).

17  Children are obliged to obey mothers for having taken mother's milk; idiomatically, it is the whole contribution of mothers to their upbringing.

18  "*Gandasa*" was first introduced in films through Sultan Rahi's character, based on a short story by Ahmed Nadeem Qasmi.

19  Prophet's cousin renowned for his legendary bravery.

20  "*Ai rah-e haq kay shaheedo, wafa ki tasweero*," a famous patriotic Urdu song, available online.

21  "*Eh puttar hatan tay nahin vikday*," a famous Punjabi war song.

22  "*A mard-e mujahid jag zara ab waqt-e shahadat hai aaya*," a famous Urdu war song, saying, "Get up O brave fighter man, the time for martyrdom has approached."

23  It reminds me of Zeba Noor, a friend and colleague of mine [Anwar Shaheen]. She was on her security duty when PIA airbus crashed in Kathmandu (Nepal). Seeing her name in martyr's list in M.R. Shahid's book was so heartening for me, as if she is alive and will remain so forever.

24  For instance, the families of three *Nishan-e-Haiders*: Major Shabbir Sharif Shaheed, Hawaldar Lalik Jan Shaheed, Major Muhammad Akram Shaheed. Additionally one can see mother of Captain Zulfikar Ali Shaheed, among thousands more martyrs. Parents of Mariam Mukhtar, the first Air Force (lady) GD pilot martyred during training, is another case in point.

25  The authors do not intend to question their beliefs, since martyrdom is a status to be accorded by God Almighty. The definition of martyrdom involves a broad range of conditions and degrees. This chapter is mainly about the popular concepts and practices.

26  It is beyond the scope of this chapter to discuss the concepts of *jehad* and *mujahid*. Basically, what people think as right, becomes their mission, so fighters of conflicting ideologies fight and die and are labeled as "martyrs" or otherwise by various groups depending on their respective ideologies.

27  Conveyed to us by Tahira Shahid Khan, author of *Beyond Honour*, Karachi: Oxford University Press.

28 Muhammad Amir Rana identifies three phases of militancy in Pakistan. In the first phase, little persuasion and religious affiliation of certain families for engaging in militancy was found; in the second phase, certain families were growing more religious and accepting militancy as a way to change the society; but in the third phase (after 2007), family is left behind; now there are found hard-liner individuals, sworn in to organizations, having a spirit of revenge and urge to change the world by their militancy (74, 81).

29 Once the Lal Masjid (Islamabad) cleric, Ghazi Abdul Rashid offered the Afghan Taliban to send women suicide attackers, but they refused to accept it, calling it un-Islamic. With the expanding network and influence of Daesh, more women are being persuaded to offer themselves as fighters, with the aim of gaining *shahadat*.

30 The war songs have boosted the image, morale, and popularity of such soldiers.

31 One Urdu short story by Sadiq Hussain suffices to show the transformation. A soldier's wife sees her young son, digging a trench, and posing as if hiding since the war was on. Her heart fills with fear. Then she receives the news that her husband was killed in war and was then honoured as a martyr. She goes out, puts his father's hat on her son's head, and gives him his father's gun (*Afsanay*, Book Home, 2012).

32 A young blind mother, living in Karachi, wished her son would grow up and conquer Kashmir. The intelligent and well-built son, now nineteen, has recently been rejected in the army selection process. This is one of those innumerable examples, where the enthusiastic youth could not get through selection, while their family was keen for it.

## Works Cited

Abbas, Ali. "Intehapasand Sargarmiyan aur Naey Rujhanaat." *Tajziyat*, no. 20, 2010, pp. 19-26.

Abbas, Hassan. *Pakistan's Drift into Extremism Allah, the Army and America's War on Terror.* Pentagon Press, 2005.

Abid, Salman. *Dehshatgardi Aik Fikri Mutal'a.* Jumhoori Publications, 2016.

Aqeel, Shafi. *Punjabi kay Panch Qadeem Sha'ir.* Anjuman Taraqqi-e

Urdu, 1970.

Akkasi, Zahid. *Sultan Rahi Pakistani Filmon ka Sultan.* Jamhoori Publications, 2010.

Ashraf, A.B. *Urdu Stage Drama Radha Kanihya say Anarkali Tak Urdu Stage Dramay ki Mukammal Tarikh.* National Language Authority, 1986.

Bloch, Lt. Colonol (R) Sikandar Khan. *Janisaraan-e Watan.* Dost Publications, 2008.

Dadi, Iftikhar. "Nuclearization and Pakistani Popular Culture since 1998." *South Asian Cultures of the Bomb, Atomic Publics and the State in India and Pakistan,* edited by Itty Abraham, Orient BlackSwan, 2009, pp. 173-94.

Devji, Faisal. *Landscapes of the Jihad Militancy, Morality, Modernity.* Foundation Books, 2005.

Evans, Suzanne. *Mothers of Heroes, Mothers of Martyrs World War I and the Politics of Grief,* McGill-Queen's University Press, 2007.

Haider, Sajjad. *Varain.* Institute of Folk Heritage, 1980.

Hamdani, Raza, editor and translator. *Razmiya Dastanain.* Institute of Folk Heritage, 1981.

Hasrat, Muhammad Younus, *Kalam Baba Farid Ganj Shakar.* Book Home, 2004.

Humayuni, Niaz, translator. *Sindhi Shairi, Qadeem-o Jadeed Shura.* Academy Adbiyat Pakistan, 1987.

Hussain, Fahmida. *Image of 'Woman' in the Poetry of Shah Abdul Latif.* Eng. Translated by Amjad Siraj. University of Karachi, 2001.

Javeid, Inamul Haq, and Amjad Ali Bhatti. *Kalam-e Sutan Bahu.* National Book Foundation, 2016.

Javeid, Inamul Haq. *Pakistan in Punjabi Literature.* Maktaba-i-Fanoos, 1993.

Jetters, Alexis, Orleck, Annelise, and Taylor Diana (eds.), *Politics of Motherhood, Activist Voices from Left to Right,* Hanover: Dartmouth College, 1997.

Khattak, Purdil, *Pushto Shairi (Qadeem aur Jadeed Shura ka Kalam).* Academy Adbiyat Pakistan, 1987.

Koreeja, Khawaja Tahir Mahmood, editor and translator. *Diwan Khawaja Ghulam Farid Bamutabiq Qalmi Nuskkha Ha'ey Qadeem.* Al-Faisal Publishers, 2002.

Kunjahi, Sharif. *Punjabi Shaeri say Intikhab.* Academy Adbiyat Pakistan, 1983.

Kunjahi, Sharif. *Kahey Farid*. Institute of Folk Heritage, 1987.

Malik, Shaheen, editor and translator. *Jindri*. Institute of Folk Heritage, 1980.

Marri, Mir Mitha Khan. *Durr-e Cheen, Jam Durrak kay Balochi Kalam ka Urdu Nasri Tarjma*. Academy Adbiyat Pakistan, 1987.

Mirza, Amjad Ayub. *Misrepresentation of Culture in Pakistani Cinema*. Book Home, 2014.

Naseer, Gul Khan. *Lahu ki Pukar*. Awami Adabi Anjuman, 1988.

Oh, Irene. "Engendering Martyrs: Muslim Mothers and Martyrdom." *Religious Ethics in a Time of Globalism*, edited by Elizabeth M. Bucar and Aaron Stalnaker, Palgrave Macmillan, 2012, pp. 69-75.

Oswell, David. *Culture and Society An Introduction to Cultural Studies*. London: Sage Publications, 2006. Print.

Rana, Muhammad Amir. *The Militant Development of a Jihadi Character in Pakistan*. Narratives Publication, 2015.

Rohila, Parto, editor and translator. *Tappay*. Institute of Folk Heritage, 1979.

Saleem, Agha, translator. *Lalan Lal Latif Kahey*. Institute of Folk Heritage, 1984.

Saigol, Rubina. *Qaumiyat, Taleem aur Shanakht*. Fiction House, 1997.

Saigol, Rubina. *Qaumparasti, Askariyat aur Sinfi Taqseem*. Fiction House, 2017.

Schleifer, Aliah. *Motherhood in Islam*. The Islamic Texts Society, USA, 1996.

Shahid, M.R. *Shaheedan-e Watan*. Al-Faisal, 2006.

Sheikh, Asad Saleem. *Dulley di Baar*. Fiction House, 2015.

Yaqoob, Qasim. *Urdu Sha'ri par Jangon kay Asraat (Tehqeeq-o Tanqeed)*. City Book Point, 2015.

Chapter Three

# Military Moms in the Spotlight: What Media Attention on Mothers in the U.S. Military Means for Public Policy

Sarah Cote Hampson

In February 2010, the story of Alexis Hutchinson–a U.S. Army cook and single mother who went AWOL rather than leave behind her infant son and deploy to Afghanistan–hit several prominent media outlets. Hutchinson's story is significant in that it sparked, for a short time, a national discussion about the issue of mothers serving in the U.S. military. Two years later, in 2012, Terran Echegoyen-McCabe and Christina Luna, both active duty service members in the U.S. Air Force, were photographed breastfeeding their children at Fairchild Air Force Base in Washington. The photo set off yet another wave of media attention on mothers serving in the U.S. military as well as public debate about the appropriateness of integrating the roles of *mother* and *soldier*.

The experiences of these women are far from unique, yet the reaction to their stories serves to highlight how relatively hidden the lives of mothers in uniform are from the public eye. In this chapter, I examine the public discourse surrounding Hutchinson's, Echegoyen-McCabe's, and Luna's stories by specifically looking at the media coverage that enveloped each of them briefly. I locate my analysis of this coverage in political science and sociolegal literature that critiques the role of public discourse in shaping public policy outcomes. I argue that the public discourse surrounding these three women serves to focus public attention on negative framing of mothers who are serving. Rather than having a public discussion about the needs of single or breastfeeding mothers in the U.S. military, the media instead focuses on such women as deviant–deviant mothers and/or deviant service members. Scholars have shown that such negative framing can have a significant impact on policy outcomes (e.g. Hancock; Haltom and McCann). I argue that negative public discourse around mothers in uniform has reinforced existing informal norms that stigmatize mothers in the U.S. military.

Although U.S. military policies on breastfeeding and deployment for new mothers have advanced in recent years, mothers who are currently serving still face a variety of barriers–both cultural and legal–to their full acceptance and integration into the U.S. military. I contend that media attention on mothers serving in the U.S. military need not be the focus of negative framing and discourse. Rather, by increasing the visibility of these women and by applying more positive framing to their stories, media attention could go a long way toward bringing about real social change for mothers in uniform.

## Connecting Public Discourse and Public Policy

For decades, scholars from various disciplines have used the concept of "media frames" to describe both how journalists organize the news and how readers decode stories. As Todd Gitlin explains, "media frames are persistent patterns of cognition, interpretation, and presentation, of selection, emphasis, and exclusion, by which symbol-handlers routinely organize discourse, whether verbal or visual" (7). Certain key words and phrases can act as symbols of larger ideas and meanings, and media's choices to use certain frames can have an effect on how readers view a particular issue. Public discourse can be shaped by how media choose to define terms, employ particular narratives, and focus on some elements of a story rather than others. How an issue is framed in the media–for example, whether drug use is discussed in the context of criminal justice or public health–is a key determinant of the direction that public discourse will take (Altheide). As some political psychologists have argued, the choice of which frames or symbols to use–or not to use–can have an effect on the reader's perception of an issue, depending on his or her own preexisting feelings (Gamson et al.; Sears). Specifically, as David Sears points out, these symbols are meant to invoke particular predispositions. For example, "busing" evokes racial attitudes, whereas the "Korean War" evoked anticommunism. "But," says Sears, "the more critical implication is that changing the symbolic meaning of any *given* attitude object can evoke a new set of predispositions.... A symbol like 'choice' might evoke predispositions that boost support for abortion, which 'murder' obviously would evoke less helpful predispositions" (129).

The literature on media framing has provided ample evidence to demonstrate the existence of media frames, but what is the potential political impact of media framing? To answer this question, I locate the analysis within a sociolegal literature connecting public discourse with how people come to think about and make decisions concerning the law, legal concepts, and legal symbols, such as "rights"–a process that in sociolegal scholarship is known as "legal consciousness." Many sociolegal scholars have found connections between public discourse, the development of legal consciousness, and the shape and direction of public policy (e.g., Bumiller; Burgess; Gilliom; Haltom and McCann; Marshall; Nielsen and Beim; Scheingold). William Haltom and Michael McCann, for instance, argue that the one significant political impact of media frames is that symbols and idea shortcuts, such as frames, shape how people construct legal knowledge. How people understand what the law is and what they think about it is largely shaped by messages they receive from the media.

Another area of communications scholarship, known as "diffusion theory," also speaks to this process of individuals forming their thinking and reaction to new ideas around them. In this literature, the media is significant to the adoption of new ideas (for instance, in the development and implementation of new public policies) through a process known as "diffusion." As Everett Rogers points out, "most individuals evaluate an innovation [or idea] ... through the subjective evaluations of near peers who have adopted the innovation." Furthermore, Rogers explains, mass media channels are more effective in forming and changing attitudes toward new ideas, since they can reach more individuals with information about the "early adopters" of new ideas (36). Once a collection of individuals have had the opportunity to come into contact with the ideas of early adopters, they can seek information that leads to decisions about whether or not to adopt these ideas themselves and pass them along. Rogers outlines five steps that lead to the full adoption of ideas in society, the first of which is the exposure to knowledge of an "innovation" or idea.

It is with the diffusion of legal knowledge that political scientists and sociolegal scholars are also most concerned, as they focus on the importance of the connections between media framing, legal knowledge, and legislative agenda-setting. This connection is documented in decades of scholarship by political scientists making similar claims to those of communications and media scholars (e.g. Iyengar and Kinder; Bennett; Edelman). As E.E. Schattschneider puts it, "In politics as in everything else, it makes a great difference whose game we play" (47). Haltom and McCann argue that the most significant impact of media framing is that the media produce prevailing currents of legal knowledge, which "have encouraged particular ideological framings of events while deterring or displacing other equally plausible interpretive frames from contesting parties" (285). In other words, some ideas or frames become more popular in the public discourse, and these ideas constitute our "legal knowledge." On the flip side, however, this means that the more unpopular ideas or frames essentially do not form our legal knowledge, and therefore do not make it to the legislative agenda. This is significant because certain groups can be effectively cut off from legislative agenda setting simply by virtue of how they have been framed in public discourse.

Further complicating the significance of discourse around mothers in the U.S. military is the fact that the military itself is arguably a unique institution when it comes to the way in which it is impacted by certain kinds of discourse. For instance, several scholars have presented evidence that a widening cultural and ideological gap exists between military and civilian society (e.g. Holsti), which makes it even more difficult for certain ideas that have taken hold in civilian society to gain traction within the culture of the U.S. military. The fact that many scholars still find evidence of a dominant "masculine culture" (e.g. Enloe) within the U.S. military–despite decades of women integrating into nearly all areas and ranks across all branches of the military–highlights the difficulty that military mothers face in making their experiences heard within this institution. An examination of how mothers in uniform are portrayed in the media is therefore important–

both in terms of exploring how their voices are heard and their stories are told as well as in terms of asking to what extent their media portrayal may impact their access to and influence on the public policy agenda.

## Methods

In order to obtain a representative sampling of how the media covered the stories of Hutchinson, Echegoyen-McCabe, and Luna, I conducted a search in LexisNexis and Access World News[1] and used their surnames to find as many references to these service members as I could. From LexisNexis, I collected twenty-seven local and national newspaper articles, sixteen magazine and online articles, seven letters to the editor, and fifteen transcripts of television and radio newscasts (a total of sixty-five sources). From Access World News, I collected twenty-four newspaper and/or newswire articles, one television broadcast transcript, and one radio newscast transcript (a total of twenty-six sources). To analyze these sources, I employed "progressive theoretical sampling"–a qualitative method of textual analysis (Altheide). Analysis involved an interpretive, bottom-up approach to concept generation, and reading each source carefully multiple times in order to gain an understanding of the dominant themes in each set of stories.[2] This allowed me to detect a dominant frame of "deviancy" that ran across the coverage of these women's respective stories. Furthermore, I noted that two types of deviancy were discussed in these stories. First, Hutchinson, Echegoyen-McCabe and Luna were portrayed as "deviant service members"–that is, media coverage ultimately framed these women as problematic in terms of their ability to fulfill their duties as service members. Second, I noted that Hutchinson, Echegoyen-McCabe, and Luna were also, in different ways, portrayed as "deviant mothers" (see Patricia Sotirin, chapter one of this volume, for a discussion of tropes of motherhood).

## Alexis Hutchinson

In November of 2009, Army Specialist Alexis Hutchinson did not report with her unit to deploy to Afghanistan. The next day, Specialist Hutchinson voluntarily gave herself up and was arrested by military police, and her then ten-month old son Kamani was placed in child protective services until her mother could arrive to care for him. As well as being an Army cook, Specialist Hutchinson was a single mother, and the father of her child did not play a role in her life or the life of her child. The Army reported that she had failed to file a valid family care plan with them, which it requires of all deploying parents. Hutchinson argued that she did file such a plan in compliance with Army regulations, but that at the last minute her mother, who was the intended caregiver, backed out of her commitment because she was caring for too many other relatives and did not feel that she could also handle an infant. Hutchinson applied for an extension to find another caregiver, but this extension was not granted, and, her lawyer said, "The day before she was forced to deploy, they told her you have a choice to make, but your duty is to get on that plane" (qtd. in Metinko). It was even suggested by Army officials that Hutchinson place her son in foster care in order to deploy. Instead, Hutchinson chose to go AWOL.

The Army does not allow single parents to enlist, but in the course of two long, ongoing wars in Iraq and Afghanistan, it is not unusual for parents to become divorced and gain sole custody, for parents to be widowed, and, as was the case with Specialist Hutchinson, for single women to become pregnant. There are an estimated seventy thousand single parents currently serving in the Armed Forces, and the Army has the greatest number of these –as many as half the total number (CNN, "Largest NATO"). From November 2009 through February 2010, when she received a "less than honorable discharge" from the Army, Hutchinson's story captured the media's attention, and a public discourse surrounding her specific case evoked more general concerns about single parents– especially single mothers–serving in the Armed Forces.

## Terran Echegoyen-McCabe and Christina Luna

In May of 2012, Senior Airman Terran Echegoyen-McCabe and Staff Sgt. Christina Luna posed in a park for a photo shoot for the breastfeeding support group Mom2Mom. Luna was pictured breastfeeding her infant daughter, and Echegoyen-McCabe was pictured breastfeeding her ten-month old twin daughters. The shoot was planned to promote Breastfeeding Awareness Month, and to "encourage more women to breastfeed, including in public," according to the group's coordinator, Crystal Scott (Geranios). Both women, members of the U.S. Air Force Reserves, and stationed at Fairchild Air Force Base, just outside of Spokane, Washington, were photographed breastfeeding in their

Washington Air National Guard Uniforms. It was this fact that caused controversy.

Soon after the photographs were posted on the photographer's website, National Guard spokesman, Keith Kosik, released a public statement noting that the women had committed a violation of uniform regulations, which prohibits the use of a uniform to promote a civilian cause. Kosik noted that the servicewomen would likely not be disciplined, but that the Guard would use this incident as an "opportunity for education" about uniform policy (Geranios). The photographs quickly went viral, gaining national and even international attention, and sparked a debate that raised questions about the appropriateness of public breastfeeding in general, and about breastfeeding in uniform in particular.

## Discourses of Deviancy

### Deviant Service Members

The first facet of Hutchinson's deviancy as depicted in the news coverage pertains specifically to her deviance from her duty. Hutchinson's deviance as a service member was discussed largely in the context of personal responsibility (and her lack of it). This lack of personal responsibility frame is one that scholars have observed in various forms elsewhere. Martin Gilens, for example, documents the racialization of welfare recipients in the media. Additionally, Gilens shows that the framing of welfare recipients as black correlates with public opinion data reflecting public perceptions of African Americans as lacking a work ethic (76). Ange-Marie Hancock's *The Politics of Disgust* goes further to highlight the link between what she calls a "public identity"–a kind of media frame–and moral judgments. Hancock argues that the public identity of the "welfare queen" as a black, single mother on welfare is a stereotype used persistently in the language employed by the media to talk about welfare recipients. The coded variables that Hancock identifies include "don't work," "single-parent family," and "system abusers."

As Alexis Hutchinson was a soldier in the service of her country, it may seem that on the one hand she could be framed in distinct contrast to the public identity of the "welfare queen." Yet Hutchinson's identity as an African American, single mother opens her up to the possibility of being painted with the same deviant brush as the welfare queen, with respect to her lack of personal responsibility and work ethic. It is this element of the welfare queen image–specifically, a lack of personal responsibility–that was used in media accounts of Hutchinson to frame her story. Hutchinson's choice to go AWOL rather than leave her child with strangers is an aspect of her story that can be framed within the context of shirking her duty. She is, thus, susceptible to being framed as just another African American who lacks work ethic. It is through this ideological construct of "personal responsibility" that Hutchinson can be viewed as a deviant soldier.

The favoured description of most news sources for Hutchinson's actions on the day of her deployment was to say that she "skipped" it. Overall, some version of this word was used thirty-five times to refer to Hutchinson's refusal to deploy. Words like "shirked" (three times) and "failed" (twice) were also used in this context, but "skipped" was by far the most widely used verb. One letter to the editor describes the sentiment behind this frame in unobscured language: "When she made the choice to join the Army, the possibility of deployment was understood. With the paycheck comes the responsibility and obligation to fulfill your duties. If you are unfit to fulfill those duties, find another job.... It is time for Hutchinson to take responsibility for her actions" (Pagano). In her CNN interview, Meredith Leyva, author of *Married to the Military: A Survival Guide for Military Wives, Girlfriends and Women in Uniform* stated, "This is the commitment you sign up for in the military. These are professionals. They need to be professional about it" (CNN, "President Obama"). These comments express incredulity at the idea of excusing Hutchinson for her deviant behavior. Host Michael Martin, in an NPR interview with Hutchinson's lawyer, also vocalized this public sentiment: "But others say that you cannot enlist in the military while this country is fighting two wars, particularly in the area in which she is serving, and not expect to deploy and not expect to have a plan in place" ("Army Mom Refuses to Deploy"). These statements question Hutchinson's commitment to her duty. The notion that servicewomen often become pregnant to avoid deployment is a common stereotype that I have documented elsewhere in my interviews with servicewomen (Hampson).

In addition to public questions about Hutchison's deviancy, the Army officials commenting on Hutchinson's actions did their best to frame her as a deviant soldier, which is not surprising given that it was in their interest to do so. Three articles quoted an Army statement as saying: "The investigation revealed evidence, from both other soldiers and from Private Hutchinson herself, that she didn't intend to deploy to Afghanistan with her unit and deliberately sought ways out of the deployment" (Dao; Lee; "Single Mom Discharged, Army Says"). Several reports also portrayed Army officials as magnanimous in their decision to settle Hutchinson's case by "other than honorably" discharging her and retracting all veterans' benefits, rather than court-martialing her. "The Army filed criminal charges last month against Hutchinson of Oakland, Calif., but a general at neighboring Fort Stewart chose to settle the case by granting her an administrative discharge rather than try her in a military court" reported the Associated Press (Bynum). "Single Mother is Spared Court-Martial," read the headline of the *New York Times* (Dao). Hutchinson was "spared" by the Army, when it could have rightfully done far worse to punish her deviance. Another CNN broadcast also indicated with its language that Hutchinson had, in a sense, "got away with it"; she was "lucky":

> **FRIEDMAN:** This is the luckiest soldier in the United States military, right now.... They give soldiers a reasonable opportunity to take care of it, and you're right, they did give Miss Hutchinson an additional period of time. While she's going to go on a dishonorable discharge and lose substantial veteran and military benefits, the fact is she could be facing court martial, she won't. She's a very lucky soldier.

> **WHITFIELD:** So, Richard, do you see the far-reaching implications, there will be other military personnel who will state the same kind of case? And there's precedence here now, they may have to follow that ruling.

> **HERMAN:** Yeah, there is precedent for this case now, Fred. She got a less than honorable discharge. She was relieved from facing a court martial which would have resulted in federal criminal charges against her. That felony conviction would have followed her through life.... She caught a good break. (CNN, "Largest NATO")

Terran Echegoyen-McCabe and Christina Luna did not face the same direct heavy criticism from the Air Force National Guard in public statements that Hutchinson had faced from the Army. This is likely because their offense was considerably less significant from the point of view of their command. Nevertheless, the women were also publicly criticized by Air Force spokesmen. Although there are no regulations specifically regarding breastfeeding while in uniform, the two airmen were consistently labelled as "wrong" while their actions were seen as a "violation of uniform regulations" by the Washington Air National Guard's spokesman, Capt. Keith Kosik. Interestingly, however, Kosik went out of his way to make it clear that the Guard was making a distinction between the women's actions as mothers and their actions as service members.

> *Military regulations prohibit the use of the 'uniform, title, rank or military affiliation to further a cause, promote a product or imply an endorsement. If you look at the press coverage that's out there right now, it has been construed as a battle against breastfeeding ... the fact is they're not being persecuted. The fact is breastfeeding was never an issue for us. (qtd. in Bannach)*

Capt. Kosik tries to make it clear that it was merely the implication that they were promoting a civilian cause that made their actions in uniform deviant. However, there is a fine line between this distinction and framing the action of breastfeeding in uniform at all as inherently problematic. Another Air Force Spokesperson, Capt. Rose Richeson, for instance, stated, "Airmen should be mindful of their dress and appearance and present a professional image at all times while in uniform" (qtd. in "Weekend AM News"). In this framing of Echegoyen-McCabe and Luna by the Air Force, it was not the women's actions that were deviant. However, once they donned the uniform, their actions became deviant–it was breastfeeding in uniform that was the problem. Richeson's words seem to imply that there is (and ought to be) a clear line between what is acceptable when one is acting as a professional and when one is acting as a mother. Indeed, the fact that no branch of the military had any regulations at the time regarding public breastfeeding while in uniform suggests that few others in the U.S. military saw the personal act of breastfeeding as one that is potentially compatible with the professional nature of the uniform.

Public commentary on the story also went much further on this point than did the official Air Force spokesmen. Crystal Scott, a military spouse who started Mom2Mom said, for instance, "A lot of people are saying it's a disgrace to the uniform. They're comparing it to urinating and defecating while in uniform" (qtd. in "Moms in the Military Create Buzz"). One woman commented in a TV broadcast that "I can't hold my husband's hand while he's in uniform, but they can expose their boobs when in uniform?" (qtd. in "Weekend AM News"). In these comments, there is no distinction made between Echegoyen-McCabe and Luna using the uniform to promote Breastfeeding Awareness Month and the women simply breastfeeding in their uniforms in public. Rather, it is clearly the blending of these women's professional and maternal identities that is the problem. "The uniform" signals to the world a certain professional identity–one that Echegoyen-McCabe and Luna violated the moment they allowed their maternal identities to be visible when they ought to have been invisible. It is through crossing this imaginary line between mother and airman that Echegoyen-McCabe and Luna became deviant service members.

## Deviant Mothers

Hutchinson, Echegoyen-McCabe, and Luna were not simply criticized for their inability to behave correctly as "professionals." All three women were also framed as unable to correctly perform their other identity–as mothers. For African American women, the "bad" mother is an image that has emerged in its current cultural context largely out of the public discourse on welfare. When welfare benefits for widows and children emerged in the early twentieth century, only so-called good mothers–widows and married women–were identified as deserving of aid. Unwed motherhood in particular became the symbol of "bad" or "unfit" motherhood in the cultural discourse (Schur; Fraser and Gordon; Ladd-Taylor and Umansky). Hutchinson's position as a lack, single mother is one that makes her susceptible to interpretation as a bad mother–one who is depended on the state rather than on a husband.

The language that questions Hutchinson's fitness as a mother is subtle, and centres largely on her deviant status as a single mother. Hutchinson is not just deviant because she is a single mother and, thus, unable to fit into the nuclear family model. Her status as a single mother in the Army renders her even more deviant because single parents are not allowed to join the Army. She can, therefore, be framed as someone who has done what she ought not to have on two counts when she had her son.

Alexis Hutchinson's single motherhood seems to have been a central point of the media coverage of her story.[3] Given that Hutchinson's difficulties stemmed from her inability to comply with Army regulations that she find care for her children, the significance of her not having a partner is perhaps understandably important to highlight. Yet several articles take a further step and pair what Ange-Marie Hancock identifies as "moral judgments" in their use of the "single mother" quality to describe Hutchinson. For example, in an opinion piece, columnist Tammerlin Drummond of the *Oakland Tribune* (the local paper of Hutchinson's hometown) writes the following: "Yet beyond all the shouting, what I see is a young woman who made a poor choice and wound up getting in over her head. The same, unfortunately, happens to many young women. They have unprotected sex, and end up pregnant and raising a child on their own. Whatever plans they had for their own lives are radically altered."

Drummond, thus, paints Hutchinson with the typical deviance frame of the single mother as someone who made a "poor" choice. Someone "raising a child on their own" cannot be as "good" of a mother as she might have been had she had the child in wedlock. This moral judgment attached to the term "single mother" potentially contributes to the bad mother frame when it is discussed in the way Drummond does here. Additionally, when single-motherhood is used as the starting or focal point of the story, its deviance takes on a greater significance.

The attribution of moral judgment to Hutchinson's mothering, however, appears more consistently in her comparison with other military mothers and single parents in the news stories. A *USA Today*, article, for example, begins, "An Army mother who refused to go to Afghanistan because she failed to get someone to care for her son wants the military to discharge her rather than enforce a policy thousands of single mothers have abided by" (Gomez). Here the author uses the term "single mother" not in direct reference to Hutchinson, but rather as a means of demonstrating that she is deviant among single mothers in the Army, who have complied with the policy. The article the focuses on this aspect of Hutchinson's story: "'There are thousands of soldiers that have similar circumstances," Fort Stewart spokesman Kevin Larson said. "They're single parents. They do the right thing. They prepare for their deployment. They fulfill their sworn duty.'" The article continues by citing statistics that back up Larson's statement and implicitly lending it further credence: "More than 30,000 single mothers have deployed to the two most recent wars, according to a study by Iraq and Afghanistan Veterans of America." A *New York Times* article used similar statements from Army officials, and, again, followed them up with facts pertaining to "problems" of pregnancy in the military. "In its statement, the Third Infantry Division noted that there were many other single parents or dual-military families in Specialist Hutchinson's unit who deployed to Afghanistan. 'They have experienced similar challenges but have been able to overcome them so they could deploy with their units,' the statement said" (Dao).

Two of the seven letters to the editor also echo and reinforce this framing of Hutchinson as a "bad mother." "I realize that personal responsibility is an antiquated idea, and this story just amplifies this. I do sympathize with the choice made by Army mom Alexis Hutchinson to refuse deployment rather than put her child in foster care. The issue, though, is that she put herself in this position," writes Mary E. Pagano from Virginia Beach. Chris Zon from Oakland is even clearer in his disgust with Hutchinson for her deviancy as a single mother: "Why should anyone feel sorry for this woman, who, as an active military personnel, chose to become pregnant, knowing she might be deployed at any time? Why didn't the reporter inquire as to the whereabouts of the father of this child, who should be taking care of his child? Why does Alexis Hutchinson not see this as her responsibility, and take responsibility for her actions?"

Echegoyen-McCabe and Luna once again did not receive the same degree of criticism of their identities as mothers in media commentary as Hutchinson did. Doubtless this has something to do with perceptions of them as white, married mothers, rather than the more socially deviant image of the black, single mother. In fact, the women were often praised in the media as "good mothers" for making the choice to breastfeed. Tamara Dietrich, commenting on the issue in the *Daily Press*, for instance says, "And, frankly, if I were in a public place when Echegoyen McCabe needed to hitch up and hook up, I'd do what I normally do in such a situation: avert my gaze and go about my own business. And silently approve of this woman for being a good mother" (Dietrich).

Nonetheless, the women–particularly Echegoyen McCabe–did receive a heavy amount of criticism for "exposing" themselves by breastfeeding in public, and this criticism was occasionally tied to their deviance as mothers. Tamara Dietrich, for instance, opens her commentary by noting the difference between how Echegoyen McCabe and Luna breastfed in the photographs.

> *The photo that kicked off the criticism is of Senior Airman Terran EchegoyenMcCabe, who hitched her Tshirt above both breasts, the better to accommodate the twin baby girls attached to them. Frankly, it's a double shot of more breast than baby. By comparison, Echegoyen McCabe's friend Staff Sgt. Christina Luna is in the same photo nursing her own infant, but discreetly covered. I'm betting that if the shot of Echegoyen McCabe weren't so ... revealing, the backlash might not be so severe.*

*Air Force Times* also ran an article about the women's story containing quotes from two other mothers serving in the Air Force. Both indicate that they had no problem with breastfeeding while in uniform, but that it was the public nature of the act that had bothered them. Said Staff Sgt. Amber Green, "Because of my own personal beliefs, I always covered up where it looked like I was just cuddling with my child without anyone noticing I was [breastfeeding] in uniform ... We are the face of all military branches and should do our best to be professional/respectful in and out of uniform." Lynda Valentine, an Air Force veteran, is also quoted as saying "Regarding the argument that breastfeeding is 'natural,' I don't think it's OK for women to 'whip out their boobs' anywhere they want any more than I think it's appropriate for guys to whip out their penises to pee anywhere they want. Yes, both are completely natural acts, but both should also be done with discretion" (qtd. in Davis). A good mother, therefore, does indeed feed her child, but she covers up when doing so. The implication is that by publicly breastfeeding and "exposing" themselves, Echegoyen-McCabe and Luna performed their motherly duty of feeding their children in a way that is deviant.

## Conclusion: What is the Proper Role of Mothers in the Military?

In the media coverage of Alexis Hutchinson, there were many occasions when her duty as a mother was distinguished clearly from her duty as a soldier. In addition to painting Hutchinson as deviant–both as a soldier, and as a mother; however, some of the media coverage also praised her for doing the right thing by putting her role as a mother above her role as a soldier. "Hutchinson should never have been put in the position of choosing between the Army way and a mother's first obligation to her child's welfare," said Suzanne Fields for the *Creators Syndicate*. This comment suggests that Hutchinson's role as a mother was her proper one and that her role as a soldier was secondary. Can one imagine a father in a similar situation being framed in this light–that children are his "first obligation"? This seems to imply that the "Army way" is somehow different for a mother than for another soldier. This reading is further validated by Field's later statement that "we can expect these women to do their duty, as women in the military always have, but when men send women to war the country has lost something very precious." In addition, *The New York Times* was the only one of my sources to carry a quote from Hutchinson's mother, Ms. Hughes, that echoed this same theme: "People have said to me: 'She signed this contract. She's supposed to go. That's her first priority'... My response is: 'I don't think so. This is her child. This is her family. This is her priority. The military is a job'" (qtd. in Dao).

Other columnists and letter writers used Hutchinson's story to question whether mothers ought to be in military roles at all. "Here is another question we should be asking: What is watching Mommy go off to war doing to some of those children?" writes Mary Eberstadt in *The Washington Post*. Eberstadt's opinion piece cuts to the real heart of the tragedy frame–the abandonment of children: "Sending fathers into military zones has been a tragedy for as long as war has been around. Sending mothers along with them–many of them the only parent a child has–is simply wrong. If we're uncomfortable staring at that picture of Specialist Hutchinson and her baby, maybe we should ask ourselves why" (Eberstadt). Similarly, Tammerlin Drummond in the *Oakland Tribune* asks, "Is sending single parents into combat something we really ought to be doing? That is the real issue, not whether Hutchinson got away with a fast one." The language of these columnists does not serve to contribute to framing Hutchinson as a bad mother, rather one who is in a tragic position–one that she should not have been in in the first place because of societal rather than an individual failure. The Rev. Jeff Wuertz's letter to the editor well illustrates the societal failure element of this frame:

> *If the reporting is accurate regarding Alexis Hutchinson, her choice to sacrifice her career and face military charges for skipping her deployment was the right one. The fact remains that when we make raising family less important than our careers, we have missed the boat God intended us to float in. If the Army actually said that her 10-month-old son would need to be put in foster care, the Army is wrong. We wonder why America is sinking. Hutchinson will certainly face many challenges in her life. Making the correct choice for her child will be honored by God.*

In these columns and letters, Hutchinson's story becomes a link to a larger, preexisting frame of women in combat: they are vulnerabl and do not belong in the masculine arena of war (e.g., Wheelright; Holland; Howard and Prividera). One example of Hutchinson's story acting as an opening to discuss women's place in the military in general is Elizabeth Rubin's *Vogue* article "Bye-Bye Baby," which takes up the tragedy angle of Hutchinson's story to discuss the heartbreak of servicewomen in general who must leave their children to deploy. Rubin does this through interviews with several servicewomen with children who talk about the difficulties of leaving children behind. "Not even the Soviets, Israelis, or Iraqi Baathists have sent mothers of infants and toddlers to the front lines like we do," observes Rubin. The article's depiction of women in combat is firsthand, and allows the women's voices to come through genuinely. She quotes them about aspects of their jobs that they enjoy and aspects they struggle with, which do not involve their children but are professional. Yet through her statement comparing the U.S. deployment of mothers to other countries and through her comment that "few have studied the effect that all this warring is having on children whose parents are repeatedly deployed," Rubin helps to reinforce the frame that women's first duty is to their children and that their place in the Armed Forces is still an awkward one.

Furthermore, the framing of Hutchinson as part of the larger discourse of women in the military also occasionally took a tone of concern about how women's incursion into the military was causing problems."

The *Philadelphia Inquirer*, for example, ran an article titled "Women in the Ranks: There Are More in the Military Than Ever Before, Not Infrequently Coming under Fire. Yet the Homefront Keeps Calling." The story begins with a discussion of Hutchinson's case, but then turns its focus on the specific difficulties that women in the Armed Forces face versus their male counterparts. For example, the article discusses the problem that pregnancy poses to servicewomen and the military alike: "The military's response to pregnancy also is still evolving. Advocates for female service members are urging longer post-birth deployment deferrals for the 10 percent of military women who become pregnant each year. Critics say maternity leaves and months-long deployment deferrals hurt unit readiness." The article also features an interview with author Kingsley Browne, who wrote the book *Co-Ed Combat: The New Evidence That Women Shouldn't Fight the Nation's Wars*–a title that speaks for itself in terms of its advocacy of the framing of women as out of place in the military (Davis). In a similar vein, the CNN broadcast of Hutchinson's story raised questions about whether Hutchinson being discharged rather than court martialed might have installed a "precedent"–the implication being that other women with children might now try to "skip" deployment without fear of court-martial (CNN, "Largest NATO").

Hutchinson's story demonstrates how public discourse and negative media framing of military mothers may possibly lead to public policy decisions that restrict the further inclusion of women in the military. The Center for Military Readiness, for instance, submitted a statement for a House hearing on women serving in land combat in 2013 that cited similar arguments about "pushing young women and mothers" who are "reluctant" to go into combat (Center for Military Readiness). However, it is also possible to see through Echegoyen-McCabe's and Luna's stories how public discourse may be positively impacted by spotlighting the experiences of military mothers for a time.

As noted above, although Echegoyen-McCabe and Luna did receive a great deal of criticism–both as airmen and as mothers–for their decision to be photographed publicly breastfeeding while in uniform, these women also received a great deal of public support for their decision as well. Kelly Allison Pickering in the *Denver Examiner,* for instance, takes issue with Air Force spokesman Capt. Rose Richeson's statement that "Airmen should be mindful to ... present a professional image." Pickering asks: "Is breastfeeding unprofessional?" Pickering's article goes on to quote Echegoyen-McCabe saying that she is proud to wear her uniform while breastfeeding, and concludes: "Many support these photos, saying that women in the military (and in other careers for that matter) can work and breastfeed. They can multitask. They can be loyal to the military and also to their children." Moreover, Jo Ashline in the *Orange County Register* asks, "Why are we okay with the idea that soldiers can take another life while in uniform but cannot sustain one via breastfeeding?" Both columnists question the seemingly natural distinction made in other articles on the story between Echegoyen-McCabe's and Luna's identities as service members and mothers. Rather, these columnists wonder why the two identities cannot coexist (see Elle Kowal, chapter seven, and Naomi Mercer, chapter eight, this volume, for personal experiences navigating motherhood and the military with respect to nursing and caring for small children).

Although there are still no official policies in any of the U.S. military branches that explicitly regulate breastfeeding while in uniform,[5] huge strides have been taken in recent years toward improving conditions for breastfeeding mothers in the military. In fall of 2015, for instance, the Army finally released a policy on breastfeeding–the last service branch to do so. The media coverage of this new policy included numerous photos of soldiers breastfeeding in their Army uniforms.[6] Since 2012, other military mothers have also spoken up in the media and have posted photographs of themselves breastfeeding in uniform.[7] The struggle for acceptance and recognition as mothers and service members is far from over for women like Hutchinson, Echegoyen-McCabe, and Luna. Yet their stories bring attention to the needs and experiences of mothers serving in the U.S. military, and impact the legal consciousness, and, ultimately, the policy decisions of Americans on issues that affect other women who serve. Hutchinson's story shows that the media spotlight can bring with it a negative discourse around military mothers–that some might use children or pregnancy to "skip out" on their duty. But Echegoyen-McCabe's and Luna's stories also show that sometimes the spotlight can also bring with it a chance to discuss policy gaps and to highlight the needs of military mothers. Media coverage of the experiences of mothers in uniform can, therefore, also offer a chance for others–civilian and military alike–to hear their stories. Media coverage can, for a time, render visible the everyday, often invisible experiences of mothers in uniform.

Echegoyen-McCabe's and Luna's photographs, however explosive, may have opened the door to normalizing the image of a woman breastfeeding in uniform. By being photographed breastfeeding in uniform, Echegoyen-McCabe and Luna (whether intentionally or not) put themselves forward as early adopters of the idea that breastfeeding while in uniform is normal. As diffusion theory suggests, knowledge formation is the first step toward the implementation of new ideas. The media spotlight on breastfeeding in uniform almost certainly allowed for the introduction of the idea that breastfeeding while in uniform may be normal to many to whom this idea had never occurred. Such normalization can result in shifts in public discourse, which question the status quo and, ultimately, lead to the possibility for policy change. Indeed, it is possible to observe some resistance to the dominant deviancy discourse in the words of some columnists commenting on Echegoyen-McCabe and Luna's story. Discourse, in other words, has not only the power to constrain and limit access to the public policy agenda, but also the power to introduce new ideas that resist dominant frames. Its ever-shifting, mutually constitutive relationship with public policy means that discourse is not only a way in which mothers in uniform might find themselves being oppressed, but might also seek empowerment and inclusion. Giving mothers in uniform a voice is even more important in light of the culture of masculinity that still dominates the U.S military. If the stories of mothers in uniform are never heard, then their experiences are rendered invisible. In sum, if public discourse can indeed have a significant impact on the public policy agenda, then perhaps what is needed are more opportunities for mothers in uniform to have their experiences brought into the public eye and their voices heard.

### Endnotes

1   These are both databases that contain newspaper articles, wire and broadcast transcripts from a large number of media sources.

2   For more on interpretive research design, see also Schwartz-Shea and Yanow.

3   Some of the news pieces focused on Hutchinson's single-parent status more than others, though the majority (72 percent) of all articles and newscast transcripts and three out of the seven letters

to the editor either contained a reference to her single-motherhood in the headline itself, or in the first sentence of the report. In addition, all but one of the news stories (not including the letters) mentioned the fact at least once.

4   According to the latest information from the *Breastfeeding in Combat Boots* blog (Roche-Paul). Policies do exist in all branches regarding time and space to pump or breastfeed, but do not contain specific information about how uniform regulations should be taken into account with regard to breastfeeding.

5   See, for example, CNN's coverage, which included a photograph of ten soldiers breastfeeding in uniform in a public park–perhaps purposely reminiscent of Echegoyen-McCabe's and Luna's photo (Grinberg).

6   Air Force Reserves Staff Sgt. Jade Beall, for instance, in 2015 (Bologna).

## Works Cited

Altheide, David. *Qualitative Media Analysis*. Thousand Oaks: Sage Publications, 1996.

"Army Mom Refuses To Deploy." Tell Me More. National Public Radio, 20 Nov. 2009.

Ashline, Jo. "Moms in the Military Create Buzz after Breastfeeding in Uniform." *Orange County Register 31* May 2012: n. pag. Print.

Bannach, Chelsea. "Fairchild Moms in National Spotlight: Photos Show Breastfeeding Servicewomen in Uniform." *The Spokesman Review*, 1 June 2012, p. 1A.

Bennett, Lance. *News: The Politics of Illusion*. 4th ed. Longman, 2001. Print.

Bologna, Caroline. "Air Force Mom Breastfeeding In Uniform Is A Stunning Look At Military Motherhood." *The Huffington Post*, 12 Mar. 2015, www.huffingtonpost.ca/entry/jonea-cunico-military-breast feed_n_6856762. Accessed 5 Jan. 2018.

Geranios, Nicholas. "Breastfeeding Photos of Military Moms Stir Debate." *Associated Press* 1 June 2012.

Bumiller, Kristin. *The Civil Rights Society: The Social Construction of Victims*. Johns Hopkins University Press, 1992.

Burgess, Susan. "Gender and Sexuality Politics in the James Bond Film Series: Cultural Origins of Gay Inclusion in the U.S Military." *Polity*, vol. 47, no. 2, 2015, pp. 225-48.

Bynum, Russ. "Army Discharging Single Mom Who Refused Deployment." *Associated Press*, 12 Feb. 2010.

Center for Military Readiness. "CMR Submits Statement for Record of House Hearing on Women in Land Combat." Center for Military Readiness, 27 Aug. 2013, www.cmrlink.org/issues/full/cmr-submits-statement-for-record-of-house-hearing-on-women-in-land-combat. Accessed 5 Jan. 2018.

CNN. "President Obama in China; The AIG Bailout; New Breast Exam Guidelines; Killings at the Canal; Where Presidents Hu and Obama Meet and Where They're Split; Why We May Pay More in Taxes or See Smaller Refunds; Safe Social Networking; Shocking Numbers of Hungry Americans, According to Agriculture Dept.; Palin's Quest To Be Taken Seriously Falls Flat for Some Conservative Women." *CNN Newsroom*.17 Nov. 2009.

CNN. "Largest NATO Offensive of the War in Afghanistan; A U.S. Marine and British Soldier Die in a Major NATO Offensive; Deadly Explosion at Popular Bakery in Western India; Obama Assures Haiti Funds Will Not Stop the Flow of Other World Aid Programs." *CNN Newsroom*. 12 Feb. 2010.

Dao, James. "Single Mother Is Spared Court-Martial." *The New York Times* 12 Feb. 2010, www.nytimes.com/2010/02/12/us/12awolmom. html. Accessed 5 Jan. 2018.

Davis, Carolyn. "Women in the Ranks; There Are More in the Military than Ever Before, Not Infrequently Coming under Fire. Yet the Homefront Keeps Calling." *The Philadelphia Inquirer*. 10 Dec. 2009.

Davis, Kristin. "Uniform Dilemma." *Air Force Times*, 11 June 2012, p. 22.

Dietrich, Tamara. "Bad to Breastfeed in Uniform?" *Daily Press*, 10 June 2012, p. A2.

Drummond, Tammerlin. "Drummond: Country First or Child? An Even Tougher Choice for Single-Parent Soldiers." *Contra Costa Times*, 16 Feb. 2010.

Eberstadt, Mary. "Mommy's War." *The Washington Post*, 26 Feb. 2010.

Edelman, Murray. *The Symbolic Uses of Politics*. 2nd ed. University of Illinois Press, 1985.

Enloe, Cynthia. *Bananas, Beaches and Bases: Making Feminist Sense of International Politics*. 2nd ed. University of California Press, 2014.

Fields, Suzanne. "Sending a Woman for a Man's Work." *Creators Syndicate*, 18 Feb. 2010.

Fraser, N., and L. Gordon. "A Genealogy of Dependency: Tracing a Keyword of the US Welfare State." *Signs*, vol. 191, 1994, p. 309.

Gamson, William, et al. "Media Images and the Social Construction of Reality." *Annual Review of Sociology*, vol. 18, 1992, pp. 373-93.

Gilens, Martin. *Why Americans Hate Welfare: Race, Media, and the Politics of Antipoverty Policy*. University Of Chicago Press, 2000.

Gilliom, John. *Overseers of the Poor: Surveillance, Resistance, and the Limits of Privacy*. University Of Chicago Press, 2001. Print.

Gitlin, Todd. *The Whole World Is Watching: Mass Media in the Making & Unmaking of the New Left*. Berkeley: University of California Press, 1980.

Gomez, Alan. "Army Investigates Soldier Mom; Lawyer: Baby Not Being Used to Shirk Duty." *USA Today*, 18 Nov. 2009.

Grinberg, Emanuella. "Army Issues New Breastfeeding Policy." *CNN*, 2 Oct. 2015, www.cnn.com/2015/10/02/living/army-breastfeeding-policy-feat/index.html. Accessed 5 Jan. 2018.

Haltom, William, and Michael McCann. *Distorting the Law: Politics, Media, and the Litigation Crisis*. University Of Chicago Press, 2004.

Hampson, Sarah Cote. *Rights in the Balance: Working Mothers and the Limits of the Law*. Stanford University Press, 2017.

Hancock, Ange-Marie. *The Politics of Disgust: The Public Identity of the Welfare Queen*. New York University Press, 2004.

Holland, Shannon. "The Dangers of Playing Dress-up: Popular Representation of Jessica Lynch and the Controversy Regarding Women in Combat." *Quarterly Journal of Speech*, vol. 92, no.1, 2006, pp. 27-50.

Holsti, Ole R. "A Widening Gap Between the U.S. Military and Civilian Society? Some Evidence 1976-96." *International Security*, vol. 23, no. 3, 1999, pp. 5-42.

Howard, John, and Laura Prividera. "Rescuing Patriarchy or Saving 'Jessica Lynch': The Rhetorical Construction of the American Woman Soldier." *Women and Language*, vol. 27, no. 2, 2004, pp. 89-97.

Iyengar, Shanto, and Donald Kinder. *News That Matters: Television and American Opinion*. University of Chicago Press, 1987.

Ladd-Taylor, Molly, and Lauri Umansky. "Introduction." *"Bad" Mothers: The Politics of Blame in Twentieth-Century America*, edited by Molly Ladd-Taylor and Lauri Umansky, New York University Press, 1998, pp. 1-28.

Lee, Henry. "Mother Who Refused Duty Is Discharged; Military." *The San Francisco Chronicle*, 12 Feb. 2010.

Marshall, Anna-Maria. *Confronting Sexual Harassment: The Law And*

*Politics Of Everyday Life.* Ashgate Pub Co, 2005.

Metinko, Chris. "Oakland Army Mom Refused to Go to Afghanistan because of Son." *Contra Costa Times*, 13 Nov. 2009:

Nielsen, Laura Beth, and Aaron Beim. "Media Misrepresentation: Title VII, Print Media, and Public Perceptions of Discrimination Litigation." *Stanford Law and Policy Review*, vol. 15, no. 1, 2004, pp. 237-66.

Pagano, Mary E. "Duty Calls [Letter to the Editor]." *The Virginian-Pilot*, 2 Dec. 2009.

Pickering, Allison. "Air Force to Nursing Moms: 'Aim High', except When Breastfeeding in Uniform." *Denver Examiner* 6 June 2012: n. pag. Print.

Roche-Paul, Robyn. "Breastfeeding in Uniform." *Breastfeeding in Combat Boots*, www.breastfeedingincombatboots.com/. Accessed 5 Jan. 2018.

Rogers, Everett M. *Diffusion of Innovations.* 5th ed. Simon & Schuster, 2003.

Rubin, Elizabeth. "Bye-Bye Baby." *Vogue*, 2010, p. 380.

Schattschneider, Elmer E. *The Semi-Sovereign People: A Realist's View of Democracy in America.* Cengage Learning, 1975.

Scheingold, Stuart A. *The Politics of Rights: Lawyers, Public Policy, and Political Change.* 2nd ed. University of Michigan Press, 2004.

Schur, Edwin. *Labeling Women Deviant: Gender, Stigma and Social Control.* Temple University Press, 1983.

Schwartz-Shea, Peregrine, and Dvora Yanow. *Interpretive Research Design: Concepts and Processes.* Routledge, 2011.

Sears, David. "Symbolic Politics: A Socio-Psychological Theory." *Explorations in Political Psychology*, edited by Shanto Iyengar and William McGuire, Duke University Press, 1993, pp. 113-49.

"Single Mom Discharged, Army Says." *CNN*, Feb. 2010, www.cnn.com/2010/US/02/12/georgia.soldier.mom/. Accessed 5 Jan. 2018.

Weekend AM News. ABC KTNV, Las Vegas, NV. N.p., 2 June 2012.

Wheelright, Julie. "'It Was Exactly Like the Movies!' The Media's Use of the Feminine During the Gulf War." *Women Soldiers: Images and Realities*, edited by Elisabetta Addis et al., St. Martin's Press, 1994, pp. 111-134.

Wuertz, Jeff. "Put Child First [Letter to the Editor]." *The Virginian-Pilot*, 1 Dec. 2009.

Zon, Chris. "Not Even Reporting [Letter to the Editor]." *Contra Costa Times*, 26 Nov. 2009.

Chapter Four

# Connecting the Past and Future through Contemporary Discourses of Motherhood and Militarism in Canada: *Bomb Girls* and *Continuum*

Nancy Taber

In Canadian culture, mothers and the military are largely presented as dichotomous concepts. For example, there is a yearly appointment of a National Memorial Silver Cross Mother to represent all mothers whose children have died in military service (Veterans Affairs Canada, "National Memorial"). Her tenure begins just before the National Remembrance Day ceremony on 11 November, which is broadcast nationwide. Viewers watch as a grieving mother, in civilian clothes, lays a wreath at the base of the National War Memorial, surrounded by uniformed military personnel (see Patricia Sotirin, chapter one, this volume, for a discussion of American Gold Cross mothers, and Udi Lebel and Gal Hermoni, chapter five, for a discussion of maternal bereavement in the Israeli context). The only other time when Canadians may think of mothers and the military is likely when a local soldier dies and there is an article in the newspaper indicating that his or her mother received a Memorial Cross medal. In this way, mothers (and mothering) are represented as outside the military organization, and only important to acknowledge when children die (see Sotirin, chapter one, for a discussion of other types of military mother tropes in the American context). Furthermore, mothering is reified as a gendered and embodied concept by the fact that until 2008, only mothers, not fathers, were honoured in this way[1] (Veteran Affairs Canada, "Memorial Cross").

Popular culture is slightly more nuanced. There are only a few Canadian programs set in military and militaristic contexts. These include fictional television series, such as *Bomb Girls*, *Continuum*, and *The Border*; the television documentary *Border Security: Canada's Front Line*; and, a radio-play, *Afghanada*. In some of these programs, there are female protagonists; however, in most of them, mothers are absent or tangential. *Bomb Girls* (Global, a division of Shaw Media Inc.) and *Continuum* (Showcase, a division of Shaw Media Inc., also airing on Syfy in the United States) are exceptions, as they take up mothering in complex ways.

This chapter focuses on the two protagonists who are mothers. Lorna Corbett (*Bomb Girls*) is the shift matron for Victoria Munitions factory in the Toronto, Ontario, area during the Second World War. She has two sons fighting overseas and a teenage daughter who lives at home. She is also a motherly influence to the women she supervises at the factory as they build bombs for the military. Kiera Cameron (*Continuum*) is a police officer with the paramilitary Vancouver City Protective Services (CPS) in 2077. She time travels to 2012 with terrorists who escape at the moment of their execution. The program shifts from future to present (Kiera's past) as Kiera attempts to get back to her own time in order to be with her son. Failing that, she aims to protect the timeline so he remains safe in the future. Both Lorna and Kiera are positioned within gendered and militaristic expectations.

This chapter considers motherhood "as social and as fluid a category as fatherhood" (Scheper-Hughes 232-33), wherein "the concept of 'mother' [and mothering] is not a singular practice but is always context bound" (Abbey and O'Reilly 14-15). It explores how although maternal thinking may facilitate a politics of peace (Ruddick, *Maternal Thinking*; O'Reilly, *Rocking the Cradle*), it can also concomitantly facilitate a politics of war, violence, and militarism. It uses feminist antimilitarist theory (Enloe) to explore how the television programs challenge gendered representations while supporting militaristic ones. In this chapter, I further explain how mothering and militarism interconnect; discuss my use of public pedagogies; detail my methodological approach; provide an analytic summary of the television programs *Bomb Girls* and *Continuum*, including media reviews for both and scholarly research for the former (I could find nothing on the latter); and, explore the themes that emerged. I conclude that these fictional programs, with one set in the past and the other in the future, are connected through real-life contemporary discourses of mothering and militarism, with resultant implications for Canadian society (see Anwar Shaheen and Abeerah Ali, chapter two of this volume, for a discussion of mothers and martyrs in the Pakistani popular culture context).

## Public Pedagogies, Militarism, and Mothering

As Canadians participate in local memorial services, view the National Remembrance Day ceremony, read newspapers, and engage with popular culture, they are taught, through these public pedagogies, how mothering and the military connect at a societal level. Carmen Luke argues that "learning and teaching, in my estimation, *are* the very intersubjective core relations of everyday life. They exist beyond the classroom, are always gendered and intercultural" (7, emphasis in original). More recently, Jake Burdick and his colleagues, in their exploration of the complexities of the concept of public pedagogies, define the term as "focusing on various forms, processes, and sites of education and learning occurring beyond or outside formal schooling" (2). In this chapter, I focus on popular culture as pedagogy in ways similar to Kaela Jubas and colleagues who explore television and film, as my analysis entails two television programs. Additionally, as two of the contributors to *Popular Culture as Pedagogy: Research in the Field of Adult Education* attest (Robin Wright and Gary Wright, in their examination of *Doctor Who*), fans' interaction with television goes beyond the programs themselves, and can include fan fiction and Internet communities. Both *Bomb Girls* and *Continuum* have extensive official websites with episode guides, cast bios, trailers, and interviews. They have also inspired fan fiction. Additionally, *Bomb Girls* connects to the actual women who inspired the program, to their local area, and to a contemporary organization conducting a fundraising legacy campaign. It also has a *Save Bomb Girls* webpage. *Continuum* has fan pages, wikis, and a graphic novel, as well as a petition to save the program on Change. org. Clearly, these programs go beyond the screens on which they are played, and bring militarized mothering into the daily lives of viewers.

Cynthia Enloe's work is grounded in a feminist antimilitarist stance wherein militarism is understood to be wrapped up in patriarchy and to privilege hegemonic masculinity over femininity and other forms of masculinity. She describes militarism as "a belief in hierarchy, obedience, and the use of force" wherein citizens "adopt militaristic values ... and priorities ... see military solutions as particularly effective ... [and] see the world as a dangerous place best approached with militaristic attitudes" (4). Militarism is not subsumed by militaries, although it is interconnected with them; militarism exists in the daily life of civilians who may have no direct link to a military organization. For instance, when I look around my small suburban city of St. Catharines, Ontario, Canada, I see people dressed in camouflage fashion, playing with toy guns, entering a paintball arena, going to the theatre to see war movies, and lining the Highway of Heroes.[2] I myself am also wrapped up in militarism because of my previous service as a military member (see Taber, "Learning How to Be a Woman" and *Ruling Relations, Warring, and Mothering*); my negotiations with my teenage son about playing video games based on aspects of war; and even my position as a faculty member in a university named for Major-General Sir Isaac Brock, otherwise known as the Hero of Canada due to his death in the War of 1812 (see Taber, "Generals, Colonels, and Captains" and "Military and Academic Gendered Organizations"; Code et al.; see Morten Ender, chapter six, Elle Kowal, chapter seven, and Naomi Mercer, chapter eight, in this volume for contributions that focus on personal experiences).

Militarism in the series of *Bomb Girls* and *Continuum*, as a whole, is present in several ways. *Bomb Girls* is directly connected to the military and to war, in that the characters are building munitions to be used in the fight. The characters are worried about loved ones overseas, train for air raids, must pass security clearances, express hatred for the enemy, and believe in the war (with a few nuanced exceptions). They wear uniforms (overalls and coloured turbans to keep their hair covered and demarcate their shifts, which are named for colours), are subject to a hierarchy, and are expected to be obedient. In *Continuum*, in 2077, a militaristic police force (City Protective Services, CPS) keeps the peace, conducts raids, carries out executions, and is beholden to the corporations that rule it. Trials are automated, and judgment is instant. Police officers are called Protectors, but they appear to protect the corporations over the citizens. Surveillance is present in citizenship chips, which are injected into citizens, wearable technology that enables instant communication, and the projection of propaganda onto the sides of buildings. Militarism carries over into 2012 through a clear cut belief in good and evil, constant fighting and gun battles, the hunting down of fugitives, and the hierarchy of the police force that expects obedience.

The focus on mothering for the characters of Lorna and Kiera is interesting in that it offers a lens to explore how militarism and mothering intersect. Sara Ruddick explores how mothers themselves are not necessarily peaceful, or good, but that the practice of mothering can inform a politics of peace. She explains that "preservative love," a key component of mothering, "is an *activity* of caring or treasuring creatures whose well-being is at risk" ("Preservative Love and Military Destruction," 240, emphasis in original) but that "toward one group of combatants, however, a mother is not reliably non-violent, namely the families and children of her own "'enemies'" (244). She also states that "mothers are militarists. Some mothers ... fight in defense of their homeland or in civil revolutionary struggles to bring justice to their children. Self-defense and armed revolutionary justice can seem a direct expression of preservative love, as long as we allow the use of violence in any cause" (256). Lorna and Kiera, I argue, are militarists at the same time as they are caring mothers. Their "maternal thinking is provoked by the work of caring for particular biological children in particular historical-social contexts" (Ruddick, "Maternal Work" 105). This context is, in Lorna's case, in wartime. In Kiera's, it is in a violent futuristic world whose timeline is in jeopardy.

Over the last few years, I have watched the two seasons of *Bomb Girls*, as well as the television movie, and the four seasons of *Continuum*. In conducting this research, I rewatched each episode and the television movie, as I searched for instances of mothering, which I defined as invoking the word "mother" (or a version of it) or child/children; interaction between a mother and child/children; and caring labour performed by a mother toward her own child/children and to those in her care–labour that includes "preservation, growth, and social accept-ability as constitutive of maternal practice" (Ruddick, *Maternal Thinking*, 22) as well as attentive love (Ruddick, "Preservative Love and Military Destruction").

I transcribed these instances and analyzed them from a feminist antimilitarist perspective, using Donald Polkinghorne's "analysis of narratives," which "results in descriptions of themes that hold across the stories' moving 'from stories to common elements'" (12). I searched for how mothering intersected with militaristic values (i.e., hierarchy, obedience, force, viewing the world as dangerous, and an "us versus them" mentality), priorities, and actions. I have previously used this type of analysis in my research exploring the life histories of military mothers (Taber, "You Better Not Get Pregnant"), and found it useful in thematically framing their stories. In this case, I am analyzing scripted television programs instead of interviews (which were then constructed into life stories in a narrative analysis, see Taber, "A Composite Life History"). The forms differ while the method and theoretical perspective correspond.

## Bomb Girls

*Bomb Girls'* website describes the Canadian program, which aired from 2012-2013, as the following:

> *Set in the 1940s,* Bomb Girls *tells the remarkable stories of the women who risked their lives in a munitions factory building bombs for the Allied forces fighting on the European front. The series delves into the lives of these exceptional women from all walks of life– peers, friends and rivals–who find themselves thrust into new worlds and changed profoundly as they are liberated from their home and social restrictions.*

The factory portrayed in the program, Victory Munitions, "is an amalgam of two real munitions plants: the General Engineering Company of Canada (GECO) plant in Scarborough and the Defence Industries Limited (DIL) plant in Ajax. The establishment of the Ajax plant was what led to the creation of the town after the war" ("Ajax," para. 2). The award-winning program aired in multiple countries, did well in the ratings, and received positive critical reviews (Taylor). However, it was cancelled after two seasons (2012 and 2013), because of "a business model driven by simulcasts of American shows" ("Ajax" para. 4). As one columnist explained, "*Bomb Girls*, a show that was at its heart a story about the empowerment of women at a time when they still lived sheltered lives, was never going to attract the broad audience of Global imports like *Hawaii Five-0* or *Elementary*" (Stinson, para. 8). Nonetheless, part of *Bomb Girl*'s appeal came from "a strong following among young women charmed and intrigued by the story of how their grandmothers fought to get jobs and respect" (Taylor, para. 6). *Bomb Girls* is a unique window into the lives of Canadian women in the Second World War, whose stories, in many ways, have been hidden from history and popular culture. The series ended with a television movie in 2014, the aim of which was to "ensconce *Bomb Girls* as an iconic show ... [in order to] kee[p] the title alive ... [so] it will have a future'" (para 13). The program is still available through the Global TV app, on the Global website, and on DVD.

Lorna Corbett, the main character, is played by Canadian-born Meg Tilly. Although there are other characters on the program who are mothers, none of them are main protagonists. Furthermore, Lorna's character is centred on her motherhood to the girls at the factory, her daughter, her sons, and the unborn child she miscarries. In real life, Tilly has spoken about the importance of her own motherhood, as she herself: "left her acting career behind in the '90s, with the exception of doing movies of the week when she needed money, because she wanted to concentrate on raising her three children. She had trust issues with leaving them in someone else's care, and she didn't want to live with regrets" (qtd. in Hampson, para. 12). Her bio likewise states, "After a busy decade and a half, Tilly stepped away from acting to focus on her family, raising three beautiful children. In that time, she also wrote four critically acclaimed novels. With her children grown and after an absence of 17 years, she has returned to acting" ("*Bomb Girls* Cast," para. 3). None of the other cast bios mention children.

Joan Sangster explores how although *Bomb Girls* is one of the few contemporary television programs focusing on working-class women, it also "misrepresents the lives of most working-class women" (202). (Carmela Patrias makes a similar argument with reference to racial minorities.) Furthermore, the main protagonist is Gladys Witham, a society rich girl who does not need the work. Regardless, Sangster argues that "we need more mass media efforts like *Bomb Girls*: they allow us to encourage our students to think about the relationship between mass media, representation and working women, to raise questions about the agency of working women, and perhaps eventually tell different stories about the past" (210). In particular, "the wartime setting" of *Bomb Girls* "provided the producers with the *licence* to tell the stories of women on the factory floor" (200, emphasis in original), as viewers might have been less interested in the stories of women factory workers in any other context. As well, I argue, the program provides an interesting opportunity to explore how militarism intersects with gender and motherhood.

## Continuum

*Continuum's* website describes the show as follows: "When the group of fanatic terrorists known as Liber8 escaped their planned execution in the year 2077, they vaulted back in time to the year 2012, sweeping dedicated CPS Protector, Kiera Cameron along with them." *Continuum*, which aired from 2012 to 2015, is available on the Showcase website and on DVD. Unlike *Bomb Girls*, which was unique in its focus on Canadian history and working-class women's lives, *Continuum* has been successful because, as its creator, Simon Barry, said, "it looks like a quote-unquote American show" (qtd. in Genzlinger, para. 4). Emma Ellis, a *Wired* columnist, defines *Continuum* as "a classic time-travel story that is also sort of a police procedural. But the twist (and the fun) lies in what initially seems like *Continuum's* most annoying quirk: the 'high-concept' corporate stuff" (para. 3)–in that corporations rule through a Corporate Congress after the collapse of government. A group called Liber8 fights against this corporate rule that has taken away its citizens' freedom, but it is unclear if they fit into the category of "freedom fighter" or "terrorist" (Genzlinger). Genzlinger explains that "the show's deliberate ambiguity has fans debating on chat boards whether 'Continuum' is a pro-business, right-wing series or the opposite. And Kiera, as Season 1 progresses, gradually confronts the possibility that she is fighting for the wrong side." As the seasons advance, it is clear that the program as a whole problematizes notions of justice, democracy, and freedom in its critique of militarized corporatism.

Kiera Cameron, played by American actress Rachel Nichols, has a character description stating she is "a tall striking beauty" who is "a police officer" and "a dedicated wife ... and mother." Her "separation from them [her family] will cause her a great deal of pain and longing to get 'home'" ("Continuum: Cast," para. 1). Indeed, Genzlinger argues that it is "Kiera's angst ... about the husband and son she left behind in 2077 [that] giv[es] a personal dimension to the classic time traveler's worry about whether intervening in the past will alter the future" (para. 9). Ellis describes Kiera as "a rare ass-kicking female protagonist who is also nurturing and family-oriented, but she's also the most unreflective and self-obsessed character to ever travel through time" (para. 8). Of the program as a whole, Ellis writes that "it features a female lead with a distinct and multi-dimensional personality, and a refreshingly diverse cast who are given the same consideration. It's also an interesting, and interestingly Canadian, take on issues like big business and terrorism" (para. 18). The program was sold to fifty countries (Genzlinger). Upon the announcement of its cancellation after its third season, it wrapped up with a shortened fourth season. There is also the possibility of its continuation in another format (Avalos).

In my analysis, I focus on tensions between Kiera's desire to return home (to her future timeline) to be a mother to her son and her work as a Protector to defend the timeline. The program provides a lens from which to explore how Kiera as a character moves from a militaristic police officer believing in a stark contrast between right and wrong supporting the status quo, and one who questions it (which culminates in the latter half of season three).

## Thematic Elements

There are several common elements relating to mothering and militarism in Lorna's and Kiera's lives as well as diverging ones. They relate to the intersecting themes of performing militarized mothering and caring for others. The examples and quotations to which I refer below are exemplars; the programs are imbued with the themes.

### Performing Militarized Mothering

Lorna and Kiera are, in many ways, militarized mothers. For both characters, "self-defense and armed revolutionary justice"–in the form of fighting the Germans in the Second World War (Lorna) and Liber8 in 2077 as well as from 2012 to 2015 (Kiera)–are "direct expression[s] of preservative love ... [through] the use of violence in any cause" (Ruddick, "Preservative Love and Military Destruction" 256). The characters accept a need for hierarchy and obedience (although Kiera resists these elements from 2012 to 2015, but not in 2077) and force. Lorna and Kiera are workers in militarized organizations that are replete with regulations and hierarchical obligations, and engage in violence toward others.

They both view the world as a dangerous place, where it is either us (the Allies for Lorna; CPS, the Vancouver police force, and properly behaved citizens for Kiera) or them (the Axis powers for Lorna; Liber8, Kellog, and the corporations for Kiera). Lorna initially denigrates an Italian man, Marco Moretti, claiming that he is a security risk because of his ancestry: "an Italian building bombs, might as well lay out a welcome mat for Mussolini" (season one, episode one, "Jumping Tracks"). When her husband, Bob, a disabled war veteran from the First World War, accuses Lorna of "helping to kill someone else's boys" by working in a munitions factory, she retorts that she is "protecting my own" (S1E1). Later on in the series, when she is asked to speak at an Armistice Day (now called Remembrance Day) ceremony, she explains that "We have two sons overseas, facing dangers I can't even know the shape of, and here we are, building the bombs that make them strong" (S1E5, "Armistice").

Kiera believes in the execution of Liber8 members, even when others question it. She states that "they'll all just be dead, and we can move on with our lives" (S1E1, "A Stitch in Time"). When she travels back in time with Liber8, she immediately attempts to catch them. She delivers one of the members, Lucas Ingram, to the police, stating "One down, seven to go" (S1E1). She later threatens the lives of Lucas's ancestors in order to force him to give her information. When Liber8 breaks Lucas out of prison, Kiera says that "they're [Liber8] soldiers, starting a war that they already lost once" (S1E1). She is committed to her cause throughout, as she states at the beginning of season four that "I accomplished my mission. Stopped Liber8, prevented whatever future they might have built and I made sure that you will never build the broken future that I came from" (S4E1, "Lost Hours"). For the remainder of season four, Kiera's focus shifts to stopping Kellog, who is described as "a half-mad war lord" in an alternate future. When this is accomplished, she turns her attention to stopping the corporations from taking over. The entire plot of the series is focused on Kiera ("us") against a "them," with the "enemy" changing throughout the series. Interestingly, although this friend-foe binary preserves the dichotomy of good versus evil, it also contests it, as the two poles switch and replace each other. As one character states, "One man's terrorist is another man's freedom fighter. But how do you switch from one to the other?" (S1E6, "Times Up").

Both characters are willing to sacrifice their own happiness to support the greater good. Lorna ends her Armistice Day speech by stating, "You can't say we don't pay a price. Sometimes, you know a thing's right. What's a few sacrifices on our part, when we stand to win back the happiness and freedom we deserve" (S1E5, "Armistice"). When speaking with a reporter–Dottie Shannon, played by Rosie O'Donnell, who is working on a story about the women at the factor–Lorna explains, "My work's all I know. Raised three children. Kept this house together through the lean years." Dottie observes that Lorna's attention has simply shifted from the children to the factory, and Lorna replies, "I need to stay useful." When Dottie asks, "and if it [the war] should ever end?" Lorna says, "maybe then, it'll be my turn" (S2E9, "Something Fierce").

Kiera struggles with the need to stop Liber8 (and, later Kellog and the corporations) from harming people and with her desire to return to her own time: "I want to get home.... More than anything. But I can't let thousands of people die, even if there's a small chance I might be able to change what's happening" (S1E10, "Endtimes"). As the series progresses, the tension between her goals increases, as she explains: "It's getting harder and harder to choose which path to take. Which decisions are the right ones. I want to do right by everyone, without sacrificing what I need." When asked, "What do you need?" Kiera replies, "It doesn't matter." She is willing to "stop him [Kellog] at all costs" (S4E3, "Power Hour"). In the series finale, Kiera states the "mission priority" is not to return home but to "destroy the machine and the portal." Only once the mission is achieved will she consider her own future. She explains, "if it's my time, we'll find out one way or another. But either way, change of plan" (S4E6, "Final Hour").

For Lorna, "patriarchal motherhood" (O'Reilly, "Outlaw(ing)") is entwined with militarism, as women are continually devalued, and the men in their lives work to control them. When Harold Akins, the factory supervisor, approaches Lorna after she watched two airmen walk into his office, she fears she will be given bad news about one of her sons. She is visibly upset and then relieved when Harold says he needs her "help telling Edith her husband died." When she asks, "so, my sons are alive?" Harold responds, "Of course. Yeah. You women always think the worst" (S1E1, "Jumping Tracks"). Lorna is continuously arguing that her workers are skilled: "we've proved we're as capable as men" (S2E12,

"Blood Relations"). When a detective investigates a death, Lorna fears her workers will not be treated fairly: "we women, the jobs we do, he thinks it perverts a girl. He's a man who hates us" (S2E12). At the same time as Lorna challenges gender roles, she also reinscribes them. She tells Dottie, "I used to think you were uppity, marching into a man's world. Until I started working there myself" (S2E9, "Something Fierce"). When one woman brings her baby to a "day nursery" and states, "I wish they'd thought of that before the war," Lorna replies it is "sad ... [to] go through so much to make a child and give it to someone else" (S2E2, "Roses Red"). Furthermore, she believes women should act in socially acceptable ways, which I describe further in the section on caring labour below.

Kiera's embodiment as a woman is less of a plot point, yet, at the same time, her status as a mother is continuously present. In a flashback near the beginning of season one, during a blackout caused by an attack by Liber8, Kiera holds and kisses her baby, Sam. Greg, her husband, tells her, "If you really want to do something about them [the terrorists], you should join the CPS. They're recruiting. With your military service you'd be a lock for Protector." Kiera responds, "Well, I have always wanted to," and Greg tells her "I'm ready when you are." Kiera states, "I know. But let's be honest, it's gonna take more than a few blackouts to tear me away from my most important job," which is being a mother (S1E4, "A Matter of Time"). In the next episode, Kiera meets Lily, her future grandmother. She tries to convince her not to have an abortion in order to preserve the timeline: "having a baby doesn't mean giving up on your dreams. A child can add to them." Kiera continues, "when I found out I was pregnant I didn't think I was ready, either. I was fresh out of the military and starting a new career. Having a child was the last thing on my mind." However, the outcome was a good one, as she and her then boyfriend, Greg, were married (S1E5, "A Test of Time"). At the end of the season, viewers learn that Greg was not quite so accommodating, especially when he challenges her promise to tuck their son, Sam, into bed every night because of her job: "You promised to be honest with him. We both know the job, the nights you're not gonna make it home. Don't make promises you can't keep." Kiera replies, "That's not fair" (S1E2, "Fast Times"), which demonstrates the tension between her motherhood and her work. Finally, in the last episode of the series, Kellog, her antagonist, acknowledges his deep respect for her: "Women like you are rare. In any time" (S4E6, "Final Hour").

The connection between the themes of militarized mothering and caring for others is perhaps best exemplified by the following interaction between Kiera and her son. It occurs when Kiera is leaving him in order to protect him, by providing security for the execution:

> Sam: Mom? Are the bad guys attacking us again?
> Kiera: No. The bad guys are in prison. And pretty soon they'll never be able to hurt anyone ever again.
> Sam: Do you have to go?
> Kiera: Yeah. It's my job.
> *Sam hands Kiera a toy soldier.*
> Kiera: For me?
> Sam: For tomorrow. In case you need backup.
> Kiera: Thank you. (S1E1, "A Stitch in Time")

Throughout the series, Kiera is shown with the toy soldier. She holds it in her hand and carries it with her as she mourns her separation from him. When she attempts to accept the fact that she may never see him again, she puts it away in a drawer.

## Caring for Others

Lorna provides caring labour for her own children, the girls on her shift, and her husband. She is concerned with their "preservation" and "social acceptability" (Ruddick, *Maternal Thinking* 22) while engaging in attentive love (Ruddick, "Preservative Love and Military Destruction"). With her daughter, Sheila, Lorna keeps the concept of social acceptability continually at the forefront, striving to ensure her daughter dresses properly, acts like a lady, and dates someone of her own culture and race. This social acceptability extends from the mundane–"Sheila, must you chomp gum?" (S2E11, "Kings and Pawns")–to life decisions–"Don't waste your affections, Sheila. Don't throw your youth away on a man with no future to offer" (S2E11). When Lorna tells Sheila, "I only want what's best for you," Sheila tells her to "Stop. Stop mothering me. Live your own life" (S2E11). Earlier, Lorna defends her intrusions in Sheila's life by stating, "You can't ask a mother to sit and watch someone hurt her child" (S2E8, "Where There's Smoke").

With the girls on her shift, Lorna fiercely fights for their preservation (fighting for their safety in the workplace as well as their right to be treated with respect and without harassment) and social acceptability (encouraging them to act and dress as ladies while making a good impression on visitors). Preservative love and attentive love are connected through the vital need for social acceptability. In the first episode, when one of her workers on the Blue Shift, Vera Burr, is seriously hurt in an accident at the factory, Lorna demands that the doctor "do that surgery on Vera." She argues, "You can't let her leave here deformed. It will destroy her future ... Vera is a soldier ... you will show her the same respect ... you do the soldiers ... you do your best, for that girl" (S1E1, "Jumping Tracks"). After another accident caused by a faulty munition, Lorna's workers are blamed. She contests the belief that her girls are subpar by arguing "It could have as easily been the men" (S1E2, "Misfires"), and works to ensure her girls are "suitably cha-peroned," as it is her job (S1E4, "Bringing up Bombshell"). She makes it clear to Harold about what is and what is not "appropriate workplace behaviour" (S1E4). She engages in after-hours workshops to give "tips for juggling work and home" and to "make the factory more appealing to girls" (S2E3, "The Enemy Within"). When she finds a new worker on a bench of the changing room early one morning, she asks, "Where did you sleep last night?" Upon learning that the worker lost her housing assignment, Lorna invites her home, and says, "No girl of mine sleeps in a bus station" (S2E5, "The Harder we Fight"). She tells Gladys Witham, another one of her workers, "if you need a sympathetic ear, ever, I'm always here for my girls" (TV movie, *Facing the Enemy*). Lorna states that she is "a mother...defending my own" (S2E5, "The Harder we Fight").

Lorna's preservative love eventually results in her being fired. After an explosion kills a worker, she tells Harold's boss, "you also have to answer to us." She continues, "we need to shut this place down until we can find out what caused that explosion. Because until we know every life here is in danger." She then states, "Someone died. How many more have to die before you." Harold encourages Lorna to back down, and she says "what, be quiet? Not anymore. I insist on a full investigation.... the workers are my responsibility" (*Facing the Enemy*).

For Kiera, caring labour is almost entirely absent. In a few flashbacks, she engages in attentive love with her son. She feeds him, tucks him into bed, and throws him a birthday party, but preservative love is prominent. Kiera works to preserve his safety from Liber8 by trying to defeat them, to return to her own timeline, and to protect the future. Throughout, she throws herself into her mission against Liber8 in order to cope with the loss of her family. She says, "I have a husband and a son. And right now, I'm confronting the possibility that I may not make it back to them." She continues, "The only thing that's going to get me through this is finding a way to believe that my being here is for a reason. That what I'm doing will somehow help my family in the future while I'm here in the present" (S1E2, "Fast Times"). Kiera is haunted by the possibility that her actions may endanger her family instead of protecting them: "I have a little boy and a husband that I'm likely to never see again. If I don't do everything right while I'm here, they may never exist" (S1E9, "Family Time").

Kiera often expresses her desire to get home and preserve the future: "You want to protect the time line? Send me home. I can prevent Liber8 from ever coming to 2077. I can make sure none of this ever happens! I can make things right. And then I will destroy the device, and nobody will ever use it again. That's all I've ever wanted. To put the pieces back together, and return to my family!" (S2E13, "Second Time"). In the final season, she argues that she has done enough: "I accomplished my mission. Stopped Liber8, prevented whatever future they might have built and I made sure that you will never build the broken future that I came from." She argues, "It's time for me to focus on myself. What I want." Kiera continues, "I want to go home, Alec, and I need you to send me" (S4E1, "Lost Hours"). In the series finale, she says, "If there's even the slightest chance that I can be with Sam again, I'm willing to risk everything" (S4E6, "Final Hour").

For Kiera, attentive love and preservative love are largely presented as a dichotomy, which is epitomized at the end of the series finale. Kiera returns to a peaceful future, and is met by a changed Alec Sadler (who was once the catalyst for the Corporate Congress). Kiera asks Alec, "Sam. Is he here?" She looks around and realizes that there are police, not CPS. Alec says there was "no collapse, no uprising, no revolution." Kiera responds, "No Corporate Congress." Alec tells her, "It's because of you Kiera." Kiera sees her son across a park and thanks Alec: "You've given me the greatest gift." When she starts to approach Sam, another woman sits down beside him. Alec explains, "We thought you died that day [when she walked through the time machine in hopes of returning to the future] ... we steered civilization inspired by your sacrifice." Kiera realizes that in this timeline, she was never Sam's mother. Alec says, "This is the price for making the world a better place. This Sam will grow up in a world free of violence, free of revolution, free of corruption. His future is bright. And it's because of you, Kiera. It's the price of love. Real love. You'll understand, in time" (S4E6, "Final Hour").

## Conclusion

These programs are commendable in that they represent mothering as a complex practice. However, they promote a narrative wherein mothering is largely militarized and gendered, as it is threaded through with elements of violence, sacrifice, and patriarchy. In Lorna's case, social acceptability is a key element of preservative love and attentive love (Ruddick, *Maternal Thinking*, "Preservative Love and Military Destruction"), which limits her freedom, and that of those she loves, to performing gender in expected and traditional ways, even as they work in nontraditional roles. Enloe's notion of "'feminine respectability'" (43) is similar, as she explores how it can serve militarized corporate interests by guiding women into certain types of work and forms of behaviour. In Kiera's case, attentive love is separated from preservative love, which implies that women cannot engage in both, particularly if they work in a masculine militarized context–similar to one of the findings in my research with military mothers (Taber, "You Better Not Get Pregnant") that "women must choose between career and family" (336) (see also Kowal, chapter seven and Mercer, chapter eight, this volume, for personal experiences that illuminate the difficulty in combining military life with motherhood).

Both these programs have continuing legacies. In 2014 (CBC Radio) and 2016 (Agar), a radio program and news article respectively argued that Veronica Foster, who was known as Ronnie, the Bren Gun Girl (the Canadian precursor of Rosie the Riveter), should be honoured on Remembrance Day. The Town of Ajax, through its "Ajax Bomb Girls Legacy Campaign," published newsletters from 2013 to 2015, which taught residents that in the First World War, Defence Industries Limited employed seven thousand women and precipitated the founding of the town of Ajax. The newsletters include stories of real Bomb Girls. The town is still raising money for a statue.[3] Fans are still posting on

*Continuum* message boards to ask questions about the plot and debate how the characters might have fared if the program continued.[4]

These articles, radio programs, and websites keep the programs alive for viewers. They may also pique interest in the programs for those who may accidently come across them. As such, it is important to consider what these programs and their resultant artifacts, as public pedagogies, teach viewers and citizens about mothering and militarism. A focus on learning through popular culture can help to engage with, and challenge, the ways in which mothering is reified and militarized, as well as to open up space for new ways of understanding mothering. Perhaps in this way, it will be possible to, as Andrea O'Reilly argues, "re-envisio[n] and repositio[n] 'mother' from a noun to a verb ... [in order to create] a 'feminist ethic of care' paradigm" ("Outlaw(ing)" 28). Lorna and Kiera demonstrate that mothers and mothering provide interesting plots and dilemmas. The historical and futuristic settings give license (borrowing from Sangster) to explore how mothers negotiate their public and private lives, which shows that they are not discrete contexts but are interconnected. Lorna and Kiera are both "ass-kicking" (Ellis) in varying ways, as they work to protect and care for those they love. As such, by watching *Bomb Girls* and *Continuum*, and focusing on how the protagonists mother, viewers can see how "mother" indeed becomes a verb through which the characters problematize gender and militarism.

## Endnotes

1   Members who served after 2001, and are living as of 2008, can now choose three people to receive the award.

2   A stretch of Highway 401 in Ontario down which the funeral convoys of soldiers killed overseas travel, which is broadcast on local news networks.

3   At the time of writing this chapter.

4   At the time of writing this chapter.

## Works Cited

Abbey, S., and A. O'Reilly. "Introduction." *Redefining Motherhood: Changing Identities and Patterns*, edited by S. Abbey and A. O'Reilly. Second Story Press, 1998, pp. 13-26.

Agar, J. "How Women Helped to Win Second World War." *Toronto Sun*, 2015, www.torontosun.com/2015/11/09/how-women-helped-to-win-the-war. Accessed 28 Mar. 2016.

"Ajax War history Inspires New TV Show." *Oshawa this Week*. 3 Jan. 2012, www.durhamregion.com/community-story/3500999-ajax-war-history-inspires-new-tv-show/. Accessed 24 Mar. 2016.

Avalos, R. "Continuum: Creator Teases Potential Spin-Off and Film." *TV Series Finale*, 19 Oct. 2015, tvseriesfinale.com/tv-show/continuum-creator-teases-potential-spin-off-and-film-38841/. Accessed 28 Mar. 2016.

"Bomb Girls." *Global*, 2016, www.globaltv.com/bombgirls/. Accessed 24 Mar. 2016.

"*Bomb Girls* Cast: Meg Tilly as Lorna Corbett." *Global*, 2016, www.globaltv.com/bombgirls/. Accessed 24 Mar. 2016.

Burdick, J., et al. "Breaking Without Fixing: Inhabiting Aporia." *Problematizing Public Pedagogy*, edited by J. Burdick et al. Routledge, 2014, pp. 1-11.

CBC Radio: The Current. "Famous across Canada as 'Ronnie the Bren Gun Girl,' meet Veronica Foster." *CBC Radio: The Current*, 10 Nov. 2014, www.cbc.ca/radio/thecurrent/income-splitting-unapologetic-abortion-and-the-threat-of-sand-mining-1.2907259/famous-across-canada-as-ronnie-the-bren-gun-girl-meet-veronica-foster-1.2907266. Accessed 28 Mar. 2016.

Code, M., Landry, A., B. Reader, and N. Taber. "'He's Obviously Important': Student Perceptions of a Military General as a University Namesake." *Review of Education, Pedagogy, and Cultural Studies*, vol. 38, no. 3, 2016, pp. 1-16.

"*Continuum:* Cast. Kiera Cameron (Rachel Nicholas)." *Continuum*, 2016, http://www.syfy.com/continuum/cast/kiera-cameron/4 Accessed 28 Mar. 2016.

"*Continuum:* Main." *Continuum*, 2016, Accessed 28 Mar. 2016.

Ellis, E.G. "Wired Binge-Watching Guide: *Continuum*." *Wired*. 2 Mar. 2016, www.wired.com/2016/02/binge-guide-continuum/. Accessed 28 Mar. 2016.

Enloe, C. *Globalization and Militarism: Feminists Make the Link*. Rowman & Littlefield Publishers, Inc., 2007.

Genzlinger, N. "They're from the Future, and Canada." *The New York Times*. 10 Feb. 2013, p. 20.

Hampson, S. "Meg Tilly as She is, Not as You'd Imagine." *The Globe and Mail*, 28 Mar. 2013, www.theglobeandmail.com/arts/television/meg-tilly-as-she-is-not-as-youd-imagine/article10530917/. Accessed 22 Mar. 2016.

Jubas, K., N. Taber, and T. Brown, editors. *Popular Culture as Pedagogy: Research in the Field of Adult Education*. Sense Publishers, 2015.

Luke, C. "Introduction." *Feminisms and Pedagogies of Everyday Life*, edited by C. Luke, State University of New York Press, 1996, pp. 1-27.

O'Reilly, A. "Outlaw(ing) Motherhood: A Theory and Politic of Maternal Empowerment for the Twenty-first Century." *Hecate* vol. 36, no. 1/2, 2010, pp. 17-29.

O'Reilly, A. *Rocking the Cradle: Thoughts on Motherhood, Feminism and the Possibility of Empowered Mothering*. Demeter Press, 2006.

Patrias, C. "Race-Based Discrimination in *Bomb Girls*." *Labour/Le Travail*, vol. 75, 2015, pp. 195-99.

Polkinghorne, D. "Narrative Configuration in Qualitative Analysis." *Life History and Narrative*, edited by J. A. Hatch and R. Wisniewski, The Falmer Press, 1995, pp. 5-23.

Ruddick, S. "Maternal Work and the Practice of Peace." *Journal of Education*, vol. 167, no. 3, 1985, pp. 97-111.

Ruddick, S. *Maternal Thinking: Toward a Politics of Peace*. Boston: Beacon Press, 1989.

Ruddick, S. "Preservative Love and Military Destruction: Some Reflections on Mothering and Peace." *Mothering: Essays in Feminist Theory*, edited by J. Trebilcot, Rowman & Allanheld, 1983, pp. 231-62.

Sangster, J. "*Bomb Girls*, Gender, and Working-Class History." *Labour/Le Travail*, vol. 75, 2015, pp. 200-10.

Scheper-Hughes, N. "Maternal Thinking and the Politics of War." *The Women and War Reader*, edited by L.A. Lorentzen and J. Turpin, New York University Press, 1998, pp. 227-33.

Stinson, S. "Cancelled Global Series Bomb Girls Gets a Goodbye, at Least." *National Post*, 27 Mar. 2014, http://nationalpost.com/entertainment/television/cancelled-global-series-bomb-girls-gets-a-goodbye-at-least Accessed 28 Mar. 2016.

Taber, N. "A Composite Life History of a Mother in the Military: Storying Gendered Experiences." *Women's Studies International Forum*, vol. 37, 2013, pp. 16-25.

Taber, N. "Generals, Colonels, and Captains: Discourses of Militarism, Higher Education, and Learning in the Canadian University Context." *Canadian Journal of Higher Education,* vol. 44, no. 2, 2014, pp. 105-17.

Taber, N. "Intersecting Discourses of Gender: Military and Academic Gendered Organizations." *International Journal of Lifelong Education,* vol. 34, no. 2, 2015, pp. 230-46.

Taber, N. "Learning How to Be a Woman in the Canadian Forces/ Unlearning It through Feminism: An Autoethnography of My Learning Journey." *Studies in Continuing Education,* vol. 27, no. 3, 2005, pp. 289-301.

Taber, N. *Ruling Relations, Warring, and Mothering: Writing the Social from the Everyday Life of a Military Mother.* Dissertation. University of South Australia, 2007.

Taber, N. "'You Better Not Get Pregnant While You're Here': Tensions between Masculinities and Femininities in Military Communities of Practice." *International Journal of Lifelong Education,* vol. 30, no. 3, 2011, pp. 331-48.

Taylor, K. "Why Fans of Cancelled TV Show Bomb Girls Are Fighting Back." *The Globe and Mail,* Apr. 26. 2013, www.theglobeandmail.com/ arts/television/why-fans-of-cancelled-tv-show-bomb-girls-are-fighting-back/article11571558/ Accessed 22 Mar. 2016.

"Ajax Bomb Girls Legacy Campaign." *Town of Ajax,* 2012, http:// honourajaxbombgirls.ca Accessed 22 Mar. 2016.

Veterans Affairs Canada. "Memorial Cross." *Veterans Affairs Canada: Memorial Cross,* 2015, www.veterans.gc.ca/eng/remembrance/medals-decorations/memorial-cross Accessed 25 Apr. 2016.

Veterans Affairs Canada. "National Memorial (Silver) Cross Mothers." *Veterans Affairs Canada: National Memorial (Silver) Cross Mothers,* 2015, www.veterans.gc.ca/eng/remembrance/memorials/books/silver Accessed 25 Apr. 2016.

Wright, R.R. and G.L. Wright. "Doctor Who Fandom, Critical Engagement, and Transmedia Storytelling: The Public Pedagogy of the Doctor." *Popular Culture as Pedagogy: Research in the Field of Adult Education,* edited by K. Jubas et al., Sense Publishers, 2015, pp. 11-30.

Chapter Five

# Public Grief Is Maternal: The Gendered Discourse of Israeli Military Bereavement

Udi Lebel and Gal Hermoni

## Introduction

Since the establishment of the State of Israel in 1948, Israeli society has formed a number of military bereavement communities–each a sub-culture competing over modes of representation and processing of loss in the public sphere (Lebel, "Postmortem"). These are, in fact, epistemic communities who define the behavioural expectations from its members, and act de-facto as "policy communities" (Mack, "Civil") and "memory communities" (Meyers, "Israeli") in the public sphere.

Studies of psychosocial or sociopolitical contexts of military bereavement in Israel have focused on the behaviour of bereaved families, especially bereaved parents, regarding four main aspects: bereaved families' projection of their social activism on their emotional state and processing of their loss; the effect of their public activism on the formation of Israel's security policy; their sociodemographic profile as indicative of their public activism; and an analysis of the discourses promoted by bereaved parents. A further attribute of Israel's "national bereavement regime" (i.e., the social constructs and expectations forming legitimate modes of representing loss in the public sphere, both in terms of the discourse and in terms of behaviour (Lebel, "The 'Grief Regime'") has yet to be investigated–namely, the fact that the bereavement communities functioning within it are exclusively led, formed, and operated by bereaved mothers and not by bereaved fathers.

Fathers whose sons have died in military service, especially those fathers who had already held public leadership or national positions, have kept their grief private, which has reproduced of hegemonic gender relationships, regardless of the nature of the discourse or activities carried out by bereaved mothers. We argue that although feminine activism in the public sphere is perceived as a tool for political empowerment and feminist resistance, Israel's national bereavement regime reproduces the traditional balance of powers between men and women in the dominant culture (see Anwar Shaheen and Abeerah Ali, chapter two of this volume, for a discussion of mothers and martyrs in the Pakistini context).

## Aims and Structure

The first goal of this chapter is to present the epistemic bereavement community as an arena for motherly activism in Israel. The chapter will follow the emergence of what we call four "loss communities"–each forming a subculture that materializes military bereavement processing and representation modes in the public sphere. These communities were formed spontaneously and voluntarily by bereaved mothers whose sons died during their military service. In terms of sociohistorical development, each of these communities is "freer" than its predecessor. Although the first loss community conformed to institutional expectations, those that followed have become more and more covert.

The chapter's second goal is to attempt to explain why only bereaved mothers have embarked upon social activism, whereas bereaved fathers tend to keep this biographical detail within the private sphere and to avoid public activism based on the fact that they are bereaved parents. As we will show, in Israeli public leadership (in the army, politics and culture), there was no shortage of men who were bereaved fathers. However, the public was not aware of this part of their identity. We will try to explain this phenomenon using the psychocultural approach to loss as well as the psychoanalytic theory of gender differences. Both theories show that women in the the conclusion that the emergence of women in the public sphere based on their trauma and loss is by definition a sign of weakness and victimhood, thereby lacking legitimacy for gaining "leadership capital" (Lebel and Hatuka, "Israeli Labor"). Therefore, only those who lack this type of capital from the start–namely, women–would allow themselves to enter the public sphere using the moral capital of trauma and bereavement. Conversely, men, who are positioned higher in the leadership capital regime, would prefer to maintain a powerful image–thereby omitting the bereavement component from their public identity.

We commence our analysis by describing Israeli society's four main epistemic bereavement communities: the hegemonic bereavement community; the political bereavement community; the military accident bereavement community; and the Zionist-religious bereavement community. These four communities offer fertile ground for motherly activism, even though Israeli public leadership has always included men who choose to hide their bereavement. In the second and final part of the chapter, we review possible explanations for the exclusivity of motherly use of bereavement in the public sphere in an attempt to explain the gendered differences of the politics of bereavement.

## The Hegemonic Model of Bereavement: Heroic Victimology

After the establishment of the state and the war over its independence, Israel's first Prime Minister and Minister of Defense David Ben Gurion (1886-1973) understood that the hegemonic model of bereavement served to communicate to bereaved families what exactly is expected of them by the establishment in terms of their behaviour in the public sphere (Lebel, "Postmortem").

This model is based on an ethos of masculinity: it includes the demand for emotional restraint, avoidance of exposure of pain and sorrow, and an acceptance and recognition of the necessity of their sacrifice. But Ben Gurion's words, as well as those of other Israeli political and cultural leaders, on issues of bereavement and loss, were directed mainly toward the bereaved mother. Although there was no shortage of bereaved fathers, it was the mother who became the main target of the hegemonic model of bereavement. An example for this can be found in Ben Gurion's opening remarks during an event marking the publication of *Parchments of Fire*–a series of books commemorating the fallen soldiers of the War of Independence:

> *I know that the wideness of the soul, the nobility and loyalty as*
> *well as the bravery of these sons and daughters did not come*
> *from nowhere ... maybe fathers also have some part, but I am*

> *confident that a very large part, maybe the greatest part, is due*
> *to the mothers ... the Jewish mother, who has educated her sons*
> *in this spirit, will not only know sorrow for the loss of her dear*
> *one ... but she will also feel happiness and pride in knowing that*
> *she has given such sons to her nation.*

Ben-Gurion then clarifies that he intentionally speaks to the mothers and not the fathers sitting before him: "I am convinced that with all the pain, especially of the mothers, the mothers in particular, because their pain in the deepest ... I know that you feel a sense of human and Jewish glory to have had such sons" (Ben Gurion, "Speech"34). Similar words can be found in Ben Gurion's many references to the mothers of enlisting and serving soldiers, while he nearly ignores their fathers.

One such phrase has become a corner stone of Israeli military discourse: "May every Jewish mother know that she has put her son under the care of commanders who are up to the task."

Even today, this phrase can be found posted at entrances to army bases and adorning the diplomas of graduates of junior and senior officer courses. This famous phrase comes from a message extended by Ben Gurion to army commanders: "It is not enough for the commander to know his job, he must love humankind ... and especially must evoke trust in the soldier and in the soldier's mother" (qtd. in *Davar*). Once again, Ben Gurion identifies the mother, and not the father, as the central actor in Israel's army-society relationship.

This tendency was also applied by later political leaders, including Ben Gurion's opponents. For instance, Menachem Begin (1913-1992), leader of the *Herut* political movement, also focused on the bereaved mother when referring to matters involving loss and bereavement: "The heroism of the Jewish mother, who has offered her son on the altar of Israel's war of existence and freedom, is the saint from whom Israel will draw, also in the days ahead, the strength to continue standing against our enemies" (qtd. in Lebel, *Politics of Memory*, 123). The public image of the bereaved mother became the face of the hegemonic model of bereavement. Mothers have served as both recipients and creators of the bereavement discourse: both when they were expected to fit the required top-down bereavement code and when they initiated the establishment of *Yad LeBanim*–Israel's representative organization of bereaved families that still operates today–as a result of their bottom-up activities.

In an open letter to the press written by a number of bereaved mothers whose sons died in the War of Independence, they approached all bereaved mothers, who had not met each other yet, with a proposal to establish an institution for commemorating their sons:

> *We hereby approach all bereaved mothers in Israel who have given their nation the apple of their eye ... we are approaching you and you only, because our sorrow that annihilates the soul and the body can only be felt by a mother who has also suffered this tragedy ... we approach you with a proposal to unite, so as to establish a memorial for their sacred memories ... to contact each and every bereaved mother via the press... to encourage the mothers and to help them resume their lives. (qtd. in Shapira)*

This letter by bereaved mothers has led, with the support of the ministry of defense, to the establishment of a representative organization, which until this day still forms a central commemoration umbrella for all Israeli Defense Forces (IDF) fallen soldiers.

The woman who served as role model for the hegemonic model of bereavement was Rivka Guber, a bereaved mother whom Ben Gurion referred to as "the mother of the sons"–marked as the ideal type of the Israeli bereaved mother and as the ultimate normative typecast of the bereaved mother in Israel. Rivka Guber (1902-1981) was a perfect match, in the eyes of the Israeli establishment of the time, to serve as a symbol representing the "family of the bereaved." She belonged to the correct political party of the time (the Labour Party), was a *Moshav* member, and was active in the women organizations of the *Histadrut*. In her youth, she enlisted in the British military, and encouraged her sons, even before the establishment of the state, to enlist in the Jewish Brigade and later in the *Hagana* underground movement (which later became the Israeli Defense Forces). After losing both her sons in the War of Independence (Efraim died on 26 March 1948 and Zvi on 8 July 1948), she dedicated her time to promoting a range of initiatives of national significance–including increasing immigration, establishment of schools and libraries, establishment of new settlements, and more (Lebel, "War Opponents").

The transformation in her public status–promoting her from a local to a national hero–took place after David Ben Gurion had read the *Book of Brothers* (Guber), which she wrote about her sons. It was a book fitting the hegemonic discourse of bereavement and was laden with meaning and implications of their death, devoid of any anger for her loss, and filled with a desire to continue to fulfill national-collective goals. Immediately after reading the book, Ben Gurion requested to meet her: I do not know whether there is anywhere in Israel–in our times or throughout history–a mother like the mother of these two sons. Her words are unlike any other in world literature" (our emphasis, *Thoughts*). Ben Gurion transformed the book into a largely distributed educational text, and the ministry of defense funded many translations and prints of it in Israel and worldwide. "The unique thing about this book," Ben Gurion lectured, "is the image of the mother shining from its pages. The mother's words will forever stand as the epitome of heroism and loyalty of the Jewish mother. She succeeded in expressing the feelings of many mothers in Israel" (Ben Gurion, *Davar*). On another occasion he wrote: "This book contains something more noble and precious even than the noble and precious deeds of the brothers ... fortunate is the generation having such mothers amidst it. Maybe this is the truest and deepest secret of the huge 'miracle' that has happened to our nation in this generation." He added that although the name of the book is *Book of Brothers*, he believed it should also be called the "*Book of the Mother*" (Ben Gurion, *A Letter*).

Guber was perceived as the epitome of the Israeli bereaved mother. Many public events were held in her honour, and were attended by senior government officials. On every ten-year anniversary of the publication of her book, a public conference would be held, attended by public figures, including the president and ministers. On remembrance days, she would often be interviewed over the radio and would be invited to speak during national ceremonies alongside the prime minister (Lebel, "War Opponents"). We believe that her work and her position have formed the guiding principles in terms of the status of bereavement in society in general and the status of bereaved mothers in particular, within the hegemonic model of bereavement:

a. The bereaved mother as constantly identified with bereavement. She always remembers that her public status is formed by the loss of her son and that she must serve as a public agent for his memory. This is the foundation of the public legitimacy for her work, and, therefore, there is no legitimacy for shaking it off. At all times and at every event, Rivka Guber was always wearing black, and everything she spoke about always related to the dead and the fallen.

b. The bereaved mother as an ethical authority. She is perceived in public as an "opinion leader" (Weimann) and as possessing "moral capital" (Lamott). In 1951, Rivka Guber was offered a place in the *Mapai* political party, and over the years, she took part in various committees on culture and education policies. On 31 May 1978, his first day as president of the State of Israel, Yitzhak Navon, in a symbolic gesture, dedicated a part of his day to visiting her. When Menachem Begin won the general elections and became prime minister in 1979 he invited Guber to take part in a small delegation that attended the Israel-Egypt peace accord signing ceremony. In 1969, Guber was awarded the Israel Prize for her life's work in education and immigrant absorption. Guber was invited to voice her opinions in many media channels on a range of national issues, such as the peace accord with Egypt and the resulting need to evacuate settlements.

c. The bereaved mother as myth. Based on the hegemonic bereavement model, the bereavement discourse must be apolitical, sacred, and pure. In 1958, Israeli writer Yehoshua Bar Yosef (1912-1992) dared to write a novel titled *Story of the Four*, which was based on the character of Rivka Guber. Bar Yosef, however, gave her human attributes, including sexuality, and described the implications of the loss of her sons on her life, such as insomnia and alcohol consumption. As a result, Bar Yosef was ostracized by many official institutions; his stories ceased to be printed in newspapers. Publishers refused for years to accept his manuscripts. He was publicly denounced by Ben Gurion and many others in Israel's intellectual leadership (Lebel, *Ben-Yosef*).

d. Public-media presence of the bereaved mothers. More so than the fallen soldiers themselves, their bereaved mothers became well known to the general public. They became, in Althusser's words, a part of the ideological state apparatus. Rivka Guber's funeral was organized by the Ministry of Defense's Soldier Commemoration Unit, as if she had been a fallen soldier herself. She was even buried at the military area of the Kfar Warburg cemetery in an official ceremony attended by the state's leaders and by school children who arrived by organized busses.

e. Dis-trauma–The antivictimology discourse of the bereaved mother. Bereaved mothers who functioned within the hegemonic bereavement model adopt a discourse of stoicism and heroism. They attribute meaning and productiveness to their loss, and acceptance their fate. They have an absence of anger toward the nation's leaders and outwardly express the trauma they experienced following their loss.

f. Bereaved mothers embark upon social activism following their loss. They exchange their trauma for moral and symbolic capital and penetrate the public discourse by carrying the flag of their loss and bereavement.

## The Political Model of Bereavement: Political Victimization

Following the Yom Kippur War (1973), and especially during the first Lebanon War (1982), a political bereavement model began to take shape, opposed to the hegemonic bereavement model. What had begun as a sporadic attempt by individual bereaved mothers was eventually transformed into a new military loss subculture and an epistemic bereavement community–led by bereaved mothers.

On 18 October, 1973 a few days following the loss of her son Yosef, Tikva Sarid from *Kibbutz Beit Hashita* published a newspaper article in which she demands the resignation of Minister of Defense Moshe Dayan (1915-1981). In her article titled "Dayan Must Go," Sarid writes that "The IDF was not prepared nor ready for this war. The Minister of Defense is responsible for not having informed the government of the severity of the situation. He is responsible for each of these horrendous crimes of omission" (38). Following Sarid's column, other mothers began to act in a similar manner, mostly individually and spontaneously, although some of the activities were collective and organized. One such example was a group of bereaved mothers who had lost their sons during the Yom Kippur War and organized to prevent Golda Meir (1898-1978), who had been prime minister during the War, from being awarded the Israel Prize.

A more organized endeavour took place during the First Lebanon War (1982) when for the first time in Israel's history a mass public protest was voiced against the legitimacy of this war while the fighting was still underway. Raya Harnik, the mother of Guni Harnik who died during the battle over the Beaufort, can be identified as the representative figure in the political bereavement discourse of the First Lebanon War. Journalist Ruvik Rosenthal, in a book about the families of the fallen soldiers of that battle, writes the following:

*After Guni died, Raya became a unique political figure ... the way
in which she appeared, her clear expression and her connection
to the battle of the Beaufort that became a symbol of the entire
Lebanon War, transformed her into the person most recognized
with the protest against the Lebanon War. Raya fitted this role.
She is willing to be exposed, knows how to express herself and
does not fret from possible responses to her actions, whether
supportive or negative ones. (112)*

Harnik became the central spokeswoman of the protest against the
War; she was invited to speak at many political rallies and was
considered an opinion leader. She wrote newspaper columns and was
regularly interviewed in the media. In particular, she became a role
model for mothers of soldiers and fallen soldiers joining the
bereavement community that was formed as a result of her work.

An example of one such movement was "Mothers against Silencing,"
initiated by Shoshana Shmueli, the mother of a soldier sent to Lebanon
for the third time. She published a letter in the press in which she
approaches parents of soldiers serving in Lebanon, and asks them to
protest the war that is futilely taking soldiers' lives. This movement was
one of the main catalysts forcing the Israeli government to withdraw
IDF forces from Lebanon to the South Lebanon security belt. Fourteen
years later, the Four Mothers organization was formed–also following a
publicist call to pressure the IDF to retreat from southern Lebanon back
to Israel.

In a column published in the *HaKibbutz* newspaper, titled "Mothers
Serving the Army," the writer called mothers of soldiers to make their
voices heard against the futile deaths of their sons in South Lebanon's
security belt. The writer of this column assumes that only mothers may
enter the public arena and act against this reality: "And do not tell me,
dear mothers, that you are being torn inside ... why do you accept this
situation, instead of demanding: do not take my son from me...we
*kibutznikim* [Kibbutz members] have always been the first to act ...
mothers, all of you out there, make your voices heard" (Eran).

Many mothers, including those who lost their sons in Southern
Lebanon, responded to the call by founding the Four Mothers
organization, which succeeded in causing decision makers to bring the
IDF forces from Southern Lebanon back to Israel and to end its presence

there. The movement pointedly approached soldiers' mothers and not their fathers, as explained by Dalia Itzik, a female government minister, who approached the prime minister when her son enlisted in the army and she feared that he would be sent to Southern Lebanon: "Until now you have heard only the voices of Generals. Today, I would like you to listen to a mother's voice" (qtd. in Segev. "A Mother's Voice" 5). The prime minister promised her that he would bring the boys back from Lebanon (Itzik, 2000).

The bereaved mothers who joined the organization used the media to influence the public agenda in ways that were previously unheard of. For example, in September 1997, hours after Eyal, son of Orna Shimoni–who became one of the leaders of Four Mothers–was killed in Lebanon, Orma decided to call the popular radio program *It's All Talk* and asked to speak live. Shelly Yacimovich, the show's host at the time, refused at first to interview a mother who had now lost her son, but Shimoni insisted she had a right to be interviewed, and that she had things to say. Eventually, Yacimovich agreed, and Shimoni used her time of live national radio to speak strongly against the IDF's continued presence in Lebanon. This interview further established a pattern in which bereaved mothers are considered legitimate interviewees moments after hearing that their sons have died and expressing their outrage toward the futile death forced upon them.

In addition, the public began to be more and more exposed to what within the hegemonic model of bereavement was supposed to remain behind the scenes: the pain and sorrow of bereavement. It is within this context that Manuela Dviri, whose son was killed in Southern Lebanon in 1998, became a public figure. Alongside her political activism within the Four Mothers organization, Dviri often spoke against the hegemonic model of bereavement and shared with the public the physical and emotional hardships of a bereaved mother, while she also refused to be tagged only by the bereaved mother role within the public sphere (Lebel, "War Opponents").

Harnik, Shmueli, Shimoni, and Dviri became the leaders of a new subculture of bereavement; they were created, promoted, and accepted by a community comprised nearly entirely of bereaved mothers, mostly belonging to the middle-high class of the Israeli political left. Harnik still speaks at leftist political gatherings, and Dviri ran for Knesset (national legislature) on behalf of a political party. Both became, after the loss of their sons, publicists in the Israeli and the international press.

The discourse of the political bereavement community may be characterized by five central attributes.

a. Collectivism of distress. The bereaved mother is one who exposes the traumatic aspect of her loss. She does not collaborate with the expectations that she should keep her feelings, pain and, sorrow in the private sphere, but rather she expressed them in the public while marking herself as victim.

b. Political victimology. The bereaved mother does not blame her victimhood on the concrete attacker (the enemy soldier) for the loss of her son in battle, but on the decision makers (prime minister, minister of defense) who sent her son to an unnecessary battle. According to her logic, they are the aggressors that need to be acted against.

c. Politicization–ascribing meaning by forming public policy. The bereaved mother can give no obvious meaning to her son's death, so she acts to transform it into something meaningful and productive. To do so, she must influence public policy in such a way that it would prevent the death of more soldiers under similarly futile circumstances in the future. Thus, she needs to become a political agent, and appropriate her loss for political action.

d. Incorporating the media. The bereaved mother can convert her trauma into moral capital to penetrate the public and media discourse. It is there that she promotes her ideological ideas, which are backed by the legitimacy of her loss and her sorrow.

## Military Accident Bereavement: Victimological Militarism

Although the mothers of the political bereavement discourse challenged Israel's official military bereavement discourse, they did so while protecting the army's hegemonic status. For instance, members of the Four Mothers organization decided to act according to what they referred to as "military immunity." According to the organization's statute, the IDF would not be targeted. "All our actions are aimed at changing the decision to remain in Lebanon, and are not directed against the IDF's soldiers."

Hence, the political bereavement mothers used their status for protesting against politicians, but not against the army. This basic rule was later abandoned by another bereavement community comprised of mothers who had lost their sons to military training accidents. The work of this community did in fact succeed in undermining the mythical status of Israel's army commanders–framed in Israeli culture as both highly professional and moral. These mothers exposed many of them as being involved in failures and cover-ups, which raised questions regarding the validity of the phrase quoted at the beginning of this chapter: "May every Jewish mother know that she has put her son under the care of commanders who are up to the task."

However, the first round of public activism following the loss of a son in a military training accident was not counter-hegemonic. Naomi Unger, the mother of Nizan who was killed in 1984 by a stray bullet during a Paratroopers Brigade special reconnaissance unit drill, decided immediately after his death that she would meet with IDF generals to ensure that the army would implement organizational changes preventing such accidents from happening again (Dromi). She even published a book that accompanied her many meetings with officers in order to raise awareness to the importance of safety in training (Unger).

In parallel, Yael German, whose son Eyal was killed in a training accident in 1987, established a group of bereaved parents (*Amichai*) that worked to eliminate the occurrence of these tragic events. The group acted in collaboration with the army, which led to the establishment of an IDF committee led by Major General Yaacov Lapidot investigating the matter and develop and implement a suitable policy (Doron and Lebel).

Both German and Unger later expressed their disappointment at the army's actions, which in essence co-opted their initiative. The Lapidot Report was never implemented, and training accidents, as well as their cover-up, continued to be a part of the army. In an interview to Sima Kadmon published in *Maariv* newspaper in 1992, German said the following:

> *For four years we believed that the army will do what is needed.*
> *The change ... ever since the publication of the Lapidot report ...*
> *we believed that if we sat still, cooperated, tried to convince,*
> *things will happen ... we chose the path of cultivation ... maybe we*
> *didn't do enough ... had we shouted, gone to the media, asserted*
> *stronger pressures, we would have prevented an accident.*

Conversely, a second group of mothers who lost their sons to military accidents formed a unique and counter-hegemonic loss community–led by the activism of Shula Melet, the mother of the soldier Amir Melet who died in what was referred to as "the net roulette." In this so-called game, a soldier in tied to an aircraft net barrier, which was then lifted off the ground while he is on it. But in Amir's case, the restraints fastened him to the net were torn, and he was thrown off; his body was flung into the air and then hurled onto the ground. Later on 30 March, 1992, he died in hospital. Melet decided to investigate the accident herself. She visited the base, interviewed soldiers, crossed testimonies, and contacted family members of previous soldiers who were killed in similar circumstances–and which had not been exposed to the public. She found that this game was actually a ceremony part of the organizational culture of the base and that additional lives had been lost this way in the past. Her investigation showed her just how superficial the military police investigation actually was and how, in fact, the case was covered-up while concealing testimonies and falsifying facts. She published an ad in the *Yad LeBanim* publication for bereaved parents, *Sia'ch Shkulim* ("bereaved parents discourse"), in which she reached out to other bereaved families whose sons were killed in military accidents, and she has called on them to organize and work together to eliminate these tragedies (Doron and Lebel).

On the one year anniversary of her son's death, Melet organized the first rally of its kind in her city: dozens of bereaved parents gathered on a makeshift stage in the presence of the media, and expressed, for the first time publicly, their demand to remove the investigation of accidents from within the IDF and lead to a civic examination.

Melet presented the military system as one that covers up tragedies and accidents, and she mentioned the names of commanders whom she believed should be dismissed from the army for their role in these accidents. At that time, Leah Zuriano, whose son died in a helicopter accident, joined Melet's leadership of the organization. In a letter to military journalists, she writes the following:

> *Have we lost our minds wanting justice to be heard? Yes.*
> *The blood of my son calls to me from the ground and I will not*
> *be silenced until the Knesset legislates a law that takes*
> *investigation, prosecution, judgment and punitive rights from*

*the hands of the military authorities in cases involving the death*
*of soldiers in training accidents. We have already paid the price*
*of silence. But the rest of the public must not forget that they are*
*not immune! Our struggle is not a personal one, but should be*
*a public struggle of all parents in this country*
*(qtd. in Lebel, "What Have" ).*

After Melet committed suicide, other bereaved parents continued her work. Zuriano swore on Shula Melet's grave that she will continue to promote her goals: "The response raised by your tragic death has promoted the cause for which you have fought. We promise you, on your grave, that we will not relent. With the empowerment that you have given us during your life and with the public response raised by your death, we will achieve our goal of extracting the investigations and judgments from the IDF" (qtd. in Lebel, "What Have").

The bereaved mothers began carrying out new practices that were then unheard of in Israel, all of which served to undermine the sanctified myths of national bereavement:

e. Military victimology. Shula Melet set out to form a close group of parents who feel that the army is to blame for the death of their sons, which led them to adopt a confrontational approach toward the military. Lea Zuriano has stated the following: "When Gili was killed Shula Melet came to the Shiv'a on her own accord ... today when there is a tragedy I immediately pick up the phone and call the family, and brief them: tell them what they need to do, send representatives, tell them they should get a lawyer immediately, that they should not accept the army's version, they should ask questions ... I immediately extend my experience to new bereaved families" (qtd. in Lebel, "What Have"). These bereaved mothers attend Shiv'as of soldiers killed in military accidents not only to give support and participate in the sorrow of the families, but also to convince and to direct newly bereaved mothers to public activism.

f. Marking the army as the aggressor. These bereaved mothers have identified senior IDF officers as responsible for their loss and as those against whom their struggle should be directed. This involves doing everything in their power to stop the advancement of these officers in military ranks as well as to transfer their authority to investigate accident to a civil authority. This idea was expressed in the name of the movement established by Shula Melet: the movement of the oppressed.

g. Public and judicial initiatives. Melet, Zuriano, and other bereaved mothers acted toward the establishment of public committees to investigate and expose the truth behind the deaths of soldiers in accidents and tragedies. They often petitioned the Supreme Court and conducted other public and judicial struggles to prevent the military advancement of officers whom they believed were involved in causing the death of soldiers in accidents.

h. The image of the army–visibility and communication. Mothers took advantage of a variety of means to influence public discourse, to define training accidents as a social problem, and to identify themselves as victims of the army. For instance, a number of mothers struggled to gain permission write their own texts on the military tombstone of their sons. Some of them wished to write on their sons' tombstone that the deceased is a victim of military negligence. Mothers who had joined Shula Melet began to appear in court rooms where trials were held against officers held responsible for soldiers' deaths in operational accidents. They did this in order to be interviewed by journalists covering these proceedings, whereas many senior officers attended and spoke in defense of their counterparts. In addition, the mothers used to attend prearmy enrollment assemblies, which the army normally organizes for high school students and their parents. At these assemblies, they would distribute leaflets detailing cases in which military officers had covered up operational accidents in the past in order to spread mistrust toward the military system among the youths about to enlist and to their parents.

In her struggle, Shula Melet marked a new alternative in the relationship between parents who lost their sons in military accidents, and the military system. She and her counterparts experienced what has been described as "betrayal trauma" toward the army. They worked to transform Israeli society's perceptions of the army, considered to be society's most trusted public institution. Melet's character and her work have been commemorated in a novel written by a popular writer (Gur, *Stone for Stone*)–a fact that has further strengthened the establishment of her pattern of work as an integral part of the modes of processing loss in Israel's public repertoire.

## The Religious-Zionist Model of Bereavement: Back to Heroism–the Heroic Victimology

In recent years, the presence of nationalist-religious Israelis has been constantly growing in the IDF's combat units as well as among its junior and middle command positions. This is a new security community who began to gain power following an initiative toward the establishment of premilitary academies, mostly in Judea and Samaria, led by senior reserves officers and rabbis. These academies have served as a launching pad for pushing young nationalist-religious men to enlist in elite units and from there, as expected, on to senior positions in the IDF and in Israel's public administration.

This is a community that has positioned itself in with values such as heroism, patriotism and nationalism, and is interested in being perceived as an alternative to the neoliberal communities that have become more critical, post-modern, and even post-nationalist (Lebel, "Settling" and "The 'Immunized'"). One of the ways in which this community emphasizes its differentiation from neoliberal groups is by creating an alternative to their political discourse of bereavement. Thus, for instance, Rabbi Yosef Weizen commented on the role of religious Zionism in this context: "We have been given the task to serve on the front line. How much weakness and softness of heart would be caused to every house in Israel if we fail to heroically meet this task. We must be the remedy to the Four Mothers disease ... the dam stopping the collapse of our national standing" (qtd. in Lebel, "Postmodern" 47).

Despite substantial criticism from rabbis and officers belonging to the Zionist movement regarding the excess influence of mothers (belonging to the political bereavement model) on decision makers, it is interesting to note that also among bereaved families belonging to this community–again those who embark upon social activism–are the bereaved mothers and not the fathers.

The ultimate leader of this loss community is Miriam Peretz, who, similarly to Rivka Guber, also lost her two sons to the army. In every speech, media appearance, or lecture she gives, Peretz emphasizes that she has no anger in her heart because as her son said, "Anyone living in this country must also lovingly accept its thorns," which revived the hegemonic bereavement discourse.

Peretz became a popular lecturer. She often spoke to youths and soldiers, and emphasized the Zionist and Jewish importance of serving in the army. People also make pilgrimages to her sons' graves, and write letters to her (Magal 207). She has become a representative figure of the religious sector and also of the army. She appears in fundraising events around the world for them. Her biography, published by the most popular publishing house in Israel, was written by one of Israel's most popular children's writers (Shir) and quickly became a bestseller.

The popular media began to refer to Miriam Peretz, just as they did to Rivka Guber in her time, as "the mother of the sons" (Oshrov). She is often endowed with many titles and awards. In 2014, she was chosen to light a torch at the Israel Independence Day ceremony next to the first woman appointed major-general in the IDF. In this ceremony, individuals perceived as having national importance are honoured and recognized. *Haarez* daily newspaper listed her as one of the most influential women in Israeli society, and the Menachem Begin Heritage Center in Jerusalem awarded her its annual award for her contribution to the nation. (Other recipients included an elite military unit and attorney Alan Dershowitz who defends Israel's policy in Judea and Samaria around the world.) In 2016, she received an honorary PhD from Bar Ilan University, the academic institution associated with Israel's religious Zionist movement, for her extensive contribution to empowering bereaved families and dedicating her life to her country and society. The honorary degree was awarded to her for being "the embodiment of national strength and a tribute to the victory of spirit and faith" ("Reasons").

Toward the general elections for the twentieth Knesset, Prime Minister Netanyahu offered Miriam Peretz a seat in his party's list for the Knesset, a proposal she refused. On Election Day, Netanyahu said that Miriam Peretz would be the first person he would call after winning the election, which he did.

Similarly to other mothers in the religious-Zionist sector, Peretz symbolizes the return to the normative, hegemonic bereavement, which gives meaning to the lost lives of soldiers, which is devoid of any victimization or anger and perceives the behaviour of the bereaved mother in the public sphere as a calling and as an opportunity to become a public figure following her loss. Due to her hegemonic behaviour and the fact that she has become a political resource for the state's leaders, she has also become worthy in the eyes of the establishment and is decorated and venerated by it.

Her situation is not unique. Other religious-Zionist mothers follow a similar discourse, but here, too, bereaved mothers carried out public activism, not fathers. On 12 June, 2014, three Israeli boys were abducted in Gush Ezyon by Palestinians and murdered on that same night. In the days that followed, while the army and large groups of volunteers toured the area in an attempt to find them, the boys' mothers and fathers were widely covered by the media. But after the boys' bodies were found, the fathers resumed their anonymity, whereas the mothers quickly became social activists and well-known public figures. They managed a commemoration project for their sons and organized social initiatives in their memory–the most significant of which is the annual awarding of the "Jerusalem Award for Israel's Unity" (Abbeba and Winovski). One of them even became a host of a weekly interview program on national telvision. In 2014, all three won the award granted by the Menachem Begin Heritage Center for their resilience and strength during the abduction and after being informed that their sons had been murdered. During the 2015 general election campaign, the three mothers appeared in an Internet clip where they called for national unity (Gronich).

## Public Grief Is Maternal

We have reviewed the epistemic communities of Israel's military bereavement discourse. In all of them, mothers established the communities, led them, and took part in them, and as a result they achieved public and media exposure and have become opinion leaders (Valente and Pumpuang) and epistemic authorities (Longworth; Ward). They form the public discourse of bereavement and promote political and public agenda; the foundation of the legitimacy of their status stems from the loss of their sons in the army.

This fact is surprising as following an exploratory research we have conducted, in which we reviewed Israel's formal leadership–from the establishment of the state until today–we found that many of the country's leaders are in fact bereaved fathers, whose sons were killed during their military service, but this detail did not become a known component of their public figure. The list includes three presidents, two Knesset speakers, one chief of staff, seven major-generals and ten Knesset members and ministers. All of them tended not to openly express the fact that they are bereaved fathers, and as a result, this biographical fact did not become a known part of their public images. We will try to explain this avoidance as well as the exclusivity of mothers as leaders of Israel's bereavement discourse.

## Possible Explanations for the Exclusivity of Motherly Use of Bereavement in the Public Sphere

In their pioneering book *Men Don't Cry ... Women Do*, Kenneth Doka and Terry Martin describe a range of findings concerning the difference between men and women in terms of expressing and processing loss. Among men, from adolescence onward, self-restraint and emotional mastery are perceived as virtues. The findings also show that women are more prone to emotional expressiveness, whereas men tend toward what researchers refer to as "masculine grief," characterized by an insistence toward "mastering the environment" and achieving continuum (i.e., not letting their personal loss harm their inertia and daily functioning). The researchers conclude that men feel more committed toward "image management" (Martin and Doka 107). Since is a higher prevalence of men in leading positions in the public sphere, they tend to have a public image to defend, at a higher prevalence than women.

In the psychocultural approach, emotional behaviour, even if allegedly spontaneous and voluntary, is a product of identifying and internalizing social expectations and management of presentations of self in the public sphere (Bullhngham and Vasconcelos). William Reddy has coined the term "emotional regime," which is similar to the term "feeling rules," coined by Arlie Hochschild. Both researchers not only emphasize the fact that the discourse legitimizes individuals to express only certain types of emotions, but also that "those who fail to follow grieving norms face community sanctions" (qtd. in Martin and Doka 119).

In the classic period of ancient Athens, for example, only women held public ceremonies of ritualized mourning (Loraux). The same is true in premodern and modern Muslim society–wailing women encourage other women to express their sorrow and suffering during the funeral and after it (Gamliel).

Allegedly, in the postmodern era, changes were expected to evolve in societal gendered role division–specifically in the area of victimization and trauma. In her pioneering paper about trauma as a political tool, Anne Lamott describes a process in which today the experience of trauma grants moral capital to those who experience it, and that by way of a trauma discourse, individuals and communities (refugees, the homeless) gain prominence following struggles taking place in the public discourse.

However, we have found from our current study that in terms of the processing of loss, the gendered role division of bereavement is maintained—even when examining communities in a neoliberal and postheroic condition, such as that of bereaved families pertaining to the political bereavement model. The face of those communities are always women, and in our case mothers. Even if they adopt an antiestablishment political discourse, in terms of gendered relationships, they reproduce the hegemonic condition that exclusively identifies woman in the public sphere with their trauma and loss.

To explain this phenomenon, we turn to Freud and Lacan's psychoanalytic theory on sexual differences. This theory identifies the mother, which lacks a penis, as "lacking while identifying the father, which according to the son has castrated his mother, with power and force. As both the penis and the castration are imagined, according to the same theory, society replaces the "penis" with "phallus." As explained by Lacan, in a phallocentric society the idea of castration is an abstract concept symbolizing loss of power.

These ideas may also serve to explain the gendered differences of the politics of bereavement. According to Lacan, one of the cultural embodiments of the phallus is the fetus in the women's womb and the offspring she will give birth to. This fetus/offspring was given to her by the man as an extension of his phallus. This is the symbolic functions of sexual relations, which may simultaneously compensate and reproduce the women's positioning as castrated and lacking, as missing the phallus. The fetus, for the mother, is an alternative phallus, and the loss of the son is also a state of castration of a symbolic loss of power. But the woman, who from the start is perceived as castrated and lacking in power, is the only one that has the privilege to use this fact in the public sphere. The man, in contrast, if identified in the public sphere with the loss of his son will as a result loose his image of potency, his power, and his uncastrated existence.

Thus, rather than the inclusion of the bereaved mother in the public sphere serving as an act of female empowerment or feminist resistance, in reality it serves as a tool for her reproduction and perpetuation as castrated, which may explain the cultural acceptance of these women within and by the hegemonic social order. Not only is the hegemonic social order not threatened by them as such, but their condition, in fact, further ratifies their being essentially castrated and devoid of symbolic and concrete power.

## Conclusions and Recommendations for Future Research

Following are two central conclusions of the current study which may be further elaborated by continued research:

a. Disenfranchised grief: when examining the psychocultural contexts of the study of bereavement, most studies focus on the concept of "disenfranchised grief" (Doka)–that is, the price paid by those whose loss is not recognized or supported by the public discourse. The current study points to the complexity of this phenomenon: the bereaved fathers, whose loss is excluded from public awareness, apparently pay a personal price, yet they are better represented in the public sphere.

b. Leadership capital and political structure of opportunities: the bereaved mothers presented here have correctly identified the political structure of opportunities and understood that they have the power to convert their trauma and loss into moral capital by which they would be able to penetrate the public and political discourse (Helms). However, this phenomenon, too, deserves a more complex analysis: the use of the political structure of opportunities may have enabled bereaved mothers to become public figures, but the extent of leadership empowerment and leadership capital, which they can acquire based on their position as bereaved mothers, is limited. It appears that different bases of legitimacy can deliver different levels of leadership capital. For bereaved mothers, this means the ability to become informal leaders (opinion leaders and discourse creators in civil society) but not a part of the formal public leadership, which is reserved for those who do not base their public status on victimization and trauma.

The second Lebanon War was perceived as a failure, and evoked civil protest and an investigation committee. A soldier returning from the war published a letter titled "An Open Letter to Mothers." As was understood in retrospect, during the days of the war, soldiers were not provisioned sufficient food, equipment, weapons, and training. The battles themselves were conducted in a deficient manner, a fact that led to many casualties. The soldier did not direct his letter to the prime minister or the minister of defense, or to the chief of staff or to the commander of his brigade. He directed it at those whom he believed might in future offer a remedy for his complaints–mothers. "Dear mothers," he writes. "Cry out for your sons who are still serving as warriors in the army, because no one will protect them for you" (Roni). According to the writer, only mothers to soldiers can embark upon a public protest to help their sons.

This belief is not limited only to this soldier; it is shared by some of the founders of Israel's feminist-academic discourse. Following Operation Protective Edge (2014), during which Israel fought the Hamas organization in Gaza, the Faculty of Humanities at Tel Aviv University organized a conference titled "How to Think about War." Faculty members from Israel's left wing complained that during the war, Israeli discourse had become filled with propaganda, and become nationalistic and noncritical (Scoop). The operation was carried out by the IDF at a time in which a large percentage of its soldier, commanders, and casualties, belonged to the Zionist-nationalist community–a fact that led to the hegemonic discourse adopted by mothers of soldiers and of those who lost their lives during the war.

One of the speakers at the conference in Tel Aviv University was Dr. Dana Olmert from the Department of Literature, who discussed the absence of public criticism toward the death of soldiers, a situation that in the past would have created an antiwar discourse. Olmert is the daughter of former Prime Minister Ehud Olmert, and she herself is an activist in Israel's leftist groups and in Israel's LGBT community. In her talk, later published as an article in *Haaretz* newspaper titled "Where Are the Mothers?", Olmert spoke with nostalgia of the 1990s, when mothers to soldiers and to fallen soldiers took part in what we refer to above as the political bereavement community–mothers who use their political victimology status to publically delegitimize the IDF's actions and to stop the fighting. In the article, Olmert laments on the absence of mothers who refuse to send their sons to fight: "Although it has been proven time and again that military attempts to solve the conflict are futile" (Olmert, "Where").

It seems that during periods of expectations to change the country's security policies, even if these expectations originate from the critical left wing, they are directed toward soldiers' mothers, and mostly toward mothers of soldiers who have died during their military service. Even Olmert accepts how entering the public sphere based on the status of victimization and trauma is a path exclusively reserved for mothers. Although some of these mothers may act to promote a political agenda (i.e., peace and not war), they will still, nevertheless, be acting within the confines of a gendered worldview.

## Works Cited

Abeba, D., and R. Winovski R. "The Winners of the Jerusalem Award for Israel's Unity Have Been Declared." YNET, 28 Apr. 2015, www.ynet. co.il/articles/0,7340,L-4651369,00.html. Accessed 9 Jan. 2018.

Altusser, L. *Lenin and Philosophy.* Monthly Review Press, 1978.

Ben David, S. "A Victim of Career: Causes and Process." *Delinquency and Social Deviance*, vol. 17, no. 1, 1989, pp. 5-17.

Ben Gurion, D. "Speech on the Occasion of the Publication of Volume C of the Book Parchments of Fire' 28 September, 1961." *Leaves in His Memory*, edited by R. Avinoam,: Am Hasefer, 1976.

Ben Gurion, D. *A Letter to Rivka Guber, 24 August, 1950.* Archives of the Ben Gurion Heritage Institute, file 1/c/10. 1950.

Ben Gurion, D. *Davar*, 26 March, 1951, p. 4.

Ben Gurion, D. *Davar*, 31 Oct., 1971, p. 5.

Ben Gurion, D. *Thoughts about Rivka Guber.* Archives of the Ben Gurion Heritage Institute, file 1/c/10. 1957.

Bloodgood, E. "Epistemic Communities, Norms, and Knowledge." *International Studies Association Annual Conference*, 2008, alcor.concordia. ca/~eabloodg/ISA2008ECNormsInfo.pdf. Accessed 9 Jan. 2017.

Bullingham, L. and A. Vasconcelos. "The Presentation of Self in the Online World: Goffman and the Study of Online Identities." *Information Science*, vol. 39, no. 1, 2013, pp. 101-12.

Doka, K. *Disenfranchised Grief.* Lexington Books, 1989.

Doron, G. and Lebel U. "The Politicization of Bereavement." *Panim*, vol. 11, no. 1, 1999, pp. 55-64.

Dromi, U. "So That There Shall Be No More Victims." *Haaretz*, 10 Apr., 2007, www.haaretz.co.il/1.1400914. Accessed 9 Jan. 2018.

Eran S. "Mothers in the Service of the Army." *Hakibbutz.* 6 March, 1997, p. 3.

Eyal Ben-Ari. *Mastering Soldiers.* Berghahn, 1998.

Gamliel, T. *The Aesthetics of Sorrow: the Wailing Culture of Yemenite-Jewish Women.* Wayne State University Press, 2014.

Gronich, Z. "The Three Mothers of the Abducted Soldiers in a Message of Unity." *Kikar*, 1 Jan., 2015. www.kikar.co.il/160152.html. Accessed 9 Jan. 2018.

Guber, R. *The Brothers.* Masada, 1950.

Gur, B. *Stone for Stone.* Keter, 1998.

Hochschild, A. "Emotion Work, Feeling Rules and Social Support". *American Journal of Sociology*, vol. 85, no. 4, 1979, pp. 551-73.

Kadmon, S. "Interview with Yael German". *Maariv.* 27 Nov., 1992.

Lacan, J. "The Significance of the Phallus." *Ecrits: A Selection.* Routledge, 2006, pp. 311-22.

Lamott, F. "Trauma as a Political Tool." *Critical Public Health*, vol. 15, no. 3, 2005, pp. 219-28.

Lebel, U. *Ben-Yosef Vs. Rivka Guber.* Unpublished manuscript, 2017.

Lebel, U. "Postmodern or Conservative? Competing Security Communities over Military Doctrine–Israeli National-Religious Soldiers as Counter [Strategic] Culture Agents." *Political and Military Sociology: An Annual Review*, vol. 40, 2013, pp. 23-57.

Lebel, U. *Politics of Memory.* Routledge, 2013.

Lebel, U. "Postmortem Politics: Competitive Models of Bereavement and Civil-Military Bargaining over Military Secrecy." *Journal of Modern Jewish Studies*, vol. 5, 2, 2006, 163-81.

Lebel, U. "Settling the IDF: The Pre-Military Academies Revolution and the Creation of a New Security Epistemic Community." *Israel Affairs*, vol. 21, no. 3, 2015, pp. 361-91.

Lebel, U. "The 'Grief Regime' Gatekeepers: 'Victimological Militarism' and the Symbolic Bargaining over National Bereavement Identity." *Culture and Rites/Rights of Grief*, edited by Z. Bialas et al., Cambridge Scholars Publishers, 2013, pp. 73-99.

Lebel, U. "The 'Immunized Integration' of Religious-Zionists within Israeli Society." *Social Identities*, vol. 22, no. 6, 2016, pp. 642-66.

Lebel, U. "War Opponents and Proponents: Israeli Military Mothers from Rivka Guber to Four Mothers." *Motherhood and War: International Perspectives*, edited by C. Phelan and D. Cooper, Palgrave McMillan, 2014, pp. 159-79.

Lebel, U. "What Have They Willed Us in Their Deaths? Bereavement and Time in Israel." *Memory Games: Concepts of Time and Memory in*

*Jewish Culture*, edited by Y. Benziman, The Van Leer Jerusalem Institute & Hakibbutz Hameuchad, 2008, pp. 205-30.

Lebel, U. and G. Hatuka. "Israeli Labor Party and the Security Elite 1977-2015: 'De-Militarization as Political Self-Marginalization.' *Israel Affairs*, vol. 22, no. 3-4, 2016, pp. 641-63.

Longworth, G. "Epistemic Authority." *Analysis*, vol. 74, no. 1, 2014, pp. 157-66.

Loraux, N. *Mothers in Mourning*. Cornell University Press, 1998.

Mack, A. "Civil War." *Journal of Peace Research*, vol 39, no. 5, 2002, pp. 515-25.

Magal, Y. *Srugim Ba'kane*. Yediot Acharonot, 2016.

Martin, T., and Kenneth Doka. *Men Don't Cry... Women Do*. London: Routledge, 2000.

Meyers, O. *Israeli Journalists as an Interpretive Memory Community*. Unpublished Dissertation. University of Pennsylvania, Philadelphia, 2004.

Olmert, D. "Where are the Mothers?" *Haaretz*, 26 Aug., 2014, www.haaretz.co.il/beta/1.2416493. Accessed 15 Jan. 2018.

Oshrov N. "Miriam's Song: The Story of Miriam Peretz." *Haaretz*, 13 July 2011, www.haaretz.co.il/literature/1.1180991. Accessed 9 Jan. 2018.

Peretz M. "Speech on Jerusalem's Day, at Ammunition Hill, Jerusalem." *Beit-Eliraz*, 12 May 2010, www.beit-eliraz.org.il/?page_id=250. Accessed 9 Jan. 2018.

"Reasons for Awarding Honorary Doctorate Degrees, 7 June, 2016." *Bar Ilan University* www1.biu.ac.il/hondocs. Accessed 9 Jan. 2017.

Ronel, N. and U. Lebel. "When Parents Lay Their Children to Rest." *Journal of Social and Personal Relationships*, vol. 23, no. 4, 2006, pp. 507-22.

Roni. "Letter by a Soldier Returning from the Second Lebanon War." *Technion*, 2006, http://ie.technion.ac.il/~miriams/private/. Accessed 9 Jan. 2018.

Sarid, T. "Dayan Must Go." *Maariv*, 29 Nov. 1973, p. 2.

Segev, T. "A Mothers' Voice." *Haaretz*, 18 Feb., 2000, p. 5.

Shapira, M. "Yad LeBanim–A Name That Will Forever Remain in the History of the Jewish People." *Haaretz, Letters to the Editor*, 23 Nov. 1948.

Shir. S. *Song of Miriam*. Yediot Aharonot, 2011.

Shmueli, S. "Letter to the Editor", *Al Hamishmar*. 27 April, 1983. Print.

Unger, N. *Stop the Bullet*. Tel Aviv: Ministry of Defense, 1989. Print.

Valente, T. and P. Pumpuang. "Identifying Opinion Leaders to Promote Behavior Change." *Health Education and Behavior*, vol. 34, no. 6, 2007, pp. 881-96.

Wagner, A. "Methodology and Communitarism." *Voluntas*, vol. 8, no. 1, 1997, pp. 64-88.

Ward, T. "Expert Testimony, Law and Epistemic Authority." *Applied Philosophy*, vol. 34, no. 2, 2016, pp. 263-77.

Weimann, G. "The Influentials." *Public Opinion Quarterly*, vol. 55, no. 2, 1991, pp. 267-79.

William, R. *The Navigation of Feeling*. Cambridge University Press, 2001.

# II.

# Me-Mother-Military:
# Personal Experiences

Chapter Six

# Mom Wore Combat Boots: An Autoethnography of a Military Sociologist

Morten Ender[1]

Bubba dared my mom to join the army. It was the fall of 1974, and Bubba had enlisted in 1973–an early African American volunteer to join the U.S. Army as the military transitioned from a conscription military to an all-volunteer force in 1973 (Segal). A specialist 4 (SP4) in the active army and stationed in South Korea, Bubba was a military policeman (MP). Technically, he was my stepuncle, but I had no connection to Bubba. He was on leave, visiting his sister Linda, who was my stepaunt on my stepdad's side of the family. He sat in a big chair in the living room, spitshining his black leather combat boots and military police utility belt, surrounded by the paraphanalia for shining–spread out newspaper, Kiwi black shoe polish, water in the lid, a shoepolish stained white damp rag, horsehair shine brush, and an old pantyhose for buffing. He and my mom argued about her ability to survive the demands of army life, especially the rigours of basic training. My mom was not physically active, but she wasn't unfit either. Bubba had her stereotyped though: a woman, two kids, living in the suburbs, and "getting up there" at thirty-three years of age. He vastly underestimated her tenacity.

Like many American working-class families, on Friday and Saturday nights in the 1970s, my family–mom, stepdad, baby sister, and I–would visit and spend time with family. In our case, we would visit grandparents in South Central, Los Angeles, or an uncle and aunt in Compton,

California. Uncle Raymond worked mostly construction, and Auntie Linda worked for the local government, and they had two young daughters. Linda's five younger siblings lived with them as well. Their mother had died years earlier, and their father was not present. They had moved from rural Mississippi to Los Angeles in the early 1970s, where Raymond met her. On those weekend nights, the adults drank alcohol, ate, smoked cigarettes, played cards, listened to music, danced, argued, laughed, and tolerated one another's company. We kids played cards and board games, and entertained the adults with our dance moves once they were tipsy.

On this night in 1974, Bubba was home on military leave. He captured everyone's attention with his far away experiences, travels, and military regalia and paraphanalia. Ironically, my mother proved the most intrigued by him–far more than any of us kids including three fairly typical middle-school boys who should have been enamoured with a real-life American soldier in our midst. But we had no interest. An antiwar movement and Black civil rights permeated our community along with The Jackson Five, seven consecutive NCAA basketball titles for the local UCLA Bruins (1967-1973), newly renamed Kareem Abdul-Jabbar (formerly Lew Alcindor) of the Los Angeles Lakers, and the Los Angeles Dodgers, all occupied our attention far more.

Later that fall, mom met with a military recruiter. She possessed a number of attributes that typcially would and should have disqualified her for military service, and at a minimum, she required waivers. She lacked U.S. citizenship. She had two children and a husband. She required an American high school diploma or equivalent. (Although not recognized at the time, she had completed vocational high school in Germany in business administration and had apprenticed in the family-owned company.) English is her second language, and she was approaching her mid-thirties. The U.S. Army in the mid-1970s, however, sought volunteers from all sectors of American society, as the antimilitarism in the U.S. following the long Vietnam War remained high and undermined recruiting efforts.

Mom studied for, took, and passed the general education diploma (GED) examination over multiple days. The U.S. Army required a high school diploma or GED equivalent from women but not from men. She beat the thirty-five-year-old age limit of first enlistment by two years at the time she would enter basic training. She received a waiver for having two dependent children. The waiver included a formal, signed letter of intent from a female family member who committed to caring for my sister and I while mom was separated from us for her stateside military duties–essentially a gender-specific family care plan. This letter was necessary despite my mom and stepfather having been a dual-earner couple my entire life. Furthermore, my stepfather was fairly nontraditional in his involvement in our lives. He and my mother shared the division of household labour and caregiving fairly equitably–a social novelty for African American men (Gerson).

Mom's green card granted her permanent residence status in the United States but prohibited her from doing overseas tours while on active duty in the military. She would eventually rectify this formally during her first stateside assignment in Kansas. On the Armed Forces Vocational Aptitude Battary (ASVAB) test she qualified to be a 75B-unit clerk (Brown 123-24), which was in line with her 1950s vocational education and journeyman training in Germany where she prepared to run the family business. As she enlisted in 1975, larger, macrolevel social issues shaped her opportunities. Notably, the AVF and President Richard Nixon's task force to examine the utility of an all-volunteer military, labeled the "Gates Commission," somewhat failed to anticipate massive numbers of women enlisting. The military would eventually take advantage of this unanticipated recruiting pool, especially since men inceasingly did not enlist (Segal 36-37). The movement of thousands of women in the military, especially racial and ethnic minorities, put wind in women's sails, which mutually encouraged still others to fill the ranks (Enloe, *Maneuvers*).

Looking further back, although American women served in large numbers and gallantly during World War II (Moore, *To Serve*; Moore, *Serving*), the 1948 Women's Armed Forces Integration Act provided somewhat regular status for women but kept them in the segregated women's army corps (WACs)–except for nurses and medical specialists (Segal 119). The law required that women be older than men upon first enlistement (eighteen versus seventeen), and women required parental permission if under twenty-one. (Men only needed such permissions under the age of eighteen.) Husbands and children had to show economic dependancy on the mother to receive military family-related benefits. Finally, there existed a two percent total enlisted force strength cap on the number of women allowed to serve along with a well-defined policy for their exclusion from combat.

Of course, women in the 1940s were not subject to the draft, so they were volunteers. In 1948, following the passage of the Act, 3,300 women served (Marsden 58-59), but during the Korean War (1950-1953) roughly forty-six thousand women served with only female nurses serving in the theatre of war. The two percent cap was struck down in 1967, and other provisions approaching more equity resulted. Yet only 500 WACs outside of nurses served in Vietnam (Segal 120).

Mom—tall, blond, blue-eyed, German, tenacious, and unwavering—entered gender-segregated army basic training at Fort Jackson, South Carolina toward the end of the Vietnam War in the summer of 1975, following a delayed entry program enlistment in January 1975. The delay allowed me to complete my last year of middle school at Franklin Delano Roosevelt Junior High School. At the time, I was approaching my fifteenth birthday, about to enter high school, and might have been the oldest dependent son of a brand new military recruit in America.

The 1970s proved to be a time of tumultous change and opportunity for women in the larger American society (see Gail Collins). Momentous social forces such as the women's rights movement, a counter-culture movement, an antiwar movement (and by default an antimilitary movement), the end of military conscription, and the advent of the all-volunteer force directly impacted the military. Numerous Supreme Court cases resulted in victories for women in the military at the time (Hicks Stiehm 113-33). Compounding the large scale changes, a marked ambivalent attitude toward acceptance of women in the military arose among American civilians and servicemembers (Marsden). Survey findings pointed to "uncertainty, resistance, ambivalence, both in the military community and in the general society" (Marsden 68). Major distinctions existed in the enlisted ranks between men and women with women more oriented toward equality than men (Hicks Stiehm 105). The difference among the sexes continues at this writing some forty years later (Ender et al. 77-82; Ender 87-101; Matthews et al. 241). Mom seized the social historical moment not for her progressive politics connected to the larger movements in the society (but they certainly provided the social conditions). Rather, her choices centred on much more pragmatic and microlevel concerns—for herself and her children.

This chapter is an autoethnographic study of my memories and experiences commingled and corroberated with my mother's—including her family and childhood, our move to America, life leading up to joining the military, and her military career. It is a messy, boots-on-the-ground, intesectional case study of race, class, gender, ethnicity, region, and culture. I write this autoethnographic study well into my career as a professor of sociology specializing in social psychology and military sociology. It is now twenty-one years after my mother retired as a sergeant major (E9) following twenty-two years in the U.S. Army. A career full of both informal lauding and praise by superiors, peers, and subordinates, and formal decorations, awards, badges, citations, and campaign ribbons–including among others the Legion of Merit, Meritorious Service Medal, National Defense Service Medal, Expert Marksmanship, Marksman Marksmanship Qualification Badge with Pistol, Small Bore Bar, and the Silver German Army Marksmanship Badge.

What follows is an autoethnographic link between the early influences leading me to becoming a military sociologist and my mother's military life–including her birth and childhood during and post-WWII, her adolescence in Germany, her marriage with an American soldier, and our immigration to the U.S. I follow with our brief life in the rural U.S. midwest of Kansas, an interracial second marriage and living in urban Los Angeles and Compton, California, her enlistment in the U.S. Army in her early 30s just after the advent of the 1973 all-volunteer force, and her highly successful military career in the U.S. and abroad–but a career socially constructed around traditional gender roles. This autoethnographic study is a personal narrative that features a self-consciously and reflective exploration of the interplay between my mother's life, my socialization as a civilian and military brat self, and larger cultural and social contexts experienced at the intersection of the armed forces and the larger society. The goal is to write meaningfully, socially, and evocatively about a topic at the intersection of military scholars, women, and military sociologists. In particular, I highlight the links between my career and scholarship–including courses I teach such as "Social Inequality"; "Armed Forces and Society"; and "Marriage and the Family"–my mother's career, soldiers in our homes and our lives, and the benefits and significance of the various locales in the U.S. and abroad.

## Autoethnography

This chapter is an exercise in self-reflection. Similar to an autobiography and in the tradition of many feminist scholars, I use the word "I"; the story clearly centres around my mother's U.S. Army experiences, with particular focus on twenty-two years (1975-1997). I interweave my experiences into the background of her career. Thus, I am writing a personal biography of sorts, what some have called a "deep familiarity with a subject," which has become increasingly acceptable in some circles of ethnographers (Berg and Lune 208-10). Her military career began during my teenage years and lasted well into my graduate studies in sociology. I make little attempt to be neutral or value free in this endeavour. Rather, I am a full subject in this experience and in writing this chapter. My voice is not in the background of this chapter; rather, it is out front, subjectively disclosed. I share the experiences as interactions and observations I had during this period and now but with a significant military sociological gaze.

Qualitative methodologists now refer to this form of personal narrative as autoethnography (Ellis and Bochner 739; Tomaselli et al. 347). Carolyn Ellis and Arthur Bochner define autoethnography as "an autobiographical genre of writing and research that displays multiple layers of consciousness, connecting the personal to the cultural" (739). They go on to provide a long but incomplete list of over forty terms used by social scientists to refer to similar methods, including interpretative biography and sociopoetics (739-40).

Military studies are beginning to embrace autoethnography. A lone study published in 2006 in the scholarly journal *Armed Forces & Society* called for military sociology to be more inclusive of autoethnography and to expand from the traditional positivistic model of sociological research (Higate and Cameron 219). The two authors glean their appeal from the sparse autoethnographic work done by others in military sociology and then present their own work on British veterans and their partners.

There are now three new edited volumes dealing exclusively with a social methodological focus unique to military populations (Carreiras et al.; Carreiras and Castro; Soeters et al.). Each volume is inventive and fresh in its own right. More to the point, each includes direct and indirect methodological nods to autoethnography.

Two chapters in Carreiras et al (2016) using authethnography standout and provide guidance for this chapter. First, a chapter by my mentors David Segal and Mady Segal (180-195) detail the authors' lifeworlds as conjoined military sociologists: married, teaching, and researching in the same departments across fifty years. They stress that linked lives, sharing time and space, across the life course, is not only legitimate and informative, but useful in providing insights to subjective experiences informing objective scholarship, in this case military sociology. The second chapter is from a dissertation by Ian Liebenberg where he reflects on his doctoral research with the South African Truth and Reconciliation Commission and how autoethnography is important, adds value, and "liberates research findings from imposed objectives" (50-67). So I return to Bochner who asks, "So the question is not, 'Does my story reflect my past accurately?' as if I were holding a mirror to my past. Rather I must ask, "What are the consequences my story produces?" (Ellis and Bochner 746). I will leave this to you the reader to determine. I hope this chapter contributes to an auto-ethnographic research legacy in military sociology and inspires others to reflect on their own subjective experiences and education. May it also contribute to an emerging thinking and experiences of mothers and their sons (Brillian Muhonja and Brenard).

This chapter is a postmodern ethnography of sorts, which transcends autobiography and ethnography, and links the self and society and the objective and the subjective in novel ways (Reed-Danahay 2-3) in order to highlight intergenerational occupational linkages across three generations. My method here is based on an extorted oral family herstory I obtained from my mother (and stories from my grandmother and great grandmother) commingled with my autobiographical interpretation of our family history–done mostly over a number of family Christmas visits in the American southeast. With my mother's assistance, we used the family photograph albums along with my mother's certificate of release or discharge from active duty (DD Form 214) to generate a frame and discussion of the past. Finally, my mother commented on a late draft of the final manuscript and provided substance, confirmation, nuance, and editorial input.

## The Ender Family

The first generation of the Ender clan known to significantly experience the military and war are my maternal grandparents. My mother, Ilka Maria Johanna Brown (neé) Ender, was born during World War II on 23

November, 1941 in Bocholt, Germany, the only child of Gaston and Johanna "Hanni" Ender. "Omi," as we affectionately called my grandmother, met my grandfather during his war convalescence near Bocholt in the Nord Rhein Westphalen state of Germany. My grandfather had been drafted into Hitler's Wehrmacht and soonafter received severe wounds early in the military campaign of Germany's invasion of Czechoslavakia in 1938. Serving as a radio and telephone operater (RTO), he had been dropped behind the frontlines to radio back communiqués to the rear lead elements. He was struck by mortar fire and received schrapnel in his upper right back, shoulder, and arm, and was evacuated back to Germany to recover. Later discharged, he never returned to military duties.

Gaston Ender (left) with unidentified soldier convalescening near Bocholt, Germany, during WWII, circa 1939. Personal photograph owned by the author. 22 August 2017.

Hanni came from a working-class family in Bocholt, Germany. Her father had served in the enlisted army in Germany during WWI and survived the war. We know little about his term of service. The only relic from his experience is a family heirloom–a ceremonial sabre, sash, and holster. Hanni worked as a waitress at the time, and my grandfather, like the other men of his era, spent time in the Gastätte (taverns) and liked to drink beer. My grandparents met and fell in love. They courted in Bocholt during his convalescence and did not marry until 1943 because the National Socialists (Nazis) enforced the Nuremberg Laws in Germany. The laws required German couples to prove they had no Jewish heritage before they could marry. The system was backlogged for some time, and my grandparents apparently had no patience for such bureacratic nonsense–my mother was born in 1941 (author note: my family were never members of the National Socialist German Workers' Party aka the Nazi Party).

Gaston Ender and Hanni Kruse, Bocholt, Germany circa 1940.
Personal photograph owned by the author. 22 August 2017.

Once my Opi Gaston could travel, the nuclear family moved to his hometown of Bremen, Germany. The Americans had since entered the war bombing major German cities, such as Bremen. My paternal great-grandparents, grandparents, and their newborn daughter, my mom, spent considerable time for the remainder of the war forty kilometers southeast of Bremen in the Lower Saxony region of Germany–a small, rural, countrytown surrounded by woods and hills called Kirchlinteln, where the family had a cottage. The move allowed them to avoid the bombings in Bremen. My great-grandfather, Opi Paul, owned and managed a graphics firm near the heart of Bremen–the Steintor Quarter. Privileged as they were, the family smartly stayed in the country where he would visit on weekends. Much of Bremen was levelled during the war by arial bombardments, including my great-grandfather's graphics firm. The airplane and bombing are immortalized in the film *Memphis Belle*–the name of an (in)famous WWII American B-17 bomber of which two films were made, a documentary in 1944 and a feature-length Hollywood film in 1990. The Memphis Belle bomber completed twenty-nine bombing missions including an 17 April, 1943, bombing of Bremen, Germany–likely the day the family firm was bombed.

Paul Ender (left) and Herr Kahlenberg (the company photographer) in front of the bombed out factory, Steintor Quarter of Bremen, Germany circa April 1943. Personal photograph owned by the author. 22 August 2017.

My grandfather, Gaston Ender, was born in Hötensleben, Germany, the only son of Paul and Helene "Lene" Ender (née Reimann). They moved to Bremen soon after his birth and started a company named Graphische Betriebe Paul Ender (Graphics Works or Operations Paul Ender) in the Steintor Quarter of Bremen–a famous quarter today known as the bohemian and cosmopolitan part of Bremen a few blocks from the city centre. At its height, the company employed twenty-seven people. After the war, my family and the employees rebuilt the building and the business from the ground up. After WWII, my grandparents and their daughter moved into a small four room apartment on Bismarck Strasse in Bremen, and my grandfather worked for his father for a few years. My mother and my grandmother's younger brother–Hermann "Sony" Kruse, born two months after my mom in January 1942–grew up together and learned the family graphics trade and business with an anticipation of taking it over one day. Unfortunately, the firm folded because of an accountant's embezzelment in the early 1950s following my great-grandfather's death and my great-grandmother and grandfather's inability to recoup and manage the company. My grand-father also continued to suffer greatly from his physical war injuries and died in 1968 at the age of forty-eight. With the death of my grandfather and the loss of the family business, Omi returned to her premarriage trade–waitress. She retired at age sixty-five and lived in the same apartment building until her death in 1997.

My mother had a typical post-WWII Germany upbringing in Bremen. She studied business in high school and apprenticed in the family's graphics firm. At a young age, she and her circle of friends developed a fascination with all things of popular American culture. They enjoyed learning English in school, adored Elvis Presley who was stationed in Germany as a soldier, and loved American films, especially *Gone with the Wind*. At eighteen, she met and had a relationship with an Italian expatriot a few years her senior, who worked as a bartender at a local Bremen establishment called Club 99–a defunct bar probably named after the Werder Bremen First Division professional soccer team. I am the love child of that affair. I was born in 1960. My biological father played no role in my life. In the early 1960s, at the height of the Cold War, thousands of American soldiers were stationed in Bremen and Bremerhaven. Six months after I was born, my nineteen-year-old mother met and married an American enlisted military police man stationed in Bremen, Germany, who hailed from Denver, Colorado.

## America Bound

In December 1962, my mother and I emigrated to the United States with our American G.I. soldier destined for the American midwest having acrossed the Atlantic ocean aboard a U.S. troop ship. My stepfather, his peers, and the troop ship to the United States were to be my first exposure to Americans, and they were all military.

Mom and her first husband on their wedding day at the
Bismarck Strasse apartment, Bremen, West Germany circa 1961.
Personal photograph owned by the author. 22 August 2017.

Postcard sent from my mother to her mother, 14 December, 1962, of the
USNS General Alexander M. Patch (T-AP-122) Army Transport Service troop
and family carrier ship. Personal photograph and postcard owned by the author.
22 August 2017.

After an extended visit in Denver with American stepgrandparents,
we moved to Fort Leavenworth, Kansas. My stepfather would serve as a
military guard in the United States Disciplinary Barracks–the U.S. Army
prison. Less than two years later, my mother divorced and married my
second stepfather–an African American born and raised in Leavenworth, Kansas. Both worked at the post exchange on Fort Leavenworth
and were twenty-three years old. Kansas was one of some states that
allowed for interracial marriages in 1964, as the Supreme Court case
outlawing state-based antimiscegenation would not be ratified until
1967 (Loving V. Virginia). Soonafter, we moved briefly to Wichita,
Kansas, and then Los Angeles, California, where we eventually settled
in Compton, California–at the time a racially and ethnically mixed
working-class suburb of Los Angeles. However, with the ongoing "white
flight," Compton became one of the most crime-ridden and gang
prevalent cities in America (Baker and Rivele).

By the early 1970s, mom became disenchanted with her lifeworld.
She worked in a printing factory, and my stepfather worked in a foundry.
They owned a plain and modest two-bedroom and one-bath pink house.
A basketball rim hung over a one-car garage. They had two children and
a dog named Henry Gibson. I played baseball almost year round, and

my stepdad coached me. We went to Disneyland and Knott's Berry Farm. Life for my mother had become stable but static and fairly uneventful. Novelty was in short supply, and opportunities to transcend an American working-class life seemed limited. Mom had higher aspirations. Our house was robbed a few times, and the cars were vandalized regularly. I could not leave the neighbourhood for fear of gang violence against me. My middle school was surrounded by barbed wire fencing, and we had two uniformed, gun totting security guards on campus. I left Compton for good the summer before I would attend high school. It would have been perilous for me as nongang affiliated and the only white person attending the exclusively African American and Hispanic American Manuel Dominguez High School in Compton, California. Outside of the protection of my 'hood–usually about a two block radius–at a minimum, I would have been harrassed, bullied, mugged, and possibly, given the social problems and violence, terrorized, assaulted, or worse. With a new daughter, my mom wanted better and desired adventure especially to visit her family back in Germany. I had spent a number of summers in Germany, crowdfunded by our extended kin there. As a family, we could only afford to visit once for ten days in 1972 (although I stayed the entire summer).

Family portrait circa 1972 with author in back row.
Personal photograph owned by the author. 22 August 2017.

After Bubba's challenge in 1974, mom doggedly persued the military. The army would soon become a vehicle to travel and have more autonomy. The latter especially because her second husband, like her first, became increasing authortarian, domineering, and traditional with her (not at all with me or my sister however–in fact, he was and is quiet loving). The liberations of the feminist movement creeped into our home and neighbourhood, and mom's biography would soon intersect with American women's military history.

## Army Basic Training

During the early years of the all-volunteer force, there was a quadrupling of women in the U.S. armed forces. At the time of fiscal year (FY) 1973– the year when the all-volunteer force was born–there were about 43,000 enlisted women on active duty, or about 2.2 percent of the total enlisted force. By the end of FY 1975, there were 95,000 enlisted women on active, or about 5.3 percent of the force. At the end of FY 1978, 117,000 women constituted 6.6 percent of the enlisted force; and in December 1980, 151,000 women made up 8.8 percent of the enlisted force (Department of the Army; Segal 120).

Mom enlisted in the U.S. Army in the summer of 1975 along with 19,069 women that year. Her first duty station after basic training and quelling her husband's trepidation was Fort Leavenworth, Kansas, essentially returning to his birthplace and hometown. That summer, she sent me to Michigan to be with my godmother and her childhood friend–Ingrid (for my safe-keeping as my drift into juvenile deliquency during the school year increased, including gang-banging, and would have likely magnified during the hot summer months with fifty percent less parental supervision). She left for basic training at Fort Jackson, South Carolina, and then on to the now defunct Fort Benjamin Harrison in Indianapolis, Indiana for advanced individual training (AIT) in her military occupation specialty (MOS) field. In basic training, her young peers nicknamed her "Mama" because of her age. She thrived, and she loved it and all the women–Blacks, whites, and Hispanics, all connected with the anomalous blond-haired, blue-eyed, thirtysomething who spoke both with a German accent and Black-street dialect. Culturally, she was an ecletic mix of a privileged, middle-class German upbringing and some hip, urban Black experience–enlisting straight out of Compton, California.

Before her graduation from AIT, she picked me up from Michigan and brought me down to Indianapolis for a few days before driving to our new home in Leavenworth. I met all her peers and because this California kid had grown his blond hair far out and was fifteen, many of the newly minted GIs at the noncommissioned officers (NCO) Club mistook me for a girl–a couple of them asked me to dance–to everyone's amusement. It was my fifteenth birthday, and I was embarrassed but comforted by all the newly minted and mostly Black, female, amd junior enlisted troops. I was closer to their age than they were to my mother's. They all clearly respected, adored, and loved my mom and embraced me. For many, she was probably their first white friend and peer. She resonated with young troopers, especially minorities, and they with her. It would become a pattern throughout her career.

Indeed, her caregiving role, protecting my sister and I, and being older with an American working-class sensibiliy seemed to intesect nicely and extend well into the army. Scholars note that in the mid-1970s, the U.S. military had a relatively limited national security threat and the cultural values of the time promulgated rhetoric that supported a future equality for women in American society despite military women overtly being relegated to combat service support positions (Gereben Schafer et al. 7-13; W. Segal 761-62). The socially constructed gender roles hindered women in the military in general (Lucas and Segal 157), but they served my mother particularly well as she moved to her first duty station in Kansas.

## Fort Leavenworth, Kansas

Fort Leavenworth, Kansas, is a wonderful place to grow up in its own right–safe, stable, and family centric. More for me, after experincing the violence and terror of gangs in Compton, Leavenworth turned out to be emancipatory. Living there had additional benefits. I was an army brat and related to many civilians offpost in my stepfather's hometown–connected to both townies and basers. My step-greatgrandfather had a three-hundred acre farm ten miles outside of town, but the fourteen children had long abandoned it for living in the city. I could hunt, fish, and farm on the rural land one weekend and do all things suburban high schoolers of the 1970s did the next. The film *Dazed and Confused* captures the zeitgeist of the entire era best from my vantage point–a film written and directed by Richard Linklater, who was born two months before me in 1960. Released in 1993, it is a coming of age film set in the suburbs of Austin, Texas, in 1976, and is often praised for its "anthropological" gaze. Specific to Leavenworth, my high school classmate later wrote about the youth of our town and the drug scene in *Rolling Stone* magazine (Van Parys 256-59). Another classmate, singer-songwriter Melissa Etheridge, is a Leavenworth native and international recording artist who shares tales of our hometown in her music (DeCurtis).

I lived in multiple worlds–on-post and off-post. We lived off-base for my first year of high school. Mom was a private first class and did not qualify for on-post housing. She wanted the on-post stability and security–especially given her souring on again/off again relationship with my stepfather, which began to undermine her personal and emerging professional goals.

Despite her marriage, mom thrived as unit clerk for the 205th Military Police Company at Fort Leavenworth. Nothing happened in the company unit without her knowledge. Research showed the company to be the "social horizon" of most soldiers in the U.S. Army at the time, and it provided the symbolic boundary of social cohesion and culture for NCOs (Moskos 66-67). Her commanders respected and trusted her. She became a Girl Friday–an efficient, faithful, and committed low-level female office assistant performing a broad range of duties–to the senior leadership–a clearly sexist and perhaps demeaning but practical role that would pay dividends later in her military career and beyond.

Unlike the two officers' experiences that are shared in this volume (Elle Kowal, chapter seven, and Naomi Mercer, chapter eight), mom never directly competed with men or found herself in traditional, male-dominated units. Her jobs were relatively safe from competition and harassment. Furthermore, her maturity and personality elevated her status beyond mere unit clerk. Her geniune love of and enthusiasm for the army resonated with subordinates, peers, and senior leaders. She went native. Drank the proverbial kool-aid. In Cynthia Enloe's words–militarized (*Maneuvers*). The officers identified with her middle-class German sensibilities. The NCOs and junior enlisted connected with her working-class, street savviness. The former ignored the latter, and mom developed some shrewd impression management skills of her multicultured background. To some degree her embracing of military caregiving–a role criticized as being essential to freeing men for actual warfighting capabilities (Enloe, *Does Khaki*)–benefitted her because she is white, straight, Germanic, and performed a traditional role (Hillman 66).

We moved onto Fort Leavenworth in a purchased mobile home in the summer of 1976–the American Bicentennial. Symbolic of our social class boundary spanning, the unusually positioned mobile home trailer park on the military reservation was oddly situated between the historic military cemetery, the Officer's Club and Golf Course, and the edge of the enlisted housing area. The mobile-home park no long exists.

On 19 May, 1976, anticipating a permanent change of station (PCS) move to Germany, mom became a naturalized American citizen in Kansas City, Kansas. At the time, the U.S. Army would not allow green carded servicemembers to be stationed overseas. Fear of being drafted into the German Bundeswehr at the German border upon our arrival, I, too, became naturalized that day. And with neither stepfather having adopted me, I formally took the Ender name to carry on my maternal family name.

My Americanization naturalized and complete, I thrived socially in high school. I worked parttime at the Officer's Club, played soccer year-round on a travel team, and participated whole-heartedly in Junior Reserved Officer Training Corps (JROTC) where I was regularly recognized and awarded for exceptional community service. My circle of friends comprised many senior military officer and senior NCO brats whose own middle-class socialization greatly influenced me to consider and attend college.

Despite my JROTC participation and other proclivities, a handful of young, enlisted soldiers visiting our home encouraged me not to join the army. Most were working-class African and Hispanic Americans with high aptitude and ambition but few options in their community–the all-volunteer force became a way out. Unfortunately, the mid-1970s saw a decline in the quality of recruits when the ASVAB had been miscalibrated, allowing a generation of underperforming soldiers into the army (Segal 39-40). Many of the troops at our house felt disenfranchised in the enlisted ranks and wanted more for themselves but felt stuck, especially the African American males. Those voices impacted me in multiple ways–mostly in not enlisting upon graduation.

I graduated from high school in May 1978, and my sister completed her first two years of schooling. Mom received official orders for West

Germany in the winter of 1977. We lived in the trailer on Fort Leavenworth for two years.

On 4 July, 1978, we flew to Germany. My parents picked up their new car in Bremerhaven, and we spent the remainder of the summer with our German relatives in Bocholt and Bremen–the birthplaces of my mom and me. My mom's caregiving role would continue at her new unit but now with the added cultural capital of possessing a high degree of cross-cultural and cross-national competence (Hajjar 249).

## William O. Darby Kaserne Fürth, West Germany

We moved into the Kolb Military Housing area in Fürth, West Germany just off William O. Darby Kaserne in the northern Bavaria region of Germany in the early fall of 1978. Mom extended her role from Fort Leavenworth serving as the unit clerk for the 511th Military Intelligence Battalion on William O. Darby Kaserne. My stepdad and I found jobs immediately on the short-order grill at the postexchange cafeteria. I spent that fall working, befriending American dependents and soldiers, and taking a college night course in German conversation through the University of Maryland European Division. (I had grown fairly fluent in German and took advantage of college courses to earn credit.) That spring semester I enrolled fulltime at the University of Maryland Munich Germany Campus–a now defunct five-hundred-student residential college for mostly military and state department youth located on the southern outskirts of Munich near the Perlacher Forest and across the street from the infamous Stadelheim prison (Woessner and Cerny; Woessner et al.).

Like in Leavenworth, my mom, sister, and I thrived in Germany. Similar to our connections to the locals in Leavenworth, we were German Americans fluent in the language yet had the priveleges associated with being affiliated with the U.S. Army. My stepfather received priorty spouse hiring and eventually landed a well-paid wage grade position managing the commissary warehouse. My mom managed her job exceptionally well and often served as a liaison for senior army leaders and their spouses in the local community in addition to being a unit clerk. Again, her maturity garnered her respect within the military community, but her cultural capital of being fluent in German and knowing customs and traditions propelled her into situations many of her peers and subordinates could not imagine. Although her second marriage suffered–ultimately resulting in a separation in 1980 with a divorce some years later–my sister and I blossomed. We spent time with German family and friends and immersed ourselves into the military community. My sister did well in school.

## PFC Francis X. McGraw Kaserne, Munich, West Germany

I rotated between experiencing fulltime college life in Munich, Germany, working various well-paid U.S. Army jobs in and around Fürth, and travelling with friends throughout Europe, Asia, and North Africa. Notably, many young soldiers contined to come through our home both from my mother's unit and now through my exploits around Fürth, Munich, and Western Europe. Some would visit me in college. As a German American youth, familiar with Germany, I could blend in. I embraced young soldiers and stole them away from the military community many loathed, and showed them Germany from a German perspective. We would tour castles and monestaries. We would dress locally and pass for Germans in clubs and bars. In the 1970s and 1980s, many German bars, clubs, and discos sought to limit American servicemembers from patronizing their establishments. It was a response to large groups of drunken soldiers fighting with local nationals and destroying clubs (Ingraham). In more recent years, alcohol, drugs, and violence on the part of American servicemembers in Europe has declined significantly. Few places are off limits any more (Ingo).

The experiences with soldiers and children of military members began to give me insights to understanding American servicemembers. I developed an appreciation for taking care of soldiers as my mom did. We saw troopers not as some abstract mass but as individuals–America's sons and daughters (see Patricia Sotirin, chapter one, this volume). Sometimes they slept off hangovers on our couch or crashed on the floor of my studio attic room above my parents' apartment. As an NCO, my mom was the first to be called when troops in her unit got into trouble and she would pull them out of bad relationships with German women or American men, brothels in Amsterdam, or bars and jails around Germany. My mom consistently delivered more than was expected of her. I noticed.

I learned why particular soldiers enlisted, what they had left behind, where they were socially and psychologically, and where they wanted to go. I developed an empathy for them. I saw much of my mom and myself in them. I got to know them personally. There were so many young soldiers over the years. They looked like America–Black, Chicano, Native American, white, men, women, athiests, Baptists, wealthy, and poor coming from all over–Des Moines, Iowa; East St. Louis, Missouri; Albuqurque, New Mexico; Brooklyn, New York; and Portland, Maine; among other places. They had ambition and drive but few places to direct it. Sociologically, I recognized social mobility required a community of sorts–individuals willing to give social support to help you move forward. By 1980, the miscalibration of the ASVAB had been identified and corrected (Segal 40-41). Many of these young soldiers likely felt frustrated by their immediate NCO leaders–many of the latter had come into the army a level below the cognitive requirement. The former were good people just trying to navigate their narrow path to the American Dream, and the military served them as one option to pursue among few to none.

By the time we left for the United States in the fall of 1982, I had made many new friends, seen twenty-five different countries, fell a few credits short of an associate of arts degree, met my future wife, and spent considerable time with my sister substituting as a father figure. I did all this while I lived intermittantly in the long-abandonded maid's quarters in Kalb Housing Area that comprised the attic rooms of the enlisted personnel housing areas all around Germany. It was time to go back to "The World," as U.S. soldier slang referred to the United States.

## Fort Huachuca, Arizona, U.S.A.

Mom received military orders for Fort Huachuca, Arizona, in early 1982. Unhappy with a desert southwest assignment, she knew an eventual return to Germany demanded a senior NCO stateside tour. Now legally separated, mom asked my girlfriend and I to live with her for at least a year to help care for my sister. She wanted desperately to acclimate successfully to her new and demanding job of non-commissioned officer in-charge (NCOIC) of her unit. Frankly, I again took advantage of the locality of southern Arizona, enrolled in some college courses at Cochise College to study the flora and fauna of the region, hiked the mountains, and won Yard of the Month and then Yard of the Year for 1982 on Fort Huachuca–a post with one of the largest number of housing units in the Department of the Army, at roughly 1,954.

The twenty-two months at Fort Huachuca proved the most challenging and difficult for my mother. It was the first time in her military career she lacked the social capital of the locality. Mom did continue to focus on taking care of soldiers though, and her caring role became more formalized as an NCOIC. Young enlisted soldiers spent lots of time at our house on the weekends. They often slept on our couch. This continued after we left for college in the summer of 1983, and she and my sister's permenant change of station six months later to Alexandria, Virginia in February 1984, Germany again after that, and then finally landing back in Alexandria, Virginia for her final tour in the army.

My sister Ingrid (right) and an unidentified Brigadier General promoting my mom in Alexandria, Virginia or Washington, DC, circa 1983 (note the General's missing nametag above the right pocket). Personal photograph owned by the author. 22 August 2017.

## Parting Ways and a Legacy

In the summer of 1983 my girlfriend Corina and I packed our VW micro-bus and headed back to fulltime university study in northern California. She too is a German American from an army family with her own personal story. I was twenty-two years old and five years behind my high school graduating classmates. But I had a laid a foundation. We landed at Sonoma State University (SSU) where I studied sociology, and Corina double majored in anthropology and German. We chose SSU for the Mediteranian vibe–mountainous, great weather, and close to the ocean. Professor John Michael Steiner had the greatest influence on me there (in some ways bringing me full-circle). A Holocaust survivor, his life's work was the study of the Holocaust with a deep focus on former SS members in the German Wehrmacht (Steiner). His courses and mentorship encouraged my experience with and curiosity for American servicemembers. He recommended I read *The Professional Soldier: A Social and Political Portrait* (Janowitz), which with a growing interest in military sociology, easily led me to the work of his students–David Segal and Mady Wechsler Segal at the University of Maryland, where I eventually completed my graduate studies in sociology.

After earning a PhD in sociology specializing in social psychology and miltiary sociology, a two-and-half-year stint at the University of North Dakota and a semester teaching in Norway, I took a position in 1998 where I remain at this writing as a professor of sociology on the faculty in the multidisciplinary Department of Behavioral Sciences and Leadership at the United States Military Academy at West Point, New York, U.S.A. Although my military sociology writing had started long before arriving at West Point, the environment has benefitted me greatly by supporting and encouraging scholarship on American soldiers, military families, miltiary children, cadets, and military women (Ender et al. 87-102). Most of this recent work is with Michael Matthews and David Rohall, my long time collaborators, but much is owed to other colleagues including Remi Hajjar, Tom Kolditz, Ev Spain, and Bernie Banks among others. We focus on soldiers and cadets, at a minimum in the abstract, where we give voice to them and their families' experiences.

Despite some meager scholarly publications, my first love and best sense of self is as teacher. And fortunately, I've been privilaged to teach cadets for many years now. A lifetime of exposure to the military through my mother's military career continues to influence me. I owe much to those early developmental experiences. Teaching cadets is less abstract and far more visceral, since I know they will someday be responsible for a soldier, a platoon, a company, a village, a brigade, a city, an army, a war, or some nation. At the risk of sounding cliché, I see these future officers as the future leaders of America's youth–that same youth who slept on our couches in Kansas and Germany and tramped with me through the German countryside and hiked through the Huachuca Mountains of Arizona. They are my muse, my motivation. I have taught a "Marriage and the Family" course with a focus on military families for over twenty years and I taught "Military Families" as a Visiting Professor at the Universität der Bundeswehr München, Munich, Germany. I regularly teach a course on armed forces and society with a sociological gaze. My course titled "Social Inequality" draws attention to social differences at the intersections of race, ethnicity, sex, gender, religious affiliation, sexual orientations, socio-economic class, age, and (dis)ability. My "Military Films" course requires no explanation. Even my newly developed "Qualitative Research Methods" course is designed to push cadets to gain a depth of understanding about their research subjects. These and other courses I am fortunate to teach and enjoy them immensely. Indeed, nothing beats the classroom–completely in the moment with students. I feel at my best in the classroom and get tremendous personal and social satisfaction being on the teaching platform. I often sense the presence of old friends and fellow travelers and marvel at my luck. I hope my enthusiasm, organization, knowledge, communication, and concern for students' wellbeing resonates beyond their time in college. Living the dream means facilitating cadets' learning empathy for others–an empathy for life.

I continued to visit my mom and sister wherever they were stationed around the U.S. and in Germany. Indeed, I would fly to assist them when the army imposed another PCS, and my sole skills preparing family heirlooms for transport were required. Like other women in the military (Laurence), mom faced challenges but managed to progress. She had three more major moves before she retired as a sergeant major (SGM–E9) in Alexandria, Virginia. She went on to work for some former generals at Military Professional Resources, Inc. (MPRI) after a brief stint working in the gift-shop at George Washington's Mount Vernon home. Later, she served as an administrative assistant at the National Defense University in Washington, DC–less than a mile from her home. She fully retired to Florida to her own home near both the beach and her childhood bestfriend–Ingrid from Germany–where she still resides at the time of this writing. My sister did not stray far from home either. We both work in the new family "business"–the military. My sister works for the Navy in the Pentagon, and I at West Point. She married a now retired soldier–Charles–and benefits from being connected to the military. I married a German American army brat. I feel at home on military posts, even though I remain an outsider; I feel disconnected from civilians because I've spent almost half a century on or near army posts.

## Mom's Career Duty Stations, 1975-1997

Delayed Entry Program–January 1975
Compton, California

3 June 1975–August 1975
Fort Jackson, South Carolina–Basic Training

September 1975–October 1975
Fort Benjamin Harrison, Indianapolis, Indiana–AIT

October 1975–July 1978
Fort Leavenworth, Leavenworth Kansas

September 1978–September 1982
William O. Darby Kaserne, Fürth, (West) Germany

October 1982–February 1984
Fort Huachuca, Sierra Vista, Arizona

February 1984–June 1987
Hoffman Building, Alexandria, Virginia

July 1987–July 1990
Kilbourne Kaserne, Schwetzingen, (West) Germany

August 1990–January 31, 1997
Hoffman Building, Alexandria, Virginia

Master Sergeant Ilka M. Brown (née Ender) circa 1996.
She retired in 1997 a Sergeant Major (E-9). Personal photograph
owned by the author. 22 August 2017.

## Endnote

1  The views presented here are my own and do not purport to
represent the views of the U.S. Government, the Department of
Defense, the Department of the Army, or the United States Military
Academy. I wish to thank Corina Morano-Ender, the editors, and an
anonymous reviewer for their insights and assistance in the writing
of this chapter. The chapter is dedicated to the ABC Team: Axel,
Brittany, and CJ.

## Works Cited

Baker, John R. with Stephen J. Rivele. *Vice: One Cop's Story of
Patrolling America's Most Dangerous City.* St. Martin's Griffin, 2011.

Berg, Bruce L., and Howard Lune. *Qualitative Research Methods for
the Social Sciences.* 8th ed. Pearson, 2012.

Brillian Muhonja, Besi, and Wanda Thomas Bernard, eds. *Mothers and Sons: Centering Mother Knowledge*. Demeter Press, 2016.

Brown, Jerrod E, editor. *Historical Dictionary of the U.S. Army*. Greenwood Press, 2001.

Carreiras, Helena, and Celso Castro, eds. *Qualitative Methods in Military Studies: Research Experiences and Challenges*. Routledge, 2013.

Carreiras, Helena, et al., eds. *Researching the Military*. Routledge, 2016.

Collins, Gail. *When Everything Changed: The Amazing Journey of American Women from 1960 to the Present*. Little, Brown and Company, 2009.

DeCurtis, Anthony. "Melissa Etheridge: 4th Street Feeling." *Rolling Stone on the Web*, 4 Sept. 2012, www.rollingstone.com/music/albumreviews/4th-street-feeling20120904#ixzz25dEOgvPg. Accessed 30 Aug. 2016.

Department of the Army. *Department of the Army Historical Summary, FY 1975: Personnel*. 23 Nov. 2015, www.history.army.mil/books/DAHSUM/1975/ch05.htm. Accessed 30 Aug. 2016.

Ellis, Carolyn, and Arthur P. Bochner. "Autoethnography, Personal Narrative, Reflexivity: Researcher as Subject." *Handbook of Qualitative Research*, edited by Norman K. Denzin and Yvonna S. Lincoln, Sage, 2000, pp. 733-68.

Ender, Morten G. *American Soldiers in Iraq: McSoldiers or Innovative Professionals?* Routledge, 2009.

Ender, Morten G., David E. Rohall, and Michael D. Matthews. *The Millennial Generation and National Defense: Attitudes of Future Military and Civilians Leaders*, Palgrave Pivot, 2014.

Enloe, Cynthia. *Does Khaki Become You?: The Militarization of Women's Lives*. South End Press, 1983.

Enloe, Cynthia. *Maneuvers: The International Politics of Militarizing Women's Lives*. University of California Press, 2000.

Gereben Schafer, Agnes, et al. *Implications of Integrating Women in the Marine Corps Infantry*. RAND Corp, 2015.

Gerson, Kathleeen. *The Unfinished Revolution: How a New Generation is Reshaping Family, Work, and Gender in America*. Oxford University Press, 2010.

Hajjar, Remi M. "A New Angle on the US Military's Emphasis on Developing Cross-Cultural Competence: Connecting In-Ranks' Cultural

Diversity to Cross-Cultural Competence." *Managing Diversity in the Military: The Value of Inclusion in a Culture of Uniformity*, edited by Daniel P. McDonald and Kizzy M. Parks, Routledge, 2012, pp. 248-62.

Hicks Stiehm, Judith. *Arms and the Enlisted Woman*. Temple University Press, 1989.

Higate, Paul, and Ailsa Cameron. "Reflexivity and Researching the Military." *Armed Forces & Society*, vol. 32, no. 2, 2006, pp. 219-33.

Hillman, Elizabeth L. "Dress to Kill: The Paradox of Women in Military Uniforms." *Beyond Zero Tolerance: Discrimination in Military Culture*. Ed. Mary Fainsod Katzenstein and Judith Reppy. Rowman & Littlefield Publishers, Inc. 1999. 65-80.

Ingo, Jessica. "Army's New Off-Limits List for Europe Restricts Fewer Locations." *Stars & Stripes on the Web*, 11 Jun. 2005, www.stripes.com/news/army-s-new-off-limits-list-for-europe-restricts-fewer-locations -1.34441. Accessed 27 Mar. 2016.

Ingraham, Larry H. *The Boys in the Barracks: Observations on American Military Life*. Rowman & Littlefield Publishers, Inc., 1984.

Janowitz, Morris. *The Professional Soldier: A Social and Political Portrait*. The Free Press, 1960.

Laurence, Janice. "Women in the Military: Progress and Challenges." *Inclusion in the U.S. Military: A Force for Diversity*, edited by David E. Rohall, et al., Lexington Books, 2017, pp. 111-28.

Liebenberg, Ian. "Evolving Experiences: Auto-ethnography and Military Sociology–a South African Immersion." *Qualitative Methods in Military Studies: Research Experiences and Challenges*, edited by Helena Carreiras and Celso Castro,: Routledge, 2013, pp. 50-67.

Loving V. Virginia. "Loving V. Virginia: The Case over Interracial Marriage." *ACLU*, 16 Nov. 2015, www.aclu.org/loving-v-virginia-case-over-interracial-marriage. Accessed 11 Jan. 2018.

Lucas, Jeffrey W. and David R. Segal. "Status, Power, and Diversity in the Military." *Managing Diversity in the Military: The Value of Inclusion in a Culture of Uniformity*, edited by Daniel P. McDonald and Kizzy M. Parks, Routledge, 2012, pp. 149-61.

Marsden, Martha A. "The Continuing Debate: Women Soldiers in the U.S. Army." *Life in the Rank and File: Enlisted Men and Women in the Armed Forces of the United States, Australia, Canada, and the United Kingdom*, edited by David R. Segal and H. Wallace Sinaiko, Pergamon-Brassey's, 1986, pp. 58-78.

Matthews, Michael D., et al. "Role of Group Affiliation and Gender Attitudes toward Women in the Military." *Military Psychology*, vol. 21, no. 2, 2009, pp. 241-51.

Moore, Brenda. *Serving Our Country: Japanese American Women in the Military during World War II*. Rutgers University Press, 2003.

Moore, Brenda. *To Serve My Country, To Serve My Race: The Story of the Only African American WACs Stationed in Overseas During World War II*. New York University Press, 1996.

Moskos, Charles C. Jr. *The American Enlisted Man: The Rank and File in Today's Military*. Russell Sage Foundation, 1970.

Reed-Danahay, Deborah E., ed. *Auto/Ethnography: Rewriting the Self and the Social*. Oxford University Press, 1997.

Segal, David R. *Recruiting for Uncle Sam: Citizenship and Military Manpower Policy*. University of Kansas Press, 1989.

Segal, David R., and Mady Wechsler Segal. "Linked Lives in Military Sociology: Family, Research, Teaching, and Policy" *Researching the Military*, edited by Helena Carreiras et al., Routledge, 2016, pp. 180-95.

Segal, Mady W. "Women's Military Roles Cross-Nationally: Past, Present, and Future." *Gender & Society*, vol. 9, no. 6, 1995, pp. 757-75.

Soeters, Joseph, et al., editors. *Routledge Handbook of Research Methods in Military Studies*. Routledge, 2014.

Steiner, John M. *Power Politics and Social Change in National Socialist Germany. A Process of Escalation into Mass Destruction*. Mouton & Co., 1975.

Tomaselli, Keyan G, et al. ""Self" and "Other": Auto-Reflexive and Indigenous Ethnography." *Handbook of Critical and Indigenous Methodologies*, edited by Norman K. Denzin, et al., Sage, 2008, pp. 347-72.

Van Parys, Bill. "Bongs, Trips, 'Ludes, & Lines." *Rolling Stone: The '70s*, edited by Ashley Kahn, et al., Little, Brown and Company, 1998, pp. 256-59.

Woessner, Circe Olson, and Zoe Ann Cerny, editors. *Bavarian Crème: Memories from Munich Campus*. Writer's Club Press, 2002.

Woessner, Circe Olson, et al. editors. *Noch Eins!: Tales from the Terrapin Keller*. iUniverse Inc., 2003.

Chapter Seven

# Choosing Motherhood in the U.S. Air Force

Elle Kowal

*Women in the generation above me told horror stories about discrimination, and added "But everything has changed. That will never happen to you." ... Are we serving the next generation well if we tell them that everything is equal and fair when it's not?*
*(Silverberg 3)*

In a small airport in rural Georgia, a circle of Air Force cadets stood proudly in starched blue uniforms shining with silver shoulder insignia. They were there to practice flying a small plane for officer training. An older man took one look at the lone female in the group, smirked, and called out, "Why are you joining the Air Force? To marry a pilot?"

The cadet shot back, "No, to be a pilot."

That cadet was me at the turn of the millennium.

What a difference seventeen years can make. I have spent those years–including over six as a mother–as an officer in the United States Air Force (USAF). In 2000, I graduated from university with a Bachelor of Science in physics and a Bachelor of Science in mathematics and economics, and I commissioned as a USAF officer. I served on active duty in missile operations, finance, and space systems acquisitions for seven years and then transferred from active duty to the active U.S. Air Force Reserve (USAFR). I continued working in space systems acquisitions, both as a reservist and as a civilian contractor in space systems engineering. I gave birth to my children in 2010 and 2012, and in 2015, I transferred to the Inactive Ready Reserve (IRR) at the rank of major.

My career in space systems acquisitions is intellectually stimulating, mission essential, and rewarding. I excelled as an officer and thoroughly enjoyed my work, and I still enjoy my work today as a space systems engineer. Despite this, I encountered significant challenges in an Air Force defined by stereotypically "masculine" values. Women still face substantial cultural biases and institutional barriers to combining a successful military career with family and motherhood. This chapter explores how my career as a female service member in the Air Force was affected by military characteristics and policies. Specifically, issues of sex-based discrimination, sexual harassment and assault, hostile work environments, occupational segregation, and gendered policies regarding family colocation, maternity leave, deployment, and promotions all had major effects on my military career. My experience is offered here as autoethnography, which places my personal journey in the context of theory and scholarship in order to enrich critical understanding of both individual and structural issues for military women and mothers.

In this chapter, I cite fifteen different studies and reports from the past thirty years substantiating that the challenges I faced are not unique to me, but the common experience of female military members (Bastian et al.; DACOWITS 2003; DACOWITS 2015; DiSilverio; Etheridge; Evertson; Iskra; Long; Losey; Margosian and Vendrzyk; Morral; Steinberg et al.). Overall, research shows these issues are commonalities across female service members of various ranks, services, marital statuses, races and ethnicities. Where I can, I provide further detail on how different demographics are affected. My experience, representative of countless other female service members, illustrates how these challenges are resulting in many of us choosing to end our military careers. Air Force leadership is concerned about this attrition, and I highlight the recent forward momentum they have made with diversity and inclusion initiatives to address some of these issues. However, Air Force structure, attitudes, processes, and policies must shift further to overcome roadblocks affecting female military members. I recommend and discuss changes needed to remove structural inequality from the military and make it a more equal environment for female service members, including those who are mothers or are considering motherhood.

Issues relating to motherhood are directly relevant to a sizable portion of the female military population. In 2010, the year I gave birth to my first child, overall 36.7 percent of female military service members–111,327 of us–were also mothers (Clever and Segal 23). For black military women, who compose 25.6 percent of female military members, it is even more significant–46.9 percent of black female military members are also mothers (Clever and Segal 23). These statistics would be even higher, but many mothers and expectant mothers simply leave the military rather than continue to struggle with the challenges of military motherhood. The Government Accountability Office (GAO) found that fully 35.3 percent of early separations for female military members in 1993 were officially for pregnancy or parenthood (U.S. GAO, "Military Attrition" 31), and in 1998, an in-depth retention study by Penny F. Pierce found that female Air Force service members with a child under two years old were twice as likely to leave the military than other women (qtd. in Blanchard 19), although clearly more recent statistics and analyses are needed. Motherhood issues also affect military women who decide to leave the military or change their career path for family planning purposes prior to pregnancy or who purposefully decide to forgo having children because motherhood is seen as incompatible with military service.

## A Woman in the Air Force

My first assignment in 2000 was to space and missile training at Vandenberg Air Force Base (AFB), California. During training, the male officer sitting next to me liked to make jokes about women having sex with horses, despite the sign on the wall regarding the no sexual harassment policy. My pointed requests for him to stop only made him continue with more gusto. Another male officer co-worker who sat nearby told me he liked to watch my breasts when I stretched at my desk and pressured me to go out with him.

While in training, I volunteered to develop a new module for next year's students and built a training package on current satellite systems. I was surprised one day when my male supervisor ranted at me at length that women shouldn't be in the Air Force. He wouldn't stop, so I filled out a leave form requesting three days of vacation time to start immediately because it was the only way I could think of to legally walk away from the conversation. I spent those days studying for the

Graduate Record Examination (GRE) in order to apply to master's degree programs. I took the GRE and later received a master of science in development finance.

I completed nine months of training and was assigned to an operational missile squadron in Minot, North Dakota, as a deputy combat crew commander. Before I departed training, my instructors, both female, had one piece of career advice for me and my female crew partner–don't have sex with anyone for six months. We were warned that the male missileers had a network of passing "intelligence" on new female arrivals and would already be planning on dating us, but that having sex with anyone would hurt our careers. I later overheard two male co-workers in our squadron common room in Minot talking in exactly this way about a friend of mine before she arrived. They were arguing over who would date her first, despite the fact they had never met her. The way they discussed dating her disregarded any agency she would have in the matter. She dated neither of them.

On my second drive to a missile alert facility, my flight commander expounded upon his opinion that women should be in the kitchen cooking, like his wife, and not in the military. This commander was consistently disrespectful and inappropriate to the women he supervised, including inviting my then-roommate to join him and his wife in a threesome. After over fifty reports of unprofessional behaviour and harassment, he was investigated by the inspector general; however, the investigation was determined to be inconclusive, since the reports were all made by women and could not be corroborated by any men.

Later that year, my missile squadron commander called me into his office. He told me he didn't think I was "quite right" for the military, and he thought I'd do better and be happier in another career. He offered to facilitate my early departure from the Air Force. Perhaps what he found not "quite right" for the military was my biological sex. Perhaps it was more than that. This particular commander targeted two people at this time for removal from his squadron–me and another woman–and perhaps it was not a coincidence that she is black and I am of mixed heritage and ethnicity. My mixed ethnicity caused me to stand out in the Air Force in a way that I was not used to, as I grew up in the multicultural community of greater Boston. It was at times fetishized, stereotyped, highlighted, targeted, ignored, dismissed, and misunderstood, and it differentiated me as "other."

These moments during my first years in the Air Force made a lasting impression on me. Like so many other middle-class women who grew up in the 1980s and 90s, (Damaske 41), I had internalized the feminist credo "girls could do anything boys could do." I was blindsided to find out that some people, especially military leadership, still believed in 2001 that women shouldn't be in the Air Force. I had somehow lived my life thus far assuming equality of the sexes was accepted fact, when I now see that it is clearly not. Despite studying quantum physics at MIT as one of only two women in my class, and spending four years in reserve officers' training corps (ROTC) cadet training, it wasn't until I became active duty military that I personally encountered this level of blatant sexism.

These forms of sexual harassment and sex-based discrimination that I experienced–persistent unwanted sexual jokes and sexual attention, telling me I should not be in the military because I am female, not effectively addressing harassment–are common across the military for women (Morral et al. xxii). The Defense Manpower Data Center (DMDC) found that 78 percent of female service members have experienced sexually harassing and sex-based discriminatory behaviours (Bastian et al. iv). Sex-based discrimination rates affect all ranks of female service members at the same rate, whereas rates of sexual harassment and assault are highest for junior enlisted women. Even so, RAND estimates that 10 percent of the highest senior female officers still continue to experience sexual harassment. Additionally, RAND found that rates of both sexual harassment and sex-based discrimination are lower in the Air Force as compared to the other services, yet are still very prevalent (Morral et al xxi). Research on the statistics of sexual harassment and discrimination across races and ethnicities of military women has been inconclusive and should be investigated further, but thus far, it has shown differences mainly in the subtype of harassment experienced rather than the prevalence across groups (Buchanan et al 355). In Mary Ann Margosian and Judith Vendrzyk's study of military women, they found all the women interviewed experienced incidents "where men voiced their objections to women in the military" (70), most experienced a culture of sexual jokes, and nearly all were as surprised by it as I was (71).

## From Operations to Finance

The military is heavily occupationally segregated by sex. The operations occupational area–career fields that "directly employ weapon and supporting systems to accomplish the primary operational mission" (AFOCD 22)–is 96 percent male (OUSD Tables B-20 and B-28). In the U.S. Air Force, the operations occupational area consists primarily of pilot, navigator, air battle management, weapons systems, space, cyberspace, intelligence, and missile career fields. It also has the highest promotion rates of Air Force occupational areas (Lim et al xviii). Jennifer Berdahl and Celia Moore note that "a major tool for maintaining this inequality is on-the-job harassment: Women and minorities often face hostile receptions in traditionally male- and White-dominated domains" (426). All the instances of sex-based harassment and discrimination I described in the section above occurred while I was in the missile operations career field, and Vicki Schultz's legal analysis holds that this is a purposeful strategy for maintaining male domination in that field (1755).

Furthermore, "women in non-traditional positions often find themselves targets of attrition tactics used by men intent upon forcing them out" (Margosian and Vendrzyk 59). I feel this is true of my experience. My career floundered during my three years in missile operations. I was sidelined in various offices away from actual operations. My commander even went so far as to attempt to cancel my security clearance and tell others that I was leaving the Air Force, despite my legal commitment to serve for four years. Although I worked hard and won an award from higher headquarters for my role in a division office, continued marginalization in my career field was having the intended effect of derailing my career.

I used this opportunity to volunteer for everything I could–I tutored math, taught economics, was a camp counsellor, planted flowers, helped out at school carnivals, and assisted with a myriad of military ceremonies and leadership visits. Then I volunteered for a year-long position leading the base's diversity programming under the auspices of the Equal Opportunity Office. In this position, I facilitated diverse groups of volunteers committed to highlighting the contributions and heritage of female, Hispanic, Asian, Pacific Islander, Native American, and African American service members, as well as remembering and learning from Holocaust survivors. We planned and budgeted, organized events, made speeches, sang songs, brought in special guests, wrote articles, hung posters, briefed commanders, and successfully added celebration and appreciation of diversity to our base leadership's priority list. Looking back, I think it was my dedication and enthusiasm in that role that was a key factor in turning my career around. It was through this position that the base commander got to know and appreciate my work, and he subsequently passed on a positive recommendation for me to my future commander in California, his former classmate. She has supported my career ever since–first in the military and then in the civilian company we both now work for.

The second turning point was when I decided to travel fifteen hundred miles to the Air Force Personnel Center (AFPC) in San Antonio, Texas, to request a transfer out of missile operations and into the physicist career field. My request for transfer to this technical field for which I was qualified for was denied, and I was instead immediately transferred to the finance career field, as the deputy finance flight commander for Minot AFB.

Classified as an administrative career field (DODI 1312.1-1 229), finance is significantly more common for women in the military than operations. 24 percent of active-duty women, but only 12 percent of men, are in administrative positions (OUSD Tables B-20 and B-28). The hostile reception and attrition tactics of my supervisors in missile operations culminated in steering me towards a so-called woman's job, which in itself is a form of sex-based discrimination (McGinley 1163). This is consistent with Margosian and Vendrzyk's findings that in the U.S. Navy, "despite intensive training and qualification in nontraditional occupations, many women found themselves stuck in traditional roles because of their gender" (67) and Sarah Damaske's findings that "negative psychological experiences, like gender stereotyping and discrimination in male occupations, caused women's movement from male-dominated to female-dominated occupations" (Martin and Barnard 3). Gender is used here as an artificial hierarchal system constructed for the purpose of solidifying power for certain male–and away from female–service members.

Previous Air Force leadership recognized that improving female and minority participation and retention in operations is a priority. This is particularly important, they stated, because "the Air Force often draws many of its leaders from operational career fields" (James et al., "2016

Diversity" 4). In order to meet this objective, the Air Force will have to seriously and effectively address the sex-based discrimination and hostile work environment of the work culture in operations. Federal court has stated that sex-based discrimination and sexual harassment in the workplace is equivalent to putting up "a sign declaring 'Men Only'" (760 F. Supp. 1486). This has a direct effect on retention–42 percent of service members who had been sexually harassed or discriminated against in the past year said that these events had made them "want to leave the military" (Morral et al. 48).

In 2014, one missile squadron commander at Minot AFB was relieved from command after an investigation substantiated that he engaged in sex-based discrimination (Martinez). I am glad to see this behaviour taken more seriously than it was a decade before when I was there, but I believe the cultural problem of sex-based discrimination and harassment in operations extends far beyond just one man. It is part of "the 'unofficial' culture that is defined by exaggerated characteristics of stereotypical masculinity, among other things, and is linked to values and customs that perpetuate rape" (U.S. GAO, "Military Personnel" 38). Studies of female officers report that primary factors for leaving included not only discrimination, harassment, and assault, but a cultural acceptance of those practices along with mishandling of reports (Steinberg et al. 18; DiSilverio 34).

Sex-based discrimination, hypermasculine work culture, hostile work places, sexual harassment, and sexual assault are all linked on a spectrum of hostile gendered power relations. These tactics can be considered subconscious or purposeful methods of maintaining traditional occupational segregation and a male power advantage in promotions and career success (Schultz 1759). Cynthia Cockburn describes this behaviour as purposeful reinforcement of society's gendered hierarchy: "a male intervention for the assertion of power ... a warning to a woman stepping out of her proper place ... a controlling gesture to diminish any sense of power she may be acquiring" (142). Sexual assault, in particular, is a major issue in the military. RAND estimates that over twenty thousand active duty service members were sexually assaulted in the one year of their 2014 study alone, with junior female enlisted members (military grades E1–E4) having the highest rates of sexual assault (Morral et al. xviii, xix). In addition, risk of sexual assault varies among the services: for women in the Air Force, the risk of sexual assault is only 60 percent of women in the other services (Morral et al 89). This is consistent with the slightly different military culture in the Air Force, which focuses as much on airplanes, satellites, and scientific development as on brute operational strength. The DoD (Department of Defense) acknowledges that the military's problem of sexual assault has its roots in the hostile gendered military work culture ("Department of Defense" 5), and it massively affects the ability of both women and men to effectively and safely serve in the military. The very first step to combating the military's sexual assault problem is to address the toxic culture underpinning it.

After I transferred to the finance career field, I did not experience the same level of sexual harassment or sex-based discrimination issues that I had experienced in missile operations. I was grateful for the opportunity to transfer to a more accepting environment, and I quickly rose to success in my career in finance. I was rated as one of the top 5 out of 242 officers in my organization. I graduated as the distinguished graduate of my finance training class with an 100 percent academic average. I was rated on my performance reports as the number one officer in several organizations by supervisors who were very supportive of my career. I won multiple Officer of the Quarter and Officer of the Year awards and was promoted in rank and position.

After Minot AFB, I was assigned to the Space and Missile Systems Center (SMC) at Los Angeles AFB, California, as an acquisitions finance officer. I was the cost lead for negotiations for 3.1 billion-dollar rocket launch vehicle and support contracts. I was then selected as the finance lead for the rocket launch program, managing 3.3 billion dollars and leading a team of five personnel. During my career, I worked on a number of space and missile systems, including launch vehicles, the Global Positioning System (GPS), and the long-range family of missiles. It was high-powered, high-money, deeply analytical work, and I thrived doing it.

## Join Spouse

Despite our best efforts, my husband and I were assigned to different bases for three years before we got married. I was assigned to California while he was in Georgia, and then to North Dakota while he was in New Mexico. We decided to get married, thinking we would then be stationed together because of the "join spouse" program. Air Force Instruction

(AFI) 36-2110: Assignments states: "military couples may be considered for assignment where they can maintain a joint residence" (310). However, after we were married, there was no attempt to station us together. He was moved to Ohio while I was moved to California. We were stationed apart for another two years after our marriage, and then my husband received orders to New Mexico despite being qualified for multiple open engineering positions at Los Angles AFB where I worked. After one married assignment apart, I expected the Air Force to at least try to station us together this time around but they did not.

We tried to work with my husband's assignments officer at the Air Force Personnel Center (AFPC) to assign us together but did not get anywhere. Thankfully, there was a personnel change at AFPC, and my female deputy director called our new assignments officer on our behalf. A month later, my husband had orders to Los Angeles instead of New Mexico.

This experience was fresh in my mind as I met with senior leadership to discuss my career prospects. I had mentorship meetings with two military officers in my chain of command, one in the finance career field and one in acquisitions management. Both men said the same thing: that I would have to choose career or family, and that being assigned to a different base than my husband would be highly likely as my career moved forward. My husband, in his career counseling, did not receive this type of advice. Although AFI36-2110 states "military couples, like Airmen with a civilian spouse, should expect periods of separation during their careers" (310), dual military couples experience greater separation than those with civilian spouses (Reeves qtd. in Long). The Air Force was asking me to make a choice, and I chose family first.

The policy reads as if AFPC will at least attempt to station couples together. However, they are not required by policy to try, and in my experience, they did not bother. In 2006, when we were struggling with my husband's assignment, 32 percent of dual-military couples in the U.S. Army were stationed apart from each other (Bethea 5). This number reflects only those apart in that given year, but over the course of a career, it is probable that many more dual-military families will end up as part of that statistic at some point.

A clear first step toward helping mothers in the military would be to make assigning spouses together a priority and a guarantee in the regulation. 20.7 percent of U.S. active duty women are in a dual-military marriage as opposed to only 3.9 percent of men (*2014 Demographics Report* 47). Over 50 percent of married active duty Air Force women are in dual-military marriages, compared to only 12 percent of men (FY 2015). Because of this disparity, seemingly "gender-neutral" policies like this are not gender neutral in their effects. They disproportionally affect female personnel–and therefore mothers and potential mothers–more than they affect male personnel.

Female military members have lower retention and continuation rates than males (MLDC, "Officer Retention" 2; U.S. GAO, "Women in the Military" 14), and rates for dual-military women are even lower rates than for other women (Long 70). The male-female retention gap has been found to be persistent across all races and ethnicities, with no consistent differences in continuation rates found between minorities and white counterparts (MLDC, "From Representation" 2; Mundell 79). The difficulty of collocated assignments is a major factor for many female service members deciding to leave the military, and has repeatedly been cited in retention and attrition studies ever since the first females graduated from the Air Force Academy (for example: Roffey et al. qtd. in Long 40; Evertson and Nesbitt 95; Steinberg et al. 10; DiSilverio 29; DACOWITS, "2003 Report" 9). In 2003, the Defense Advisory Committee on Women in the Services (DACOWITS) found that family separation for dual-military families was a primary reason female officers separate from the military (9) and recommended "improving opportunities for the collocation of partners in dual-military marriage" (14).

In 2016, Air Force leadership finally recognized that dual-military collocation is a retention issue for the majority of married female service members, and is implementing an initiative to "ensure involuntary assignments that separate dual military families are avoided to the fullest extent practicable while balancing mission requirements" (James et al., "2016 Diversity" 2). The U.S. Navy has also similarly updated their join spouse policy recently ("MILPERSMAN 1300-1000").

It remains to be seen how these new initiatives will impact women in the military. Unfortunately, both initiatives are still limited by the caveat that being assigned together is not a guarantee. I believe it should be a guarantee. I personally believe that there are always opportunities to assign people together in a way that continues to support the mission–whether it be career broadening assignments

(Long 74), instructor assignments, retraining to another career field, or even expedited transfer to another service. For me, it was not living apart that was the hardest–we did that for many years and recently did it again while my husband deployed. For me, like other female service members in dual-military couples (Steinberg et al. 18), it was the stress of not knowing whether or not we would be stationed together the next time around or the next or the next after that. I did not want a career in which every assignment would to be a gamble as to whether our family would be allowed to stay together.

## On the Fast Track

When a surprise meeting was convened in 2008 for all officers on base to inform us that the Air Force would pay personnel–on a first-come, first-served basis–to leave (separate from) the active duty Air Force under the Voluntary Separation Pay (VSP) program (DODI 1332.43), I ran to grab an application (AF Form 780) from the stack in the back of the meeting room and didn't stop running until it was signed by my commander and delivered to the personnel office. I didn't stop to think. I just did it.

This decision may appear impulsive, but it wasn't–it had been previously formed after my mentorship meetings. Mentally, I had already accepted that the end of my career would be coming. As soon as I heard this announcement, I knew it was my time. It was the first decision of many in which I chose family over my military career.

Upon separation, I decided to transfer to the active Air Force Reserve and coordinated an assignment to an Individual Mobility Augmentee (IMA) position in my same unit. Complementing the regular fulltime dedicated structure of the Air Force, the Air Force Reserve has positions for various types of reservists–ranging from part-time to fulltime work, from traditional unit reservists to individual reservists, as described in the Air Force Reserve Handbook (42-44). "The Individual Reserve Program is composed of four categories of Individual Reservists: the IMA; the PIRR; non-participating Individual Ready Reserve (IRR) and the Standby Reserve" (AFI36-2629 4). As an IMA, I was assigned to my previous unit in order to backfill for and support active-duty personnel and government civilians. "IMA authorizations are individual military Air Force Reserve assets functioning as a total-force multiplier to augment the Air Force in war, contingency operations, and peacetime to meet National Defense, strategic national interest, and domestic objectives" (AFI36-2629 4). In practice, this meant that every other Friday, I returned in uniform to my desk in the rocket launch program office and continued to do the same work as before I left. Only this time, I supported the new rocket launch finance lead–assisting her and filling in for her and my supervisor, the launch and range program control chief, when they took vacations. For my fulltime job, I became a systems engineer in a civilian company and worked in the GPS program office one floor down in the same building.

I continued to do well in the Air Force and was promoted early to major through a program for "exceptionally well qualified candidates" as delineated in AFI36-2504 (14). I was a young major, on top of my world. I lived in an apartment directly on the beach in Los Angeles with a back door that opened onto the sand; I rode my bike on the Strand and went surfing each weekend with my husband. As a systems engineer, I made over six figures before I was thirty and travelled internationally to Australia and Luxembourg on business. I loved putting on my uniform and being part of the military. I was respected; my glowing officer performance report said I was "on the fast track."

I found this piece of paper the other day while I was decluttering and laughed. On the fast track to where? Motherhood? Morning sickness?

## Pregnancy

I had no idea I would be a mother within a few years. It wasn't my plan; I was "never having kids." I felt no rush with regards to my career because I had plenty of time. I had just been promoted to major. I had years before I had to think about my next promotion to lieutenant colonel. I submitted a polished application to the Air Force master's program that prepares officers for lieutenant colonel, optimistic that I would be promoted the same as I had been before–early and easily.

These career plans were derailed when I became unexpectedly pregnant. I miscarried at the end of my first trimester. I lost my first baby but gained something else: a deep desire to have a child. This was surprising, and yet hauntingly familiar of my mother's story–she was also "never going to have kids" and then went on to have four children and five miscarriages.

My husband received orders to move to a new assignment in Florida, and I felt that one of the main benefits of being a reservist was that I could move with him. I kept my reserve assignment in Los Angeles, and, after much legwork and networking in Florida, arranged to work three weeks on base in Florida and two weeks in Los Angeles annually. In my civilian career, I continued performing my same job supporting GPS in Los Angeles while working from home full time in Florida.

The day we arrived in Florida, I found out I was pregnant again. It was a take-no-prisoners, no-holds-barred kind of pregnancy. *Hyperemesis gravidarum*–persistent and severe vomiting leading to weight loss and dehydration (Oxford Dictionary)–hit me four days after we arrived, on my thirty-second birthday, and lasted until the minute my daughter was born. I was sitting at my makeshift desk in our empty house–a plastic patio chair and my laptop on a card table–dialed into an all-day conference call on modernized GPS equipment, and I remember thinking, *I just can't sit up anymore.* I slid to the floor and listened to the rest of the call from under the table and chair.

Because of the hyperemesis, all I could do was lie in bed and throw up–approximately ten times per hour. I was too sick to work, even from bed. After being threatened by the human resources director in the company I worked for that I would likely be fired if I took any disability leave, I started taking antinausea medications around the clock to enable me to work throughout my pregnancy. This reduced my vomiting to a more manageable amount every day and enabled me to eat some food. I was still very nauseous, dizzy, and weak, so I worked mostly from bed.

Fearing career repercussions, I hid my pregnancy from my co-workers as much as possible. While in Los Angeles for reserve duty, I had a daily morning routine. I set my alarm early so I could stumble to the bathroom and throw up. I lay down in the shower and continuously vomited while the water flowed over me. When I was able to stand, I finished showering, put on my uniform, went to work, shut the door to my office, and threw up in the trashcan.

## Birth and Maternity Leave

When I was six months pregnant, I was selected to attend the prestigious fulltime Air Command and Staff College master's program in Montgomery, Alabama, which I had applied for pre-pregnancy, a program limited by regulation to the "best qualified" (AFI36-2301 16). I was gratified to be selected as one of the top 24 percent of eligible officers (Grever), and attendance would virtually guarantee my next promotion. Despite this, I turned it down.

Before becoming pregnant, I would have been there in a heartbeat. It would have been another assignment apart from my husband, but we had done that before, and it felt worth the sacrifice for this major career goal. Now that I was pregnant, it was much more challenging. As one fellow military mom put it, "being in the Army wasn't that tough last year, but now that I have brought children into the world, it has become the toughest thing ever."

There was no flexibility in the timing of my attendance for this career milestone. Since my husband was required to complete his military commitment in Florida, in order to attend, I would have had to move and live without him. I would be alone in a new place for my third trimester, birth, and the first six months of my child's life, becoming a single working parent with my newborn in childcare. At the time, Air Force maternity leave for vaginal births was only six weeks, although that has recently changed to a much-needed twelve weeks (James), and parental (paternity) leave was and still is only ten days (AFI36-3003 48).

Similar to many other military women, I felt that only six weeks of maternity leave was not enough. My main concern was that I did not feel comfortable putting a six-week old into daycare. "Inadequate maternity leave was reported as a major challenge for women in the Military Services" (DACOWITS, "2015 Report" 77). This felt especially true when the Family Care Act authorized three months of unpaid maternity leave, which I was able to take from my fulltime civilian job. I chose to decline this school opportunity and instead schedule my military duty after my civilian maternity leave. I only had this option because I was on an individual billet in the reserve and not on active duty. Active duty women giving birth at the time had no flexibility: the choice was either putting their six-week-old newborns in childcare, along with the possibility of deploying while their children were babies, or separating from active duty altogether. Thankfully, for many military mothers, the new policies providing twelve weeks of maternity leave and a one-year exemption from deployment now make that choice less harsh.

There was a distance-learning program available that, while neither prestigious nor selective, was open to all Air Force majors (AFI36-2301 23). I signed up for it and kept my books next to my nursing chair while on unpaid maternity leave so I could study while I nursed. The reality was that I was too brain dead and exhausted to do so. The minute I started reading, I nodded off. My daughter was up every hour or two at night for years, as was my son after her. I was depleted from pregnancy, birth, miscarriage, and from a complete and total lack of sleep. All I could do during my maternity leave was breastfeed and care for my newborn. I never finished the program, and my supervisor believed this was the main reason I was not promoted to lieutenant colonel during my later promotion board.

I would have appreciated the option to defer my in-residence selection until ready and able to attend. A guaranteed option to postpone important promotion preparation milestones such as this as well as promotion boards, and a less structured approach to promotion requirements and timelines would be beneficial to parents as these often occur during key childbearing years (Evertson and Nesbitt 3). Currently, the Air Force officer promotion system is a very structured "up or out" process (AFI36-2504 and AFI36-2501) delineated by law in the Defense Officer Personnel Management Act (DOPMA). Former Secretary of Defense Ashton Carter stated that this "'one-size-fits-all' approach" is too rigid and asked Congress for authority for flexibility in this system, including allowing military officers to voluntarily defer promotion boards, as I recommend (Carter, "The Next Two" 2). Unfortunately, it does not appear that Congress is on board with this approach (Shane).

## Motherhood

I continued my career in the Air Force Reserve, now as a mother. When I had to travel for reserve duty in Los Angeles, I took my daughter and a family member with me to watch her. I pumped breastmilk in my office, my director's office (when he wasn't there), in empty computer labs, and in storage closets. During a bomb threat and evacuation, I hand-expressed into a water bottle in the bathroom. I breastfed over lunch when possible (see Sarah Hampson, chapter three this volume, for a discussion of the stigmatization of breastfeeding military mothers, and Naomi Mercer, chapter eight, for personal experiences with respect to being a nursing military mother). I was at my desk in uniform the day after my second miscarriage, dazed but working. I made sure I performed my annual tour before I was due with my son. I made it work.

Then, a new deputy director decided I needed to either travel to Los Angeles for all of my duty time or formally transfer my assignment to Florida where I lived. We chose to transfer, and it took years of hands-on effort to get through the administrative hurdles of doing so in accordance the process in AFI36-2115. Once my assignment transferred, I started my reserve duty in Florida, and while I was on active reserve duty, I was laid off from my civilian job. Shortly thereafter, my husband was reassigned to Ramstein AFB, Germany.

Once in Germany, I became a stay-at-home mom to two little children who wanted me in a way I could barely understand. Every second of every minute of every day, they wanted me to hold them, comfort them, talk to them, and focus only on them. I was still assigned to my unit in Florida, and there were many administrative items that I was required to complete in order to stay current in the reserve system in accordance with the Guide for Individual Reservists. Despite my best efforts, I ran into roadblock after roadblock trying to complete these required items in Germany because I was still assigned to a unit in Florida, and it was not clear to anyone the process by which to do them from overseas.

The Air Force had a need for a finance reservist in Germany, but I couldn't transfer my position here until the administrative issues were resolved, and I couldn't handle the administrative issues because I wasn't assigned in Germany. It was a catch-22, and, exhausted from being a still-breastfeeding stay-at-home mom of two nonsleeping children, I wasn't able to make any headway.

Although Air Force Instruction (AFI) 36-2115 states it "seeks to prevent the loss of valuable personnel because of relocation," (12) in practice, I did not see any evidence of this. I found the reserve reassignment process to be an overly long and incomprehensible experience. It took almost four years of actively trying to be reassigned to my husband's base in Florida before my reassignment was finalized, and by that time, we were already in the process to move to our next base in Germany.

Transfer of reserve assignments disproportionately affects female service members. Overall females transition from active duty to the reserve at a higher rate than males (DACOWITS, "2003 Report" 8). It seems like the more family-friendly option (Iskra, *Women*, 139), with more flexible possibilities for part-time work, volunteer-only deployments, and greater control over your own location. Darlene Iskra's study of female general and flag officers found that those who transferred from active duty to the reserve chose to do so because of family concerns, including concerns about being stationed with their spouses (Iskra, "Breaking" 167). This included female service members who made this decision with foresight even before marrying or having children because they were looking toward the future (Iskra, "Breaking" 168). This is consistent with my own experience and the experiences of other female reservists as well (DiSilverio 28).

Those of us that do transfer to the reserve for this reason then have to keep transferring our positions within the reserve every few years to keep up with our active duty spouse's assignments. Over 20 percent of female Air Force reservists are married to active duty Air Force personnel, compared to only 3 percent of male Air Force reservists. So although there are many fewer female personnel in the Air Force Reserve (we comprise only 26 percent of the Air Force Reserve), there are over twenty-four hundred more of us facing this issue (FY 2014 and FY 2015). Streamlining to make this process automatic and guaranteed would be extremely beneficial to dual-military mothers in the reserve, and would make the reserve more practical for personnel trying to balance family and military service. In order to improve retention rates of mid-level female service members, I believe an official, guaranteed join spouse policy is needed for the reserve as well as for active duty.

## Inactivation

I made being a mother in the military work until my daughter was four and my son was two. This took a lot of effort, but I did it, and I'm proud of that. Then I just couldn't make it work anymore. In addition to resolving administrative issues, I was expected to perform five weeks of duty back in Florida while my husband remained in Germany. Just thinking about the childcare that arrangement would require while our family was separated across continents was daunting.

I felt constant pressure from my supervisor via email to get everything done and make it all work. One night, after the kids were in bed, I sat downstairs crying, not knowing what to do. I was stuck between the proverbial rock and the hard place, between the pressure of career and family. Finally, at midnight, in desperation, I called up the automated hotline of the Air Reserve Personnel Center in Texas. After being transferred a few times, I asked, "How and when can I leave the Air Force Reserve?"

The response was lighthearted: "Any time you want. All you have to do is send in a separation request letter." I was stunned. I thought it would be more difficult than that. Before the sun rose in Germany, I had sent in a letter requesting separation to my supervisor in Florida.

Instantly, my supervisor's tone changed. She emailed me back–we can work this out; why throw away fifteen years of hard work on a successful career? I only had five years left until retirement, but I couldn't make it until then. I had been torn down by the small but constant difficulties of being a mother in the military. I knew it was time to stop trying. In the end, my supervisor convinced me to inactivate instead of completely leaving the military.

## Nonpromotion

I remained in the active reserve while I waited for my inactivation paperwork to be processed by headquarters, which inexplicably took six months. During this time, my already-scheduled promotion board was held, and one day, I opened my email and read words that until I became a mother, I never thought I would read: "I regret to inform you that you were not selected by this board for promotion." There was a 67 percent selection rate to lieutenant colonel for the participating reserve (Dewey). Although I was neither surprised nor distraught by this notification, I was disheartened. It was sad to look back over my previously successful career and see it lead to this low point. After a decade of being ranked first on my officer performance reports, being promoted early and receiving awards, I was disappointed to find myself no longer in the top two-thirds of my peer group. I can trace my nonselection directly to the series of decisions I made purposely choosing family and motherhood over my military career, knowingly sabotaging my chances of promotion. I consciously chose motherhood over my military career, but I, like other military women (Evertson and Nesbitt 116), wish it wasn't a choice I felt I had to make.

## The Masculine Military Construct

My experience is individual, yet it illustrates the multifaceted challenges facing mothers in the military. In speaking with female friends and colleagues, I have found being unable to figure out how to combine motherhood with our military careers is a commonality that often leads women to separate from the military. This is consistent with official focus group findings: "Female officers leave because they are unable to find a reasonable work/life balance," describing military life and family requirements as "incompatible" (DACOWITS, "2003 Report" 9). It is also echoed in multiple other retention studies on female service members (Long 76; Steinberg et al. 10; Evertson and Nesbitt 115; DiSilverio 28). The same data are not found for male service members. Nancy Raiha's research on dual-military couples in the United States Army found when the work-life balance feels incompatible, it is typically the female, not the male, service member who leaves the military (qtd. in Etheridge 14).

Based on official DoD data, "the military is a male-predominated and dominated organization" (Wadsworth and Southwell 164). Carol Cohn's analysis of gendered institutions highlights that "the structure of work in military institutions is invisibly premised on male bodies and male social lives" (Carreiras 106). The challenges that affected me in my career–discrimination, harassment, occupational segregation, gendered policies, ineffectual processes, and administrative red tape– overwhelmingly and negatively affect mothers in the military in ways that male service members usually never think about (see Naomi Mercer, chapter eight, this volume, for similar experiences with respect to the masculine military culture). Systemic discrimination "refers to patterns of behavior, policies or practices that are part of the structures of an organization, and which create or perpetuate disadvantage" for a particular minority group, and it is alive, well, and vocally defended in the Air Force ("Systematic Discrimination Law").

The military is based on hegemonic masculinity–a "culturally idealized definition of masculinity" (Locke 10) that is more highly valued and thus more rewarded than other forms of masculinity or femininity (Connell). In the military, this culturally idealized definition of masculinity is embodied by operational and combat experience, mission devotion unfettered by family needs, decisive leadership, and emotional toughness–and is generally speaking, white, heterosexual, Christian, alcohol consuming, and breadwinning. By definition, hegemonic masculinity subordinates anything female or considered feminine, unmanly, or simply unaligned with the hypermasculine ideal (Connell). I am not implying that only the men have these characteristics–they are internalized and perpetuated by both men and women in the military–rather, they are embodied in the organizational structure and culture of the military, and they support and endorse traditionally idealized masculine ways of operating, while penalizing anything that deviates from them.

In line with the historical organizational structure and demographic composition of the military, our current policies and processes systemically favour service members that conform with hegemonic masculinity. "Assumptions about gender underlie the documents and contracts used to construct organizations" (Acker 139) and yet "may be deeply hidden in organizational process and decisions that appear to have nothing to do with gender" (Margosian and Vendrzyk 21). Policies and processes such as the join spouse policy and the Reserve reassignment process can be seen as outdated relics from when the military was considered an all heterosexual male force, and therefor there were no policies relating to marriage between service members (Cohn, *Women and Wars* 16-17). In this case, the assumption is that the military worker is–and has always been–an idealized heterosexual male who is either single or has a wife at home to take care of the children. Unlike motherhood, which is active, fatherhood is not an activity in this construct, but only a responsibility that motivates the military worker to be more committed to the job and the stable income it provides. Thus, having children is positively correlated with officer promotion for fathers, yet not for mothers (Asch xviii). Based on the work of Joan Williams, the ideal military worker has been formed under hegemonic masculinity as one "who is fully devoted to work without family responsibilities to infringe on work commitments" (Rehel and Baxter 3). Active mothers, with our family responsibilities, are thus categorized as nonideal, whereas childfree individuals, as well as inactive parents and passive fathers, can still access ideal status.

These policies do not simply favour one group but also purposefully discriminate against others. Drawing on Gramsci's writings on hegemony–how groups establish and hold power using organizations and methods that make the resulting hierarchical power structure seem natural and normal (Donaldson 644)–hegemonic masculinity is solidified by the "maintenance of practices that institutionalize men's dominance over women" and over subordinated masculinities (Connell 185). Hegemonic "masculinity pervade[s] organizational processes, marginalizing women" (Acker 139) in order to maintain a power differential between the sexes. In this light, policies that strongly affect those not aligning with the hegemonic ideal can be seen as purposeful and powerful attrition tactics used in conjunction with the methods of sexual harassment, discrimination, reports not being handled app-ropriately, and occupational segregation highlighted above. Dominant groups–in this case hegemonic males–write the rules, and they write rules that purposefully enable them to maintain their privileged position (Reskin 58).

## Deployment

Many of these rules are unwritten, enforced through culture and attitude. Prevailing attitudes are hegemonically masculine, supporting the majority of the military population, and these attitudes scorn anything seen as contributing less than this masculine norm, even when authorized by regulation or waiver. Similar to the civilian world, this masculine norm is to work forty-plus hours a week, with as much overtime as needed, and be willing to quickly adjust to shifting schedules and travel requirements, without being constrained by childcare needs. However, in addition to this, U.S military service is unique in that it also requires a commitment to overseas deployment–being temporarily assigned in a combat zone or combat support position for anywhere from three to fifteen months without your family–as well as to geographical relocations with or without your family, depending on the needs of the Air Force, every few years. Refusing or being unable to comply with these requirements can result in punishment and jail time. These factors make military service significantly different than working in the civilian labour force, and skew it toward a more masculine cultural norm than is standard in the civilian world–perhaps purposefully, in order to maintain the military sphere as a male dominion.

The mantra that "anyone who is not willing and able to deploy should not be in the military" is echoed from men and women alike, yet it is specious. It conflates the military with deployment and the requirement to leave your family, even though for many years in the U.S., deployment was not common for the military. Although deployment is currently a generally accepted part of U.S. military service, this is a recent phenomenon. "Most personnel in the Army did

CHOOSING MOTHERHOOD IN THE U.S. AIR FORCE

not deploy at all from 1994 through 2000" (Sortor and Polich 68), which was the period of time that I entered the military. My father-in-law had a very successful twenty-eight-year-long career in the Air Force without ever being requested to deploy. There are many different ways of "pulling your weight" in the military, regardless of deployment status. Some military members fly; some are in charge of U.S.-based missiles. Some do finance, some engineer, some maintain, some cook, some deploy, some perform more than one of these activities, and many do other tasks.

Following Cohn's analysis of invisibly gendered military standards (Cohn, *Women and Wars* 17), the ideal military worker's constant availability for deployment is falsely created as a requirement for the military job not because it is necessary for the mission but because of the underlying gendered organizational structure. As Rosabeth Moss Kanter states, "This 'masculine ethic' elevates the traits assumed to belong to some men ... to necessities for effective organizations" (22). Conflating military service with deployment sets up a system of disadvantage for mothers, women as potential mothers, and dual-military couples in the military–as well as any father that wants to take an active role in his children's life–and may be done purposefully to reinforce the gendered hierarchy (Cohn, *Women and Wars* 18; Long 73; Moss Kanter 23).

Deployment hits new mothers in the military hard, while we are still recovering from childbirth, taking care of a newborn, and possibly struggling with breastfeeding or sleepless nights. One mother who had previously deployed before having children told me the thought of deploying when her first child was a newborn was "devastating." A study of black, white, Hispanic, and mixed ethnicity female veterans of various ages and services found shared experience across diverse women–including the common theme that the difficulties of lengthy separation from their children was a causative factor in their separation from military service (Dichter and True 195). In addition to the emotional difficulties, there are logistical challenges in finding long-term childcare and struggles with family reintegration upon return. Deployment is a particularly acute and challenging concern for single mothers, who comprise over a third of all military mothers. Within single motherhood in the military, rates are higher for minorities– 47 percent of black military mothers are single–and for enlisted personnel as compared to officers (Clever and Segal 23, 25), which brings inter-sectional challenges as well.

In 2015, Secretary James recognized that the prospect of deployment after childbirth is a major factor many women consider when choosing to leave active service. In order to address this retention issue, new policy defers mothers from deployment for one year after birth. Air Force analysis concludes that this update will have a negligible impact on manning and deployment levels (James et al., "2015 Diversity" 2-3) providing further supporting evidence that the current mission does not require a structure in which every military service member must be continually ready and able to deploy. Since 2001, and 2003 in particular, U.S. military deployments have increased significantly (Belasco 9). Now that we have been in this mode of high operational tempo for well over a decade, I believe it is time to relook at the construct of continuous deployments for all and investigate other possible structures for completing the mission (Public). Instead of setting up a standard that mothers are exempt from, leadership should implement standards that work for the entire military population, without creating systemic discrimination against one group.

In her article about mothers and work-life policies, Sarah Hampson concludes, "it appears that as long as their workplace policies are structured to exempt mothers from work for family needs in ways that other workers are not permitted to be exempt, then mothers will continue to suffer from stereotypes of them as workers who are trying to shirk their responsibilities" (20). This is not just a women's issue; it is an issue for men too. Men who choose to adapt their careers for family or personal reasons–who decide to engage in active fatherhood–face career penalties as well–this "flexibility stigma" is well documented for involved fathers as well as mothers (Williams, et al., "Cultural Schemes"; Coltrane et al.; Rudman et al.).

I personally know men as well as women in the military who would appreciate more workplace flexibility–this aligns with the U.S. Navy work-life taskforce findings that the current generation of service members desire a more flexible military (Karin and Onachila 183). Flexibility is the key to air power, and as service members are always told in the Air Force, "take care of the people, and the people will take care of the mission." However, it takes more than just "slapping" flexible policies on top of inflexible masculine attitudes (Williams et al.,

"Disruptive" 8). Organizations and personnel could adapt and thrive under a more flexible people-friendly policy structure, but there needs to be a significant culture change as well.

## Recent Forward Momentum

On the positive side, the Department of Defense and the Air Force are making policy shifts that help military mothers, and the forward momentum made in the past few years under former Secretary of Defense Ashton Carter and former Secretary of the Air Force Deborah Lee James has been astonishing. The DoD's Force of the Future and the Air Force's Diversity & Inclusion initiatives aim to increase retention by "improving the quality of life of military parents so they may better balance commitments they make to serve in uniform and start and support a family" (Carter, "Force of the Future"). Recent policy changes include the following: increasing maternity leave to twelve weeks (AFI36-3003 32-33); extending fitness test exemptions for one year after birth (AFI36-2110_AFGM2016-01; temporary duty (TDY), permanent change of station (PCS), and deployment deferments exempting mothers from work-related travel including deployments for one year after birth (AFI36-2110_AFGM2016-01); starting a limited three-year sabbatical program called the Career Intermission Program (CIP) (AFGM2016-36-02); and opening up all military occupational specialties and career fields to women (Carter, "Implementation" 1).

Other initiatives that have been announced as in work but not yet codified in Air Force regulation include the following: giving women the option of separating for one year after birth (James et al., "2016 Diversity" 3); improving female access to pilot, officer (James et al., "2015 Diversity" 2), and operational opportunities (and thus leadership and promotion opportunities); requesting Congressional approval for expanded paternity and adoption leave; extending on-base childcare hours; and building additional mothers' rooms on military bases. (Carter, "The Next Two" 1).

Many of these changes support military mothers in the crucial early months and years after birth, which is often the most challenging time for balancing work and family. They also support and facilitate breastfeeding, a focus area for DACOWITS in 2015 (xv) based on WHO and UNICEF recommendations for exclusive breastfeeding for six months and continued breastfeeding until two years or beyond (WHO).

I was able to pump in my office and to bring my child with me while I travelled for work, but this was likely influenced by both my rank and occupational field, and, unfortunately, not all female military service members currently have access to these same possibilities.

Each of these initiatives supporting women and mothers in the military has been rapidly announced; in fewer than two years, they have addressed issues that I have seen affect female service members over the course of my seventeen-year career. This is a positive start to removing institutional barriers and inconsistencies, as recommended by the Military Leadership Diversity Commission in 2011 (MLDC, "Retention" xvii).

## More to Be Done

These steps help female service members immensely; however, there is so much more that can be done: cultural training on sex, gender, masculinities and respect; extended (paid or unpaid) maternity leave; more or mandatory paternity leave; equal or sharing family leave; guaranteed join spouse assignments for active and reserve members; guaranteed career intermission sabbatical programs; guaranteed dual-military reserve assignment transfers; support to reservists at their spouses' assigned locations; part-time or telecommute options; removal of family care plans through schedule coordination of dual-military travel and deployments; rethinking deployment and reassignment tempos and processes; and restructuring the promotion process to include deferment options for training and boards as well as removal of "up or out" promotion policies.

Policy enactment would have to be accompanied by straightforward and respectful processes and execution. It is crucial these policies be fully guaranteed and automatic–not subject to a supervisor's approval, "mission needs," the "needs of the Air Force," a hostile work environment, an administrative black hole, or an extensive checklist of requirements. Policy alone is not enough. As former Secretary of Defense Ashton Carter himself stated, it requires a culture shift (Carter, "Implementation" 2).

The Disabled American Veterans' report on women veterans found that "despite recent improvement efforts at VA (Veteran's Administration) and DoD, women still encounter a male-dominated system that is designed to address the needs of men." One of their key recommendations is that "DoD should aggressively pursue culture and organizational change to ensure that women are respected and valued" (Murphy 4). I cannot stress the importance of this enough. Is it possible to change persistent masculine attitudes that shape retention, the daily work environment, and promotion rates? I am not sure, but we at least need to try. Step by step, we need to continue moving in the direction of equality. The Air Force has committed to creating a better, more inclusive, environment for all of its diverse service members (James et al., "Air Force Diversity" 2). Addressing underlying structural and cultural issues affecting female military service members is crucial to that endeavour.

Before I had children, I succeeded in the military by embodying traditionally masculine attributes–I was perfectionistic, organized, mission driven, and ambitious. I worked fast, and I worked late. I travelled often. There was a lot of work to do, and I focused on getting it all done as efficiently and effectively as possible. I succeeded not only because I worked as hard, if not harder, than the men, but also because I worked like a stereotypical man (Cohn, "Wars" 238).

When I had children, something slowly started to change in me. I wasn't able to work like that anymore, and I didn't want to. I slowly realized that perfectionism is not a helpful way of living. Babies appreciate neither perfectionism nor ruthless efficiency. I began to see there was more to life than one-size-fits-all career success. Although this is in line with the values of the current generation (Karin and Onachila 183), it is out of place in rigid military culture.

Empowering women should not mean encouraging women to inter-nalize traditionally masculine values, nor does it mean exempting them from requirements that continue to be based on an idealized masculine norm. True empowerment comes from a culture that embraces a model of success reflecting the diversity of feminine, maternal, and paternal values in addition to masculine ones. It means supporting both women and men who choose to balance their personal values and strengths in their career, family, and lives.

In their Air Force Diversity & Inclusion memorandum, former Secretary James, General Welsh, and Chief Cody call diversity and inclusion "national security imperatives and critical force multipliers" and state that we need to leverage the strengths of the diverse people of the United States in order to be strategically agile and operationally relevant. "Across the force, diversity of background, experience, demographics, thought and even organization are essential to our ultimate success" (James et al., "Air Force Diversity" 1). I believe that mothers are a key part of this strength and diversity and that cultural and policy shifts within the military are required to leverage that strength.

I hope the day comes soon when military culture recognizes that mothers and other caregivers have additional responsibilities outside the workplace that are just as valid as mission duties. We need, as a society, to accept mothering, to include breastfeeding, as a crucial and valuable function. Children are carried for months inside their mothers, and once born, they remain connected through invisible cords that wrap mother and child together–together through the intense need that children have for mothering, nurturing, and nourishment. These needs should be recognized, not swept aside in the spirit of gender equality or political correctness.

Encouraging women to join the military because of the belief that increasing the number of women in the military will lead to change neglects to address the barriers women face when they do so. This leaves women who do join learning some hard lessons about reality after the fact. Women should be told the truth of the situation rather than "girls can do anything boys can do" and "you can have it all" in the spirit of female empowerment. The answer to "you can have it all," is "There's going to have to be some major changes first."

The initiatives U.S. military leadership has implemented recently are a positive start, and I hope that the focus on improvement in these areas continues into the future. Unfortunately, as Kunal Modi says, "We're not there yet." We're not even close. There is still more so much more work to be done.

## Conclusion

For me, motherhood and active service in the military proved to be incompatible. Perhaps that is because, despite excelling in my career, there has always been a part of me that did not thrive in the military. Motherhood opened me up, brought me back to myself in a hard and jarring way. I have had to honour myself to survive. I have no more leeway to accept what does not serve me. As hard as it is for me to accept, as a woman of mixed ethnicity, being in the military was not serving me, and never had served me, 100 percent. I was able to overlook this for a long time, but once I became a mother, I could not overcome the challenges I faced in the military.

Men in the military, statistically, have an easier time combining family with their career as they progress forward. Former Secretary James stated that "women leave the service at twice the rate of men during the middle of their careers" (qtd. in Losey). Of those that remain, in the top three ranks of both active-duty enlisted and officer personnel (excluding generals), men are 20 percent more likely to be married than women and the women are three to four times more likely to be divorced (FY 2015). This is simply the current reality.

The message that mothers can "have it all"–a successful fulltime military career and motherhood–is misleading and results in unrealistic expectations. Just because it is possible–if the stars align, if AFPC blesses you, if you are a superwoman–doesn't mean it is probable or even desired. There are significant institutional barriers to being a mother in the military. I found this out only as I progressed through my career. The challenges I faced are not unique to me but are felt by female military members across the services, and my intention is to provide honest information and awareness to other women that are in or thinking of joining the military and to our leadership who are crafting future military policy. "Airbrushing reality," as Anne-Marie Slaughter so accurately calls it, is not helpful to ourselves or future generations.

I believe my experience shows how powerfully institutional barriers can negatively affect a female service member's military career, especially when it comes into conflict with her family priorities. I am appreciative that military leadership is finally starting to address these issues. Continued dismantling of these barriers is needed as we move into the future in order to improve the working environment for women and mothers in the military, increase retention and diversity, and strengthen our overall force. I offer some potential policy changes, but this is only a first step–this complex issue cannot be solved by policy alone. If there is a solution, to me, it comes down to values. Once the military and society transform to value female service members and motherhood concurrent with military service–and show that through policy, process, attitude, and environment–then it will become more manageable for women to be mothers in the military; until then, it will continue to be onerous, and for many of us, a reason to opt out.

## Works Cited

760 F. Supp. 1486 (M.D. Fla. 1991). "Lois Robinson, Plaintiff, v. Jacksonville Shipyards, Inc., et al., Defendants. No. 86-927-Civ-J-12. United States District Court, M.D. Florida, Jacksonville Division. Order, Injunction and Final Judgment." *Justia*, 8 Mar. 1991, law.justia.com/cases/federal/district-courts/FSupp/760/1486/1420870/. Accessed 22 Jan. 2018.

Acker, Joan. "Hierarchies, Jobs, Bodies: A Theory of Gendered Organizations." *Gender and Society*, vol. 4, no. 2, 1990, pp. 139-158.

Asch, Beth J., Trey Miller, and Gabriel Weinberger. "Can We Explain Gender Differences in Officer Career Progression?" RAND Corporation, 2016, doi: 10.7249/RR1288.

Bastian, Lisa D., et al. "Department of Defense 1995 Sexual Harassment Survey." *Defense Manpower Data Center*, 2 Dec. 1996, www.dtic.mil/dtfs/doc_research/p18_11.pdf.

Belasco, Amy. "Troop Levels in the Afghan and Iraq Wars, FY2001-FY2012: Cost and Other Potential Issues." Congressional Research Service, 2 July 2009, www.dtic.mil/dtic/tr/fulltext/u2/a503796.pdf. Accessed 22 Jan. 2018.

Blanchard, Samantha E. "Understanding the Experience of Air Force Single Parents: A Phenomenological Study." Dissertations and Theses, Paper 621, Portland State University, 2012.

Berdahl, Jennifer L. and Celia Moore. "Workplace Harassment: Double Jeopardy for Minority Women." *Journal of Applied Psychology*, vol. 91, no. 2, 2006, pp. 426-36.

Bethea, Mearen Charlene. "The Long War and the Forgotten Families: Dual-Military Couples." U.S. Army War College, 30 Mar 2007, www.dtic.mil/get-tr-doc/pdf?AD=ADA469184. Accessed 22 Jan. 2018.

Buchanan, et al. "Comparing sexual harassment subtypes among Black and White Women by Military Rank: Double Jeopardy, the Jezebel, and the Cult of True Womanhood." *Psychology of Women Quarterly,* vol. 32, no. 4, 2008, pp. 347-61.

Carreiras, Helena. "Gender and the Military: A Comparative Study of the Participation of Women in the Armed Forces of Western Democracies."*Academia*, Mar. 2004, www.academia.edu/18059073/Gender_and_the_Military_A_Comparative_Study_of_the_Participation_of_Women_in_the_Armed_Forces_of_Western_Democracies. Accessed 22 Jan. 2018.

Carter, Ashton. "The Next Two Links to the Force of the Future." 9 June 2016, *U.S. Department of Defense*, www.defense.gov/Portals/1/ features/2015/0315_force-of-the-future/Memorandum-The-Next-Two-Links-to-the-Force-of-the-Future.pdf. Accessed 22 Jan. 2018.

Carter, Ashton. "Implementation Guidance for the Full Integration of Women in the Armed Forces." *U.S. Department of Defense,* 3 Dec. 2015, www.defense.gov/Portals/1/Documents/pubs/OSD014303-15.pdf. Accessed 22 Jan. 2018.

Carter, Ashton. "Force of the Future: Strengthening Family Benefits." *Facebook*, 28 Jan. 2016, www.facebook.com/notes/us-secretary-of-defense/force-of-the-future-strengthening-family-benefits/156281 9974040427/. Accessed 22 Jan. 2018.

Clever, Molly, and David R. Segal. "The Demographics of Military Children and Families." *The Future of Children,* vol. 23, no. 2, 2013, pp. 13-39.

Cohn, Carol. "Wars, Wimps, and Women: Talking Gender and Thinking War." *Gendering War Talk*, edited by Miriam Cooke and Angela Woollacott, Princeton University Press, 1993, pp. 227-46.

Cohn, Carol. *Women and Wars: Contested Histories, Uncertain Futures.* Wiley, 2012.

Coltrane, Scott et al. "Fathers and the Flexibility Stigma." *Journal of Social Issues*, vol. 69, no. 2, 2013, pp. 279-302.

Connell, R. W. *Gender and Power: Society, the Person and Sexual Politics*. John Wiley & Sons, 15 May 2014.

Cockburn, Cynthia. *In the Way of Women: Men's Resistance to Sex Equality in Organizations*. Cornell University Press, 1991.

Damaske, Sarah. *For the Family?: How Class and Gender Shape Women's Work*. Oxford University Press, 2011.

Dewey, Cindy. "Lt. Col. Promotions Announced." *Air Force Personnel Center*, 28 Aug. 2015, www.arpc.afrc.af.mil/News/Article-Display/ Article/614281/lt-col-promotions-announced/. Accessed 22 Jan. 2018.

Dichter, Melissa E. and Gala True. "This Is the Story of Why My Military Career Ended Before It Should Have" Premature Separation From Military Service Among U.S. Women Veterans." *Affilia: Journal of Women and Social Work,* vol. 30, no. 2, 2015, pp. 187-199.

DiSilverio, Laura A.H., "Winning the Retention Wars: The Air Force, Women Officers, and the Need for Transformation." *Air University Press*, August 2003, media.defense.gov/2017/May/05/2001742915/-1/-1/0/

FP_0011_DISILVERIO_WINNING_RETENTION_WARS.PDF. Accessed 22 Jan. 2018.

Donaldson, M. "What Is Hegemonic Masculinity?" *Theory and Society, Special Issue: Masculinities,* vol. 22, no. 5, 1993, pp. 643-57.

Etheridge, Rose M. "Family Factors Affecting Retention: A Review of the Literature." *U.S. Army Research Institute for the Behavioral and Social Sciences, Research Report 1511,* Mar. 1989, www.dtic.mil/get-tr-doc/pdf?AD=ADA210506. Accessed 22 Jan. 2018.

*Evertson, Adrienne F., and Amy M. Nesbitt.* "The Glass Ceiling Effect and its Impact on Mid-Level Female Officer Career Progression in the United States Marine Corps and Air Force." Naval Postgraduate School, Mar. 2004, hdl.handle.net/10945/1711. Accessed 22 Jan. 2018.

Fiscal Year (FY) 2014 Report. "Air Force Personnel Center. Interactive Demographic Analysis System (IDEAS)." *United States Government,* usa. gov. Accessed 22 Jan. 2018.

Fiscal Year (FY) 2015 Report. "Air Force Personnel Center. Interactive Demographic Analysis System (IDEAS)" *United States Government,* usa. gov. Accessed 22 Jan. 2018.

Grever, Steve. "AF Releases Officer, Civilian Developmental Education Board Results." *Air Force Personnel Center,* 21 Oct. 2010, www.afpc.af. mil/News/Article-Display/Article/422776/af-releases-officer-civilian-developmental-education-board-results/. Accessed 22 Jan. 2018.

Hampson, Sarah Cote. "Mothers Do Not Make Good Workers: The Role of Work/Life Policies in Reinforcing Gendered Stereotypes." Western Political Science Association Meeting, 28-30 Mar. 2013, Hollywood, CA. Paper presentation.

"Infant and Young Child Feeding," *World Health Organization (WHO),* Sep. 2016, www.who.int/mediacentre/factsheets/fs342/en/. Accessed 22 Jan. 2018.

Iskra, Darlene M. "Breaking Through the "Brass" Ceiling: Elite Military Women's Strategies for Success." *University of Maryland,* 2007, hdl.handle.net/1903/7734. Accessed 22 Jan. 2018.

Iskra, Darlene M. *Women in the United States Armed Forces: A Guide to the Issues.* ABC-CLIO, 2010.

James, Deborah Lee. "Extending Maternity Leave." Memorandum for All Airmen, 9 Feb. 2016.

James, Deborah Lee, et al. "2016 Diversity & Inclusion (D&I) Initiatives." *Air Force, 30 Sep. 2016,* www.af.mil/Portals/1/documents/.

Accessed 22 Jan. 2018.

James, Deborah Lee, et al. "2015 Diversity & Inclusion (D&I) Initiatives." *Air Force, 4 Mar. 2015, www.af.mil/Portals/1/documents/ SECAF/FINALDiversity_Inclusion_Memo2.pdf. Accessed 22 Jan. 2018.*

James, Deborah Lee, et al. "Air Force Diversity & Inclusion." *Air Force*, 4 Mar. 2015, http://www.af.mil/Portals/1/documents/SECAF/ FINAL Diversity_Inclusion_Memo1.pdf. Accessed 22 Jan. 2018.

Karin, Marcy L. and Katie Onachila. "The Military Workplace Flexibility Framework." *Labor and Employment Law Forum*, vol. 3, no. 2, 2013, pp. 153-96.

Locke, Brandon Thomas. "The Military-Masculinity Complex: Hegemonic Masculinity and the United States Armed Forces, 1940-1963." Dissertations, Theses, & Student Research, Department of History, University of Nebraska, August 2013, digitalcommons.unl.edu/ historydiss/65/. Accessed 22 Jan. 2018.

Long, Valarie A. "Retention and the Dual-Military Couple: Implications for Military Readiness." Virginia Polytechnic Institute and State University, 15 Jan. 2008, vtechworks.lib.vt.edu/handle/10919/31025. Accessed 22 Jan. 2018.

Losey, Stephen. "Air Force Secretary's Diversity Plan Will Mean Quotas, Critics Say." Air Force Times, 9 Mar. 2015, www.airforcetimes. com/education-transition/jobs/2015/03/09/air-force-secretary-s-diversity-plan-will-mean-quotas-critics-say. Accessed 22 Jan. 2018.

Martinez, Luis. "Air Force Fires Two Nuclear Missile Commanders." *ABC News*, 3 Nov. 2014, abcnews.go.com/US/air-force-fires-nuclear-missile-commanders/story?id=26669590. Accessed 22 Jan. 2018.

Margosian, Mary Ann B. and Judith M. Vendrzyk. "Policies, Practices, and the Effect of Gender Discrimination on the Integration of Women Officers in the Department of the Navy." *Calhoun, 8 Mar. 1994, calhoun. nps.edu/bitstream/handle/10945/43045/policiespractice00marg. pdf?sequence=1. Accessed 22 Jan. 2018.*

Martin, Phiona, and Antoni Barnard. "The Experience of Women in Male-Dominated Occupations: A Constructivist Grounded Theory Inquiry." *SA Journal of Industrial Psychology*, vol. 39, no, 2, 2013, doi: 10.4102/sajip.v39i2.1099.

McGinley, Ann C. "Creating Masculine Identities: Bullying and Harassment 'Because of Sex.'" *Scholarly Works*. Paper 18, 2008, scholars. law.unlv.edu/facpub/18. Accessed 22 Jan. 2018.

Military Leadership Diversity Commission (MLDC). "From Represen-
tation to Inclusion: Diversity Leadership for 21st-Century Military Final
Report." 15 Mar. 2011, diversity.defense.gov/Portals/51/Documents/
Special%20Feature/MLDC_Final_Report.pdf. Accessed 22 Jan. 2018.

Military Leadership Diversity Commission (MLDC). "Officer Retention Rates Across the Services by Gender and Race/Ethnicity." Issue
Paper #24, *Homeland Security,* Mar. 2010, www.hsdl.org/?view
&did=716147. Accessed 22 Jan. 2018.

Military Leadership Diversity Commission (MLDC). "Retention."
Decision Paper #3, *Homeland Security*, Feb. 2011, www.hsdl.org/?view
&did=716005. Accessed 22 Jan. 2018.

Modi, Kunal. "Man Up on Family and Workplace Issues: A Response
to Anne-Marie Slaughter." *The Huffington Post,* 12 July 2012, www.
huffingtonpost.com/kunal-modi/man-up-on-family-and-work_b_
1667878.html.

Morral, Andrew R. et al. "Sexual Assault and Sexual Harassment in
the U.S. Military: Volume 2. Estimates for Department of Defense Service
Members from the 2014 RAND Military Workplace Study." *RAND
Corporation,* 2016, www.rand.org/content/dam/rand/pubs/research_
reports/RR800/RR870z2-1/RAND_RR870z2-1.pdf.

Moss Kanter, Rosabeth. *Men and Women of the Corporation.* Basic
Books, 1993.

Murphy, Frances M., and Sherry Hans. "Women Veterans: the Long
Journey Home." *Disabled American Veterans*, 2014, www.dav.org/wp-
content/uploads/women-veterans-study.pdf. Accessed 22 Jan. 2018.

Mundell, David J. "Study of Female Junior Officer Retention and
Promotion in the U.S. Navy." Naval Postgraduate School, *Defense
Technical Information Centre* Mar. 2016, www.dtic.mil/dtic/tr/fulltext/
u2/1027516.pdf. Accessed 22 Jan. 2018.

*Oxford Dictionary.* "Hyperemesis." 2016, en.oxforddictionaries.com.
Accessed 22 Jan. 2018.

Public, John Q. "A Closer Look at the SecAF's Diversity Initiatives."
*John Q Public,* 7 Mar. 2015, www.jqpublicblog.com/bold-or-expedient-a-
closer-look-at-the-air-forces-new-diversity-initiatives/. Accessed 22
Jan. 2018.

Rehel, Erin and Emily Baxter. "Men, Fathers, and Work-Family
Balance." *Center for American Progress,* 4 Feb. 2015, cdn.american
progress.org/wp-content/uploads/2015/02/MenWorkFamily-brief.pdf.

Accessed 22 Jan. 2018.

Reskin, Barbara F. "Bringing the Men Back In: Sex Differentiation and the Devaluation of Women's Work." *Gender & Society*, vol. 2, no. 1, 1988, pp. 58-81.

Rudman, Laurie A and Kris Mescher. "Penalizing Men Who Request a Family Leave: Is Flexibility Stigma a Femininity Stigma?" *Journal of Social Issues,* vol. 69, no. 2, 2013, pp. 322-40.

Schultz, Vicki. "Reconceptualizing Sexual Harassment." *Faculty Scholarship Series,* Paper 4973, 1998, digitalcommons.law.yale.edu/fss_papers/4973. Accessed 22 Jan. 2018.

Shane III, Leo. "The Pentagon's 'Force of the Future' plan just got trashed in Congress." *Military Times*, 25 Feb. 2016, www.militarytimes.com/news/pentagon-congress/2016/02/25/the-pentagon-s-force-of-the-future-plan-just-got-trashed-in-congress/. Accessed 22 Jan. 2018.

Slaughter, Anne-Marie. "Why Women Still Can't Have It All." *The Atlantic,* July-Aug. 2012, www.theatlantic.com/magazine/archive/2012/07/why-women-still-cant-have-it-all/309020/. Accessed 22 Jan. 2018.

Sortor, Ronald E. and J. Michael Polich. "Deployments and Army Personnel Tempo." *RAND Corporation, 2001,* www.rand.org/content/dam/rand/pubs/monograph_reports/2007/MR1417.pdf. Accessed 22 Jan. 2018.

*Steinberg, Alma G., et al.* "Why Promotable Female Officers Leave the Army," *United States Army Research Institute for the Behavioral and Social Sciences,* AD-A268 946, July 1993, www.dtic.mil/dtic/tr/fulltext/u2/a268946.pdf. Accessed 22 Jan. 2018.

"Systemic Discrimination Law & Legal Definition." *U.S. Legal,* 2016, definitions.uslegal.com/s/systemic-discrimination/. Accessed 22 Jan. 2018.

United States Air Force. "Air Force Form 780: Officer Separation Actions." 1 Apr. 2001.

United States Air Force. "Air Force Guidance Memorandum (AFCM) to AFI 36-2110, Assignments." *Air Force,* 23 Jun. 2016, www.afpc.af.mil/Portals/70/documents/Life%20and%20Career/EFMP/AFI%2036-2110.pdf?ver=2017-01-10-101210-033.

United States Air Force. "Air Force Instruction (AFI) 36-2110: Assignments." Air Force Publishing, 22 Sept. 2009, static.e-publishing.af.mil/production/1/af_a1/publication/afi36-2110/afi36-2110.pdf.

Accessed 22 Jan. 2018.

United States Air Force. "Air Force Instruction (AFI) 36-2115: Assignments within the Reserve Components." *Air Force Publishing*, 2 May 2008, static.e-publishing.af.mil/production/1/af_a1/publication/afi36-2115/afi36-2115.pdf. Accessed 22 Jan. 2018.

United States Air Force. "Air Force Instruction (AFI) 36-2301: Developmental Education." *Air Force Publishing*, 9 Jul. 2013, static.e-publishing.af.mil/production/1/af_a1/publication/afi36-2301/afi36-2301.pdf. Accessed 22 Jan. 2018.

United States Air Force. "Air Force Instruction (AFI) 36-2501: Officer Promotions and Selective Continuation." *Air Force's Personnel Center*, 24 Jun. 2016, www.afpc.af.mil/Portals/70/documents/Life%20and%20Career/Promotions/AFI%2036-2501.pdf?ver=2017-01-12-101726-643. Accessed 22 Jan. 2018.

United States Air Force. "Air Force Instruction (AFI) 36-2504: Officer Promotion, Continuation and Selective Early Removal in the Reserve of the Air Force." *Air Force Publishing*, 22 Jan. 2010, static.e-publishing.af.mil/production/1/af_a1/publication/afi36-2504/afi36-2504.pdf. Accessed 22 Jan. 2018.

United States Air Force. "Air Force Instruction (AFI) 36-2629: Individual Reservist (IR) Management." *Air Force Publishing*, 13 Aug. 2012, static.e-publishing.af.mil/production/1/af_a1/publication/afi36-2629/afi36-2629.pdf. Accessed 22 Jan. 2018.

United States Air Force. "Air Force Instruction (AFI) 36-3003: Military Leave Program." *Air Force Publishing*, 11 May 2016, static.e-publishing.af.mil/production/1/af_a1/publication/afi36-3003/afi36-3003.pdf. Accessed 22 Jan. 2018.

United States Air Force. "Air Force Officer Classification Directory (AFOCD): The Official Guide to the Air Force Officer Classification Codes." Illinois National Guard, 31 Oct. 2016, www.il.ngb.army.mil/PDFs/EmploymentForms/AFOCD%20Oct%2016.pdf. Accessed 22 Jan. 2018.

United States Air Force. "Air Force Reserve Handbook 2014." *Air Force Reserve Command*, 2014, www.afrc.af.mil/Portals/87/documents/AFR%20Handbook2014.pdf. Accessed 22 Jan. 2018.

United States Air Force. "The Guide for Individual Reservists." *Air Force Reserve Command*, 15 July 2015, arpc.afrc.af.mil/Portals/4/DRIO/TheIRGuide-1.pdf. Accessed 22 Jan. 2018.

United States Defense Advisory Committee on Women in the Services (DACOWITS). "2003 Report." 2003, dacowits.defense.gov/ Portals/48/Documents/Reports/2003/Annual%20Report/dacowits 2003report.pdf.

United States Defense Advisory Committee on Women in the Services (DACOWITS). "2015 Report." 2015, hdacowits.defense.gov/ Portals/48/Documents/Reports/2015/Annual%20Report/2015%20 DACOWITS%20Annual%20Report_Final.pdf.

United States Department of Defense. "Department of Defense 2014-2016 Sexual Assault Prevention Strategy." Sexual Assault Prevention and Response Office, 30 Apr. 2014, www.sapr.mil/public/docs/reports/ SecDef_Memo_and_DoD_SAPR_Prevention_Strategy_2014-2016.pdf. Accessed 22 Jan. 2018.

United States Department of Defense. "Department of Instruction (DODI) 1312.1-1: Occupational Conversion Index Enlisted/Officer/ Civilian." *Executive Services Directorate*, Mar. 2001, www.esd.whs.mil/ Portals/54/Documents/DD/issuances/dodm/131201i.pdf. Accessed 22 Jan. 2018.

United States Department of Defense. "Department of Instruction (DODI) 1332.43: Voluntary Separation Pay (VSP) Program for Service Members." *Executive Services Directorate*, 28 Nov. 2017, www.esd.whs. mil/Portals/54/Documents/DD/issuances/dodi/133243p.pdf?ver =2017-11-28-102301-607. Accessed 22 Jan. 2018.

United States *General Accounting Office* (GAO). "Military Attrition Better Data, Coupled With Policy Changes, Could Help the Services Reduce Early Separations." *General Accounting Office*, GAO/NSIAD-98-213, Sept. 1998, www.gao.gov/assets/160/156305.pdf. Accessed 22 Jan. 2018.

United States Government Accountability Office (GAO). "Military Personnel: Actions Needed to Address Sexual Assaults of Male Servicemembers." *General Accounting Office*, GAO-15-284, 19 Mar. 2015, www.gao.gov/assets/670/669096.pdf. Accessed 22 Jan. 2018.

United States Government Accountability Office (GAO). "Women in the Military; Attrition and Retention," General Accounting Office, NSAID-90-87BR, July 1990, www.gao.gov/assets/80/77851.pdf. Accessed 22 Jan. 2018.

United States Office of the Under Secretary of Defense (OUSD), Personnel and Readiness. "Population Representation in the Military Services: Fiscal Year 2014 (FY14). Appendix B: Active Component."

CNA, 2014, www.cna.org/pop-rep/2014/appendixb/appendixb.pdf. Accessed 22 Jan. 2018.

United States Navy. "MILPERSMAN 1300-1000 Military Couple and Single Parent Assignment Policy." *Public Navy, 12 Mar. 2016,* www. public.navy.mil/bupers-npc/reference/milpersman/1000/1300 assignment/documents/1300-1000.pdf. Accessed 22 Jan. 2018.

United States Office of the Deputy Assistant Secretary of Defense. "2014 Demographics Report: Profile of the Military Community." *Military One Source, 2014,* download.militaryonesource.mil/12038/ MOS/Reports/2014-Demographics-Report.pdf. Accessed 22 Jan. 2018.

Wadsworth, Shelley MacDermid and Kenona Southwell. "Military Families: Extreme Work and Extreme 'Work-Family.'" *The Annals of the American Academy of Political and Social Science,* vol. 638, no. 1, Nov. 2011, pp.163-83.

Williams, Joan C, et al. "Cultural Schemas, Social Class, and the Flexibility Stigma." *Journal of Social Issues*, vol. 69, no. 2, 2013, pp. 209-234.

Williams, Joan C., et al. "Disruptive Innovation: New Models of Legal Practice." *Hastings Law Journal,* vol. 67, no. 1, 2015, pp. 1-84.

Chapter Eight

# "You Can't Have a Baby in the Army!" and Other Myths of Moms in Military Service[1]

Naomi Mercer

"You can't have a *baby* in the army!" the woman said, loudly, in the waiting area seat perpendicular to mine. LAX was quieting down before the red-eye flights, including the one I awaited to take me back to New York from a trip to an academic conference in Hawaii. "You can't have a baby, in the *Army!*" she said again, changing her emphasis. Her travelling companion had shared news of their mutual acquaintance's daughter's pregnancy–a woman serving in the Judge Advocate General Corps, a lawyer with a desk job. The ladies were grey haired, and their familiarity with the military seemed thirty years out of date. The woman said it again: "You can't have a *baby* in the Army!" To me, her voice seemed to become louder and more emphatic with each repetition. I wanted her to not be so misinformed. I wanted her to shut up.

"Excuse me," I said, when I couldn't bear to hear any more. "I'm an officer on active duty in the Army. I'm also eight weeks pregnant. I get six weeks of paid maternity leave[2] when I have my baby. My prenatal care is free. I don't have to pay for the delivery in a hospital. And when I go back to work, the Army has subsidized daycare that is the best in the country. That's how you have a baby in the Army." They looked at me with shocked faces, muttered a comment or two, and changed their topic of conversation.

I recount this incident because it illustrates some of the social assumptions about mothers in military service. I am a mother in the military, having served on active duty for the past twenty-two years and becoming a mother ten years into my military career. I have exemplified, subverted, and actively defied many gendered constructions of "mother" in conjunction with the "military." My experiences range from navigating supervision of mothers, particularly single parents, before having a child myself; the timing of my career and the possibility of a baby; motherhood as part of a dual-military couple; as a divorced, single mom; as a nursing mother; as a mother remarried to a civilian man; as a mother deployed to a combat zone; as a deployed mother enmeshed in custody and child-support battles; and as a military professional who is also a mother.

## Feminism and Military Service

During the days of the Women's Army Corps (WAC), before the Department of Defense (DoD) integrated women into all branches of service as regular members in 1978, women were immediately separated from service when they became pregnant or if they acquired any dependent minor children through birth, marriage, or adoption. In 1971, the DoD amended the policy to allow married women to become pregnant and then remain on active duty after having a child. The DoD eliminated involuntary discharge of pregnant servicemembers in 1975 (Ziobro 4). Currently, a pregnant officer can resign from active duty at any time during their pregnancy as long as they have completed their initial service commitment; enlisted soldiers can resign regardless of term of enlistment. Ironically, medical care for the pregnant spouses of military servicemembers began in military treatment facilities in the 1950s (Dolfini-Reed and Jebo, 5). The barrier for women servicemembers to remain in the military while pregnant and afterward as mothers was not the lack of prenatal care and delivery facilities, but an issue of readiness: pregnant and recently postpartum soldiers cannot deploy to combat theatres. However, this barrier also reflected social attitudes toward women's–mothers'–abilities to work in military service after having children.

Whether they understand the meaning of the word feminism or not, all women in the military are feminists by virtue of believing that women belong in the military and by volunteering for service (see the introduction chapter of this volume for a further discussion of feminism). My own feminist beliefs tend to skew further left than many of my female colleagues in the military most likely as a result of my self-education as a young feminist reading second-wave and later texts in my most formative years as a child and teenager. Later, my advocacy for equal rights as a newspaper columnist developed during my undergraduate years at a private, Southern university where many of my peers were more interested in finding husbands than earning bachelor's degrees.

As an adult, my education in gender and women's studies at the graduate level has given me a heightened level of awareness of how women internalize kyriarchal norms concerning gender that I frequently encounter in other female soldiers. Elizabeth Schüssler Fiorenza defines "kyriarchy" succinctly as "a socio-cultural and religious system of domination constituted by intersecting multiplicative structures of oppression" (118). Kyriarchy represents a set of power relations forming the underlying structure of democracy as a political system in Western culture. Dovetailing with the movement among feminist theorists generally toward intersectional analysis of different axes of power and marginalization, the term "kyriarchy" is more broadly applicable than "patriarchy" because it functions as an analytic category that captures other nuances of domination and oppression beyond gender. Additionally Schüssler Fiorenza defines "kyriocentrism" as "the cultural-religious-ideological systems and intersecting discourses of race, gender, heterosexuality, class, and ethnicity that produce, legitimate, inculcate, and sustain kyriarchy" (211)–an argument echoing Kimberlé Crenshaw's theory of "intersecting patterns of racism and sexism" (1243) and other feminist theories of intersectionality (1241-99). Even when I could not link my actions and reactions to specific aspects of feminist theory, I have spent the majority of my life, from my teenage years to my present middle age, believing in the equality of women and recognizing the ways in which that equality is denied on individual and institutional levels.

Only after recently reading maternal scholar Andrea O'Reilly's latest book, *Matricentric Feminism: Theory, Activism, and Practice*, could I actually put a name to the type of feminism that has guided me as a feminist. O'Reilly argues the following:

*empowered mothering may be characterized by seven themes:*
*the importance of mothers meeting their own needs; being a*
*mother does not fulfill all of a woman's needs; involving others in*
*their children's upbringing; actively questioning the expectations*
*placed on mothers by society; challenging mainstream parenting*
*practices; not believing that mothers are solely responsible for*
*how children turn out; and challenging the idea that the only*
*emotion mothers ever feel towards their children is love. (69)*

A career in the military as a woman and a mother directly contradicts the patriarchal institution of motherhood through refuting the biological essentialism, naturalization, and normalization of mothering, among other assumptions, to only women (14) (see the introduction chapter of this volume for a further discussion of the ways in which motherhood and the military intersect). O'Reilly's characteristics of empowerment of mothers, primarily women but applicable to any caregiver, have helped me to empower myself and to empower the others who mother in my spheres of influence.

All of these things add up to not only the mother I have become, but the kind of officer and leader whom I have developed into as well. My experiences rest at the intersection of motherhood, feminism, and military service. The challenges and, sometimes, the opportunities these intersecting conditions create in a traditionally kyriarchal and culturally misogynist institution[3] exemplify the conditions of gender equality, or lack thereof, inside the military, and perhaps in society at large.

## Emerging Feminist Leadership

Throughout my career, I have supervised a variety of soldiers in different phases of their lives. What became for me a defining moment that has since shaped my leadership style was an incident while I was a second lieutenant and had been in the Army less than two years. On a Thursday, the day of the week generally reserved for training and when the duty day was supposed to end at three in the afternoon, my sergeant, a single mother, left to take her kids to the dentist slightly before lunch. After lunch, she had not returned, and we had a deadline for finishing a project. I could do most of it myself, but she had certain responsibilities toward its completion that had to be done that day. I called her at home and ordered her to come back to work. She did with alacrity, and we met our deadline. However, while we worked on our separate tasks, I noticed that she stopped every twenty minutes to make a phone call. I then realized she was calling her kids to check on them because she had left a nine-year-old and a seven-year-old at home alone. I was horrified. I had not communicated with her clearly about finishing the project that day and then, when I called her back into the office, I placed her in the untenable position of choosing between her job and her kids' wellbeing.

My insensitivity to her situation–not understanding that, having taken her kids out of school for their dental appointments and anticipating an early end to the work day, she would not have childcare coverage–demonstrated my own lack of empathy for someone who did not have the same flexibility in their lives that I had as a single service member with no familial responsibilities (see Elle Kowal, chapter seven this volume, for a similar discussion of how being a mother affected service in unanticipated ways). I further realized that my position as an officer, compared to hers as a noncommissioned officer, had socio-economic class implications, even though my salary as a second lieutenant was below her salary as a staff sergeant with many more years of service. I had not previously given much thought to the pressures my sergeant operated under as a single mother who was also African American (see Morten Ender, chapter six, this volume, for an examination of how race intersects with military service).

Her children did not come to any harm, and my sergeant accepted my apology with grace. As a result, my leadership style underwent a drastic change. I no longer felt compelled to imitate the "hard-charging" (read: masculinist) examples that many of my colleagues considered appropriate to display in the Army's culture. Rather, I broadened my own point of view to exercise empathy for others in diverse situations, and I decided that remembering and applying matricentric feminism– although, at the time, I had no succinct terminology but only my own instincts–was a much better style of leadership to practice.

For example, when I was stationed on Okinawa and still single and childless, one of my male soldiers was supposed to have custody of his children six months of the year. Before I arrived at the unit, the executive officer of the battalion and the headquarters commander denied the soldier command sponsorship,[4] meaning the soldier couldn't bring his kids to the island in fulfillment of that custody agreement. The executive officer was older, having served in Vietnam, and told this soldier that "We have to put up with the single moms bringing their kids because the fathers run off and there's no one else. We don't have to do that for you." In this way, the executive officer essentialized mothering to women and was not open to allowing a man to step into that role for his children. The executive officer and the outgoing headquarters commander departed soon after I arrived and assumed command of the headquarters detachment; the soldier approached me within a few weeks. The discriminatory nature of denying command sponsorship to the soldier based on his gender was readily apparent, and I immediately approached the battalion commander to rectify the situation. The battalion commander was unaware that the executive officer had denied command sponsorship without bringing the case to him for the final decision. Within a month, we had the paperwork in place, the soldier had an apartment that would accommodate his children, and they were on their way to join their father as soon as their six months with their mother ended.

The gender essentialism exercised by the male officers who had denied this soldier command sponsorship so that he might have shared custody of his children was another formative experience for me. I realized that ideas of masculinity and the policing of those ideas–particularly that men should not assume the primary care of children–were just as damaging to men as to women. The military is still a bastion for masculine identity based upon one's job, in essence, as a trained killer. However, the recent opening of all military occupational specialties to anyone who qualifies, regardless of gender, will serve as a catalyst for men who have created a culture of masculinism and linked their identities as "real men" to driving a tank or shooting others from foxholes to redefine masculinity for themselves. After all, if women qualify to do the same jobs, such a masculine identity is very precariously positioned.

## Breastfeeding and Lactation Misadventures

I married another service member at the age of twenty-nine. At the time, I had been accepted into the Army's Advanced Civil Schooling program and was applying to graduate schools for a master's degree in English literature. My husband and I were not stationed together during our engagement and could not be stationed together during my time in graduate school, since I had chosen a school not located near an Army post, and he was not eligible to serve in the Reserve Officer Training Corps (ROTC) department at my university. After I finished my two years of schooling, I moved to West Point, NY, to teach at the United States Military Academy (USMA). During my first semester there, my husband was reassigned to a unit about two and a half hours away. We had been married over three years and decided we were ready to start a family, despite the weekend nature of our relationship in service to our careers. My daughter was born when I was thirty-three, before the beginning of the fall semester of my second year as an instructor at West Point.

One of the first issues that arose was my office situation, since I planned to nurse. My officemate was a man, and I was not senior enough in my department, either by rank or experience, to merit an office to myself. A civilian professor was pregnant at roughly the same time, although she delivered her baby four months before me and had the summer to establish her nursing schedule. She was scheduled to move into her own office, and I did not want to delay that perquisite for her by suggesting that she and I share an office. I was adamantly opposed to pumping in the women's bathroom as one of my colleagues from another department in our building had done, but the civilian executive officer of our department just shrugged her shoulders when I asked for accommodation and looked mystified. The medical personnel exerted an extreme amount of pressure in favour of breastfeeding one's baby and reinforced an idealization of motherhood based on the child's needs rather than empowerment of the biological mother to decide for herself what met her and her infant's needs. Yet this pressure on female servicemembers was not balanced by a supportive nursing policy. The Army did not have a policy concerning nursing whatsoever until 2015[5]; my daughter was born in 2004.

Ultimately, my officemate suggested a workable solution: we switched sides of the office so that I had the back portion (with the window and a view of the river); we arranged our bookcases in between to afford me privacy, and his computer faced the hallway wall. We closed the door when I needed to pump and he screened visitors. My officemate had two kids with his spouse, and although she stayed at home, he understood how much of a struggle nursing and pumping could be. I had no qualms that this gem of a human being would devolve into a peeping tom or find some way to expose me while I was pumping, unlike the horror stories I've heard from other working mothers. Our arrangement worked beautifully, and I still appreciate my officemate's respect, his empathy, and the sacrifice of letting me have the window view.

What did not work so beautifully was the reality of being a nursing mother while working fulltime. I had six weeks of paid maternity leave after I gave birth (AR 600-8-10, 5-5.c). I had not felt comfortable asking to use my personal leave,[6] a stockpile of sixty days, to take off the remainder of the semester. Instead, my four sections of students were designated as usual, and four other officers each taught an additional section until I was back in the classroom at the end of my maternity leave. I tried to maintain a pumping schedule that would keep my milk supply at the same level as during my maternity leave when I had such a surfeit that I usually fed the baby and also had to pump for relief, freezing the milk for later use. However, my department had scheduled my classes to fill the entire afternoon, giving me no break in between to pump; departmental and other meetings tended to be scheduled for the lunch period, but they could also migrate to other times with no predictability. I did not stand up for myself and refuse to attend what were mandatory meetings in order to keep on a regular pumping schedule, and I had not foreseen that my class schedule would be problematic. Yet because the Army did not have any sort of policy regarding accommodation for nursing mothers, no one else stood up for me either. I was afraid to ask for further accommodation mostly because I was fairly certain my request would be viewed by the leadership as an attempt for special treatment and would be denied anyway; I also did not want to invoke resentment from my cohort, all of whom were men with spouses who did not work. I tried to shift my pumping around the meetings and other events that arose but this mostly resulted in an ever-decreasing milk supply. By the time my daughter was five months old, I was no longer pumping, and she was drinking her way through the milk supply in the freezer supplemented with formula.

When I rotated back to USMA with a PhD in the fall of 2013, I was a lieutenant colonel rather than a captain or a major as I had been on my previous tour as a professor. During my initial mentorship meeting with the female officers in the department, I asked specifically if the two moms of infants had worked out their nursing arrangements. Both women used the bathroom, which was basically a stall with no space for a comfortable chair, to pump, and one had weaned her child earlier than she had wished to do so. Both officers had informed their direct supervisors, but their concerns had either stopped with the immediate supervisor or the deputy and had not been brought to the attention of the department head. I intervened with the department head. As a result, our department's policy, since our building has no additional rooms available to use as a suitable lactation space, is to place nursing mothers in a shared office. Even now, with an Army-wide nursing policy in place requiring commanders to designate private and suitable lactation space and to allow breaks for pumping based on the soldier's needs and nursing schedule, the burden seems to rest on the nursing mother to insist on accommodation, instead of the proactive establishment of permanent lactation spaces and negotiation with supervisors over timing to pump. This historical lack of accommodation and the current covert resistance to the lactation policy by making female soldiers pursue accommodation echo the millennia of denial of women's spaces and also allude to fears that women who are mothers are somehow less productive at work than men whose spouses opaquely provide these services.

The problem is more widespread than my particular workplace and requires a cultural attitude shift. An officer I mentor, whom I've known since she was a cadet, contacted me wanting to know if she was "off base" in demanding that one of her soldiers, a nursing mom with a three-month-old, go on a field exercise (a mere two days hence). My mentee, a captain in command of a company, was frustrated that the soldier, who had known about the field exercise for months in advance, had not frozen her milk or developed some other plan. My mentee was also unaware of the Army's new policy–most likely because she did not have children of her own and the policy didn't apply directly to her. To me, it seemed obvious that either my mentee's subordinates had not sat down with the soldier and come up with a workable plan out of either laziness or squeamishness, or the soldier didn't trust her chain of command to support her. Considering that the unit did not have a lactation space in their garrison building and the soldier was making trips home to nurse her child during the day, and since no other accommodation had been made for her to nurse, the soldier's skepticism seemed warranted. My mentee, ultimately, showed the compassion that I expected of her regarding that soldier's situation, and I think she will be a more sensitive leader in the future. However, her ignorance about the policy and her initial attitude demonstrates the extent of the backlash, unintentional or not, toward mothers in military settings (see Sarah Hampson, chapter three and Elle Kowal, chapter seven, this volume, for similar discussions of difficulties nursing as a military member).

## Perception of Pregnancy

In my own experiences, nursing was not the only issue that would arise before I gave birth. Unlike other parts of academe, we don't have summers off to pursue our own scholarship; military professors at USMA owe their department a summer field detail.[7] My first summer should have been spent as cadre conducting the cadets' summer training. The executive officer put my name into the pool with the information that I would be in my third trimester of pregnancy and was medically restricted[8] to an eight-hour day, could not work around substances that would be harmful to the baby, like paint or gasoline, and could not lift any object more than twenty pounds. The chain of command for summer training rejected me because they would not be able to exploit my labour for long hours–they had an expectation that they would need me to be at work twelve or more hours a day. I did fill a summer cadre slot the next summer as a personnel officer when my daughter was an infant: I worked in an office with a computer and was home by 5:00 p.m. every evening for dinner, usually earlier. I did nothing in that position that I could not have just as easily done during the last three months of my pregnancy. The refusal to use a pregnant woman for a task I could have easily done was not couched in terms of concern–I doubt there was any for my wellbeing–but in terms of the chain of command assuming that a pregnant woman could not do the job (and perhaps, some illusions about what the job would actually demand from me in terms of time and physical effort). This was, to put it baldly, discrimination, but not the kind of equal opportunity complaint that I felt I could successfully pursue, especially a year after the fact. I knew that the outcome would be a dismissed or unfounded complaint. The persons responsible for not allowing me to serve my summer field detail while pregnant would merely couch their defense in language that doing so would have been a health and safety risk rather than admitting to their erroneous assumption that pregnant women are not as productive and cannot fulfill their job requirements. I taught a summer school course instead to fulfill my summer service requirement during my pregnancy.

I had a conversation with another female instructor in my department, after I had finished nursing, about pregnancy in the Army in general. She was already the mother of two children under five. I made a, perhaps offhanded remark, that many women took advantage of being stationed at West Point to have children while they were outside the operational Army for a while. She replied that she would never be pregnant while she was in a leadership position. First, as another officer to whom I later recounted the conversation remarked, working as an instructor was hardly a "leadership" position outside of our authority in the classroom, since most of the rotating professors did not supervise others the way we regularly do in the mainstream Army. Second, I felt disturbed by the idea that soldiers or cadets should not see pregnant women in leadership positions, or at all. Given that the great majority of women in the Army are in the most fertile years of their lives–roughly ages eighteen to forty-five–during their terms of service, pregnancies are inevitable. Rather than hiding pregnancy while women fill leadership or other staff positions, the better course is to normalize pregnancy as part of women's lives, part of their careers, and a condition that the Army accommodates routinely and readily. Another friend, who had been in a command position for the birth of her first child, argued that being pregnant and giving birth while in a leadership position was ideal. Because she was the commander, she controlled much of the unit's schedule and made her own accommodation for her childcare and nursing needs.

Having a baby in the Army does have many advantages. I already have equal pay based on my rank and years of service, not on my gender. The DoD funds all of my healthcare at no cost to me, and I received exceptional prenatal care. I developed gestational diabetes in my third trimester and had immediate access to a dietician, and all of the blood sugar testing supplies were prescribed for me. I decided to pay for a doula, which most military hospitals do not provide, although some have midwives in addition to obstetricians on staff. My forty-eight hour hospital stay to give birth was not entirely free: as an officer receiving a separate rations allowance, I had to reimburse the government for the cost of my meals, totaling $16. My daughter's healthcare has also been provided at no cost to me–except for prescription glasses, a monthly premium of $13 for dental coverage, about half of the cost of her braces, and the occasional $3 co-pay for a prescription for her at a civilian pharmacy when we are not stationed near a military hospital.

## Childcare and Social Attitudes toward Working Moms

Perhaps the most obvious advantage is the military's subsidized day-care. Active duty servicemembers have priority for slots in the military's child development centres (CDC) (Department of Defense Instruction (DoDI) 6060-02). In 2005, when I first sought a slot for my daughter in the CDC at our installation, dual-military and single parents had first priority. As a dual-military service member and later a single mother during the years my daughter went to daycare, I thought at the time that first priority should go to single parents: dual-military couples tend to have better financial resources than single parents and can more easily afford a month or two of civilian daycare. In the latest rendering of CDC priorities, single parents and dual-military have third priority after the children of wounded warriors and CDC employees ("Family Types and Priorities") but are still equal. I employed a live-in nanny for my daughter's first year, and I recognize my combined household income as a captain–promoted to major a few months after my daughter's birth–married to another captain gave me enormous financial privilege for childcare arrangements. Having a nanny, since my spouse was only home on the weekends, was logistically much easier with an infant than doing what I have come to call the "daycare slog."

My daughter has received daycare services at three different military installations from shortly after she turned one-year-old until she was nearly five. My income alone, even without adding in my then-husband's income, placed me in the top financial bracket for daycare fees for all four years. I paid as low as $425 and as high as $625 a month, depending on the location, for some of the highest quality daycare available in the United States. My friends who have used civilian daycare centres tend to have paid significantly more, $700-1200 a month in the 2000s, for the same level of quality, and perhaps also when the quality is not as high, since the DoD's Childcare Program ranks first in the nation among all fifty states and the District of Columbia (Child Care Aware 8). The military offers high-quality daycare because it has to: in order to retain soldiers, their children must have care that is safe, developmentally appropriate, and affordable (Butrymowicz and Mader). Where the military could improve their daycare is by having "sick child" care available–either in a different location from the main daycare centre, or a quarantined room so that soldiers who do not have a spouse at home can continue to work if they need to do so while their child is too ill or contagious for daycare but not in need of a hospital stay.

Most importantly, for me, however, has not been the affordability of daycare but learning to let go of the illusion that only I can take good care of my kid. Through her year with a nanny and more years with a plethora of daycare providers, my daughter has felt loved and supported and has loved her caregivers in return. Today, she is a well-adjusted, thoughtful, fun-loving, academically responsible tween. I can't say that she might have turned out the same had I decided to become a stay-at-home mom–since I was past my first service commitment, I could have resigned the moment I became pregnant and walked away from the Army. The thought never entered my consciousness because I loved my job, and I was excited about teaching after my fully-funded years in graduate school. I never considered resigning despite a (male) colonel once (well, twice) telling me when I was a newlywed that "when women have babies something comes over them and they get out of the Army to stay home with their children." He was, of course, justifying the possibility of not giving me the highest rating on my evaluation, since in his mind, I would simply resign and thus would not "need" the "top block" to further my career. Once I got over the shock of this little speech (the first time), I just laughed to myself (the second time), since this knowledgeable colonel apparently did not know me or understand my personality at all.[9] His old-fashioned attitude reflected a prevalent one in American society and in the military: women are natural caregivers rather than interested in pursuing fulfilling careers of their own. Yet I have been a working mom for the entirety of my daughter's life, and other than some occasional angst over moving and making new friends every two or three years, she's happy that I work. We both know that neither of us would have been happy had I given up my career to be a stay-at-home mom.

I have faced social opprobrium from not only people in or associated with the military, particularly (female) spouses, but also from civilians, as though military service and motherhood are mutually exclusive, as the women in the airport and that paternalistic colonel, so strenuously believed. The Army unofficially promotes having children but under the outdated nuclear family model, in which spouses, who are usually women, stay at home to take care of servicemembers' children. Wives[10] avail themselves of the medical and other benefits because the gendered one-sidedness of the situation is opaque–the system enables and encourages female spouses to stay at home, though at the cost of having careers of their own (Maury and Stone 8). Being a woman in the military always-already violates traditional gender roles and kyriarchal concepts of masculinity and femininity as shown in the historical exclusion of women from combat roles that has persisted in some military career fields until the official opening of all combat arms positions and units in 2016 (Office of the Secretary of Defense). Being a mother who has career ambitions, especially in an extremely male-dominated and masculinist institution like the military, is an exponential disruption of social norms that expect women to stay home to raise their children and do not expect women to participate in the violence that military service in a combat zone may demand. I am not the type to fret over what others' think. I have, however, paid a price as a mom in the military because some of my supervisors' traditional ideas about women and motherhood have led them to make false assumptions about my competence and to devalue my contributions to my unit's mission. However, I recognize how women who came before me paid a greater price but also made the positive change I experienced possible.

When a service member happens to be a woman providing care to her children, which can take mothers away from their duties temporarily, the misogyny rears its ugly head.[11] On one occasion, my daughter was teething and, by this time, in fulltime daycare. She had a fever and was summarily kicked out of daycare for the next twenty-four hours to ensure she wasn't contagious. I had to abandon my afternoon classes to another instructor and take her home. I took her to the doctor's office the next morning to obtain a note, which would clear her for return to daycare, that the fever was the result of teething and not a communicable illness. However, the same day, my daughter also developed pink eye and had to remain out of daycare for an additional day while I administered the drops to clear up the infection. As a result, I missed two days of teaching. The course director was incensed. From my point of view, I had "banked" plenty of credit through the frequency of substituting for my (mostly male) colleagues when they had absences for conferences, emergencies, or other commitments. All of the volunteering I had done to teach others' classes meant nothing to the course director. He wanted me to activate my family care plan,[12] a set of documents meant to cover emergency situations, not routine duties, for what was essentially a nonemergency. My supervisor at the time was very supportive, and I stayed home to take care of my child. No type of sick-child daycare, civilian or military, was available in my area, and I could not have asked any of the stay-at-home spouses I knew to care for my kid at the risk of infecting their own kids with pink eye. I eventually learned that I was merely the first victim in this course director's campaign to alienate all of the women, with or without children, in the department. Yet his unwillingness to recognize that I was entitled to the teaching support of my colleagues, not only because I had earned it but because it was the ethical choice, demonstrated to me the severe disadvantages I would continue to face as a mother in the military. However, my next misogynist supervisor stands out because of the special hatred in his heart for single mothers.

## The Pitfalls of Single Motherhood

I finished my first tour at West Point having gained a child and lost a husband along the way. The husband proved to not be much of a loss since, most of the time, I had been on my own with my daughter anyway. My then-husband had been stationed a few hours away and only home on weekends for the first year and a half of my daughter's life. By that point, he had failed to advance to the next rank and was involuntarily separated from active duty. Clearly, if we had felt that one of us needed to give up our military career to stay home with our daughter, he would have been the likelier candidate. He decided to take a job overseas for what expanded to the next year and a half during which we divorced. I went from having a partner part time to not having a partner at all. I arrived at my first assignment back in the operational Army, after several years in academe, as a single mom in a unit that would deploy to Iraq in ten months' time.

My supervisor in this unit assumed, before ever meeting me, that I would not be able to fulfill the requirements of the personnel job for which I was slated. He was wrong, but that didn't stop him from singling me out for an ass-chewing at every possible opportunity, even though my male peers were not subjected to his wrath for the same alleged infractions. His erroneous assumptions about my competence did not stop him from trying to bully me into courses of action that were not the best solution but merely a demonstration of his power as my supervisor. He purposely scheduled meetings for late in the afternoon, knowing that I would need to leave part way through in order to pick up my daughter from daycare by 6:00 p.m. He scheduled a meeting, prior to physical training every day, at 5:50 a.m., for which I could barely arrive on time because daycare did not open until 5:30 a.m., and the daycare centre was a twenty-minute drive in heavy traffic from the other end of post to our unit area. I had a Blackberry and a computer at home with all of the software to do my work remotely if I needed to do so after (or before) regular work hours. Despite these capabilities, he routinely emailed or called me on evenings and weekends to demand some small item that was not yet due–he usually wanted me to come into the office, and I would have to refuse because my daughter was with me, and I did not have a babysitter who could care for my child at a moment's notice.

Let me be clear: I never missed a deadline and only rarely asked for an extension far in advance when I knew I and my subordinates could not meet a deadline. I never shirked any of the tasks this man gave me to do, even when the tasking was noticeably not within the scope of my personnel specialty and general tasking was supposed to rotate between all of the staff officers yet somehow did not. My work was not perfect, but I rarely made mistakes, and my work was always presentable. I observed that many of my colleagues on the staff were much more lackadaisical in their approach to their work and their products, yet this officer continually berated me in front of others for issues that were not my fault or even within my purview, and he gave my (male) colleagues a pass for merely showing up.

The preparations for deployment during these ten months were stressful enough without the added micro-aggressions–the "everyday subtle and often automatic 'put-downs' ... expressed toward any marginalized group" (Sue 5) that I experienced at the hands of this supervisor. The stress began to take its toll on me physically: I had lost my appetite (although I had little time for cooking appealing meals between picking my daughter up from daycare, feeding, bathing, and putting her to bed and then finishing any work that I had brought home with me) and was beginning to think I had irritable bowel syndrome. In the weeks before my unit deployed to Iraq, my weight had dropped from 110 pounds, around which I normally ranged, to 98 pounds. Psychologically, I felt immeasurably guilty that I only saw my daughter for less than half an hour in the morning before dropping her off at daycare for the next twelve and a half hours, and only about an hour and a half at night before she went to sleep. I had little difficulty meeting the actual mission requirements, but the hazing of scheduling meetings very early and very late, and the contempt and unfairness with which this supervisor treated me were a living hell. Of course, I could not pick out any singular events that seemed worthy of filing an equal opportunity complaint, which is what makes situations like these so insidious. Additionally, I knew that this officer would retaliate against me, and I was afraid that such retaliation would result in the end of my career, at fifteen years of service, and result in the loss of the Army's retirement pension and healthcare, which were the primary reasons, beyond higher education opportunities, I had remained in the Army on active duty up to that point. The threat of retaliation, which was not codified in policy at the time, and the accumulation of micro-aggressions weighed me down and I remember that year as the worst of my life (see Elle Kowal, chapter seven, this volume, for similar stories of discrimination and frustration).

Although I would categorize the experience as a hostile work environment, no sexual harassment was involved; rather, I experienced systemic gender discrimination not covered by the equal opportunity policy, except in the most general of terms (AR 600-20; Training Circular (TC) 26-6). However, even if I could have proven enough for a formal complaint, my supervisor's network as a USMA graduate and his connections with general officers far outreached mine; I would have been branded, and my career would have ended after the next promotion board. Because of my own background as part of the working poor, I was not willing to risk the financial security of a military retirement pension that I had worked so long to obtain, but was still five years out of reach.

By the time my unit did deploy, I had also developed some coping strategies in which I would approach the brigade commander directly for certain issues, rather than working through my supervisor who was responsible for writing my performance evaluations. My working around my supervisor resulted in my solution to an issue already approved as the best course of action before my supervisor could refuse my course of action based on his own biases. I had also developed a network of other women upon whom I could depend if I needed a daycare pick up or a quick reaction to a work issue. The deployment itself improved immeasurably when this toxic supervisor left for his next assignment in the fourth month. I outranked the new person in my former supervisor's position and, thus, could negotiate with him on firmer footing and refuse inappropriate tasking–besides the fact that the new person did not feel constantly compelled to exert his power over the other staff officers and conducted himself in a reasonable and professional manner. My new supervisor, the deputy commander, had very little to do with my day-to-day activities, and while he had his own hang-ups about women–that we generally didn't belong in the Army–I mostly avoided him. Ultimately, the brigade commander was responsible for the ratings on my performance evaluations, and he treated me fairly rather than relying on biological essentialism to justify poor and unfair treatment of me because of my gender.

What I learned from this awful experience, however, is that I am no longer willing to compromise my obligations to my family in order to appease some misguided sense that the Army is my first priority all the time and that my family will always be less of a priority. I will be the first to admit that on some days, and for some tasks, my work matters more–especially because of the influence that I wield or the specific tasks that I complete. As a personnel officer, ensuring that soldiers are paid, their records are correct, and that they receive their awards and evaluations is an important aspect of my job because my actions directly affect their readiness for deployment, their families' quality of life, and their individual morale. As a mentor and a leader, I take my responsibilities very seriously, complete my work in a timely manner, and set a diligent and efficient example for others to emulate. I know when my work is done for the day, what tasks can wait, and what does not need doing. As such, I recognize that, sometimes, the Army is my job, not the be-all of my identity or existence, and my family is more important.

This became clear to me when I was called in for a urinalysis test, conducted monthly in military units and at random, at 6:00 a.m. on a school day when I could not leave my daughter unattended. My chain of command expressed a range of reactions from the support of my immediate supervisor to the deputy head of my department and the company commander who both believed that a urinalysis test warranted activating my family care plan for what was a nonemergency situation. I have no reservations about taking a urinalysis; they are part of military service, and I have taken one more times than I can recall. However, I refused to alter my daughter's schedule or my caretaking arrangements without adequate notice, or to violate other policies concerning leaving children unattended in on-post housing ("Child Supervision Matrix"). I have also taken this stance in defense of my subordinates when they receive a tasking that would interfere with their family commitments and the timing could be adjusted to accommodate them. In most cases, these adjustments can be affected with no detriment to the mission and little to no inconvenience to anyone else. I find such insistence on sidelining one's family commitments for inconsequential events just because one serves in the military exceedingly dehumanizing. I will not countenance such behaviour in myself, nor in others, no matter their rank. But I also realize that I can take these sorts of actions now because my retirement pension is assured, and I know that I will not be promoted past my current rank; I no longer fear retaliation because my position and the goals I set for my Army career are secure.

The Army requires that all single parents and dual-military parents have a family care plan that provides for their children during a deployment or other emergency. This plan is audited yearly and updated every time the family moves from one duty station to another. Furthermore, battalion-level units report family care plans for all dual-military and single parents every month on their unit status reports (USR). On one occasion, when I was the personnel officer for a battalion as well as single and childless, we received guidance from higher headquarters that we needed to provide a special report on single mothers. The request was not for single parents but for single mothers. I refused to provide this information because I felt it was discriminatory: the higher headquarters already received our USR that listed the single parents (mothers and fathers) by name. The requirement seemed to result from a perception that single mothers were a drain on Army resources and a threat to readiness. I kept refusing to provide my unit's data on single mothers, with my battalion and brigade commanders' support, until the requirement quietly went away. I don't think that I was the only person to protest this report as unfair and redundant, since single parent information was already reported regularly through family care plan tracking.

Unlike many others, my assignment timing has limited me to one combat deployment. I deployed when my daughter was nearing five years of age. My family care plan for my daughter, which I was required to have and maintained from my daughter's birth until my second marriage to a civilian, named my best friend as my child's long-term care provider. A few weeks before I deployed, I took my daughter to another state, halfway across the country from where I was stationed, and left her with my best friend, her husband, and their three kids. Living with them was less of an adjustment for my daughter than for me. And, having been socialized in daycare with the same ten to thirteen other kids every day, going from an only child household to a house in which she was one of four children wasn't terribly onerous for her. I was able to record ten videos reading books aloud to her that the USO shipped, along with the book, to my daughter and that my friend played for her while she "read" the book. Before leaving, I had taught her some yoga poses to re-center herself if she felt sad or upset. Once I had an Internet connection in my room, I skyped with my daughter two or three times a week.

Some people whom my best friend encountered were shocked at my apparent unfeeling abandonment of my child at such a young age, as though I had left her on the street to fend for herself. My friend relates that people would first comment on the number of children in her charge: "Those all yours?" She would reply, "Three are my kids and one is my niece."[13] The questions would continue and my best friend would tell them that I was deployed and my daughter was living with her family for a year. The usual laments would ensue about how I could leave such a young child, with the implication that I wasn't a very good mother or had no maternal feelings toward my child–I was, in effect, violating the idealization of patriarchal motherhood by not fully devoting myself to my child and pursuing a career that took me away from her. My friend shut down that line of thinking by saying that my deployment when my daughter was five was a strategic choice so that she would be less likely to remember the year I was gone. This did not entirely bear out in reality: my daughter vividly remembers her year at her Aunt's house with her cousins; she knows, on an intellectual level, that I was not present other than my two-week leave in the middle of my tour, spent with her. However, she doesn't remember my absence as a loss or an emptiness. She was, after all, cared for, safe, and surrounded by people she loves and will have relationships with for the rest of her life. She was far too busy basking in the novelty of her situation and having fun to feel cheated. I, on the other hand, missed her terribly and spent a few weeks in a miserable fog.

One month prior to my deployment in May 2009, my ex-husband served me with papers to substantially reduce his child support payments. At the time, my ex-husband had been activated and deployed to Iraq in December 2008. I retained an attorney in the state of our divorce, Nevada, to the tune of a $3500 retainer, to address this issue. We reached a new agreement shortly before I deployed. During my two-week mid-tour leave in November 2009, my ex-husband, after first learning that I would spend the entirety of that time with my daughter at my best friend's home in South Carolina, had me served again: this time, he attempted to take full custody. I retained yet another lawyer in that state for $3500. What was supposed to be two weeks of rest and relaxation were two weeks of stress while I scrambled to assemble supporting documents and affidavits from witnesses. I also needed a letter from my commander in Iraq stating that, as a deployed soldier, I would be unable to appear at the court date set for January 2010.

My ex-husband's deployment ended in December 2009; therefore, he wanted not only custody of my daughter for the remainder of my deployment but permanently now that he lived with another woman who would provide equal if not more of the care for my daughter. When we had divorced, my ex-husband had readily given me full physical custody because of the lucrative nature of the job he had overseas at the time. He had lasted at that job an additional five months after our divorce was finalized and he had moved to a job in Tennessee, joined a Reserve unit, and then deployed in about a year's time. In the suit, I had several objections to both a temporary and a permanent change of custody. First, it was clear to me that my ex-husband only wanted custody in order to avoid paying child support and was being egged on, as it were, by his current spouse. My ex-husband had no desire to see much of my daughter prior to his remarriage and actually did not contact her for the first five months of his deployment. Second, my daughter was stable with my best friend's family, and I felt that moving her to yet another new home was excessive and ill-conceived–especially given the complications of trying to integrate a child into a new home when my ex-husband himself was returning from a deployment. I could not in good conscience send my daughter into such a morass of heightened risk factors and the potential for negative outcomes. Doing so would not be in her best interest.

Luckily, if the judge had not agreed with me on those points, he did agree that suing for permanent custody violated the Servicemembers Civil Relief Act that prevented deployed soldiers from being subjected to lawsuits that would substantially alter an existing agreement; this act has specific provisions for attempts to change custody (US Congress, Section 521). My ex-husband had thought that a statute in Georgia, in which a non-custodial parent could attain *temporary* custody of a minor child while the military parent was deployed would work in his favour (State of Georgia 19-9-3-8.2.a(8)(i)(4)(A-B)). However, because he sought a *permanent* change of custody, the judge ruled for a stay until the end of May 2010 when I would be back from Iraq and could appear in court. My ex-husband dropped the case, and my daughter remained with my best friend's family in South Carolina until after I redeployed.

However, my ex-husband served me a third time in thirteen months, days after I returned to my unit's home base in Texas, to reduce his child support payment yet again, a suit filed in the state of Nevada so at least I already had a lawyer on retainer. The upshot of all of these child support negotiations is that I receive up to the presumptive maximum amount of child support for the state of Nevada based on the range my ex-husband's salary falls within, which does not cover even a third of my daughter's monthly expenses, and I have forgiven over twenty-one thousand dollars in unpaid child support. Unlike many single parents, I have had the financial wherewithal to fight multiple court battles in addition to benefitting from job security, a future retirement pension, and little-to-no-cost healthcare. Most single parents, including servicemembers, do not have the same amount of class and economic privilege to protect them against frivolous demands from their ex-spouses. Needless to say, my relationship with my ex-husband has remained fraught.

Now that I am remarried to a civilian spouse and my daughter is school age and no longer requires daycare, after-school supervision, or evening babysitters, a lot of the stress of being a mother, particularly a single one, has fallen away. We have encountered other stressors, however, that male spouses of female servicemembers experience (Weinstock). Frequently, others assume that my spouse is the service member–a condition that I was used to as part of a dual-military couple, but very foreign for my spouse who was never before affiliated with the military. The other side of that coin–my erasure by the assumption that I am not in the military–is my husband's erasure as a male spouse. He experiences a great degree of isolation because he is not a primary caregiver to my daughter, unlike most of the other spouses, and while he may be at home during the day, he telecommutes to work fulltime. Because he does not define his masculinity through military service, and the fact that his is already feminized in the American psyche as a man of Asian descent, my spouse has very little in common with many of my male colleagues. Because he's not a stay-at-home parent, he tends to not have anything in common with other spouses, primarily female. Very rarely have we encountered another male spouse with whom my husband finds any common points of interest.

My husband's career in the technology sector to some extent enables telecommuting and being able to move with me from one post to another; however, he also travels frequently, both domestically and internationally, due to the nature of his job. He is very involved in his stepdaughter's life, and we work diligently to balance the demands of both of our professions, although I find myself in single-parent mode when he is away; my absences are less frequent. My daughter spends many an afternoon, when I'm not shuttling her to dance classes, in our post's youth services facility for middle schoolers and teens. The Youth Center is staffed with counsellors and provides age-appropriate activities–from a cooking club, to a basketball court and other sports venues, to an *a capella* choir, to a daily homework "power hour." The building is clean and well maintained, the programs are generously resourced, and the staff is just as excellent as the military's child development centres. The most common complaint that I hear from other parents is that it is difficult to tear our kids away from the Youth Center because they love being there, and home is "boring" by comparison.

I am now a higher rank than during my days as a pregnant and nursing mom, but, more importantly, I am more confident in saying no to subordinates, peers, and higher-ranking officers alike. Part of this confidence comes from the security of having served in the military for over twenty years and earning my current rank through my performance and demonstrated potential. Yet most of this confidence comes from having navigated a military career as a mother and a feminist. I have found that my boundaries for what I will and will not sacrifice for the Army still leave room for empathy and the empowerment of others.

When the officers and cadets whom I mentor ask me about timing their families, my response is to not worry about the Army and do the best thing for their marriages and the families they want to have, although in some cases that includes leaving military service when their service commitment is due for renewal or expiration. All of the mechanisms for healthcare, pregnancy accommodation, maternity leave, and, most recently, nursing accommodation and limited paternity leave are in place. The Army will function just fine during women's pregnancies, their maternity leaves, and their six months of non-deployable time. The Army cannot demote women or penalize their time in service and rank, which continues to accumulate while mothers are on maternity leave and during the additional nondeployable window (AD 2016-09). Although many women will experience some type of backlash for becoming mothers, that backlash may not necessarily be inevitable or as pervasive as it used to be. As an organization fuelled by the young, the Army turns over generations rather quickly, and gender equality is more apparent now than when I first entered the Army and even when I became a parent. Therefore, I think the best time for a woman to have a child while in military service is the time that feels right for the servicemember and her partner. The Army will survive. What we cannot predict is whether our coworkers and supervisors will accept our motherhood; some may never do so, and cultural change tends to take time. A backlash against mothers in the military still exists in some units, depending upon their leadership–and this is a leadership issue. However, progress is a long and nonlinear process.

Some of the discrimination that I underwent is certainly unpro-fessional and unethical, though, in my case, largely unprovable and not situations over which my career could have withstood the retaliation. I don't regret becoming a mother while in military service and would not change the way that the timing of my family worked out for me.

Although I don't think that anyone should face discrimination for becoming a parent, I recognize that the adversity I experienced has enhanced my empathy for others and made me a better leader and a better feminist. If other soldiers in the Army don't like the fact that women have babies, or think that mothers don't belong, they are in an ever-shrinking population (Arnhart et al.). The Army realized after the Gulf War in the 1990s that going to war without women was no longer an option, and the Iraq and Afghanistan conflicts in this century cemented women's place in all branches of the military, to include the combat arms (Office of the Secretary of Defense). Military women are of childbearing age by necessity, due to the initial enlistment into military service limited to eighteen-to-thirty-six-year-olds, and likely to give birth to one or more children, which may coincide with their military careers. Normalizing pregnancy and nursing for female service-members, and normalizing parenthood for both male and female parents, is in the Army's best interest to retain experienced and skilled soldiers.

I have suffered the consequences for standing up for myself in that I have sometimes received poorly worded evaluations, meant to be unfavourable, and I have been the target of many an "off-the-record" tirade that might have had some effect on my reaching the brass ceiling. I will not be promoted higher than my current rank–perhaps largely the result of choosing my own education over command opportunities, which demonstrates yet another bias on the part of the Army and its promotion boards. Yet when I look back at the times I didn't stand up for myself, the consequences were much more severe, if not materially then in terms of my self-respect.

I have found that motherhood and military service are not incompatible–in some ways the military makes having families very easy and having a family keeps becoming easier. Yet mothers in military service are still too often the victims of misogyny that underestimates and devalues them as both women and mothers rather than the army realizing that the conditions supportive of mothers are also supportive of fathers and families in general, as exemplified by matricentric feminism. A more supportive and family-friendly military may create a better environment for retaining skilled workers and may also lend itself to developing empathy in soldiers–a quality listed in "Army Leadership" as the most important characteristic for leaders to cultivate in themselves and their subordinates (Army Doctrine Reference Publication 3-2). This cultural shift has thus far seemed incremental but, with the gains in other areas of equality in military service–that queer persons can serve openly (Lieberman), that women can serve in combat positions and not just the administrative and logistic ones (Office of the Secretary of Defense), and that a mother with two kids can become the third woman to earn a Ranger tab (Lamothe)–this much-needed shift is gaining momentum. I have contributed to this cultural shift in myriad ways, and will continue to do so because I had a baby in the Army.

## Endnotes

1  The views expressed in this article are those of the author and do not reflect the official policy or position of the United States Military Academy, the Department of the Army, or the Department of Defense.

2  In February 2016, while I was originally composing this piece, the Secretary of Defense revised the maternity leave policy. All pregnant women will now have twelve weeks of paid maternity leave that they can take at any time during the first year after giving birth (Army Directive (AD) 2016-09). Paternity leave, which recently increased from ten to fourteen days, still has a way to go (Ryan). Paternity leave, which does not count against a service member's thirty days of leave per year, does not apply to single fathers, only married ones.

3  Helen Benedict's book *The Lonely Soldier: The Private War of Women Serving in Iraq*, which provides much of the source material for the documentary *The Invisible War*, is but one source that details the sexual assault, harassment, and discrimination that female servicemembers still face in the twenty-first century, and have been subjected to since women joined the services as nurses in the early twentieth century. For more historical analysis of the latter half of the twentieth century, see Ilene Feinman's *Citizenship Rites* and Cynthia Enloe's body of work, including *Bananas, Beaches, and Bases*; *Does Khaki Become You?*; and *Maneuvers*.

4  Army Regulation (AR) 614-30 *Overseas Service* and AR 55-46 *Travel Overseas* govern granting command sponsorship to soldiers on overseas assignments in order for their family members to join them at their duty station.

5 See AD 2015-43, published 10 November 2015, which rescinded the interim policy, AD 2015-37, published 29 September 2015.

6 Servicemembers accrue thirty days of leave per fiscal year. Servicemembers may carry over a balance of sixty days leave from one fiscal year into the next. Accrued leave over sixty days is no longer available to the service member after 30 September each year (AR 600-8-10, 2-2.b (2)).

7 Each department must provide a certain number of personnel to augment the cadre for cadets' summer field training and some departments must also utilize personnel to teach condensed courses in the summer term.

8 AR 40-501, *Standards of Medical Fitness*, 7-9.

9 I still earned the highest rating from that colonel because my performance was the best among the officers in my grade that he supervised. Obviously, since then I had a baby while on active duty and nothing "came over me" so that I felt compelled to take care of my child fulltime rather than as a working mom.

10 I mean wives of male servicemembers specifically here since female spouses comprise 95 percent of the spouses of servicemembers (Maury and Stone 5). Husbands of female servicemembers, half of which are dual military (Spell), tend to work, even if they do so from home, and the families use fulltime daycare at greater rates than families with stay-at-home moms based on CDC priorities (DoDI 6060.02 "Family Types and Priorities"). My experience with same-sex couples who have children is–a mere three years after the end of Don't Ask Don't Tell and a lack of data–sadly limited thus far, although I would assume that same-sex couples are more likely to have both partners working fulltime, even with one partner in military service.

11 For male servicemembers, the misogyny is evident in the idea that their (female) spouses must provide care for sick children and that the spouse's employment is of less significance, even for dual-military couples.

12 Family care plans–governed by AR 600-20 Command Policy and DoDI 1342.19 "Family Care Plans"–are documents assembled by dual military couples and single parents with named short-term and long-term care providers of the servicemembers' children in the

event that the soldier must deploy, particularly on short notice. Failure to maintain a viable family care plan can result in administrative separation of the service member.

13 My daughter refers to my best friend as "Aunt" and her children as her "cousins." My best friend and I are very close and are sisters in all but biology. We find it generally easier to refer to our kids as nieces and nephews rather than go through a longer explanation of our and their relationship to each other.

## Works Cited

Army Directive 2015-43. "Revised Breastfeeding and Lactation Support Policy." Department of the Army, 2015.

Army Directive 2016-09. "Maternal Leave Policy." Department of the Army, 2016.

Army Doctrine Reference Publication 6-22. "Army Leadership." Department of the Army, 2012.

Army Regulation 40-501. *Standards of Medical Fitness*. Department of the Army, 2011.

Army Regulation 55-46. *Travel Overseas*. Department of the Army, 1994.

Army Regulation 600-8-10. *Leaves and Passes*. Department of the Army, 2006.

Army Regulation 600-20. *Command Policy*. Department of the Army, 2011.

Army Regulation 614-30. *Overseas Service*. Department of the Army, 2010.

Arnhart, Lynette, et al. "Gender Integration Study." Fort Leavenworth, KS: US Army TRADOC Analysis Center, 21 Apr. 2015.

Benedict, Helen. *The Lonely Soldier: The Private War of Women Serving in Iraq*. Beacon Press, 2010.

Butrymowicz, Sarah, and Jackie Mader. "How the Military Created the Best Child Care System in the Nation." *The Hechinger Report*, 2016. hechingerreport.org/how-the-military-created-the-best-child-care-system-in-the-nation/. Accessed 13 Jan. 2018.

Child Care Aware of America. "We Can Do Better: Child Care Aware of America's Ranking of State Child Care Center Regulations and Oversight, 2013 Update." *Child Care Aware*, 2013, usa.childcareaware.org/advocacy-public-policy/resources/research/we-can-do-better-

2013-update/. Accessed 13 Jan. 2018.

"Child Supervision Age Matrix." US Army Installation Management Command, 2013, https://www.army.mil/e2/c/downloads/404075.pdf. Accessed 19 Sept. 2016.

Crenshaw, Kimberle. "Mapping the Margins: Intersectionality, Identity Politics, and Violence Against Women of Color." *Stanford Law Review*, vol. 43, no. 6, 1991, 1241-99.

Department of Defense Instruction 1342.19. "Family Care Plans." Office of the Secretary of Defense, 7 May 2010.

Department of Defense Instruction 6060.02. "Child Development Programs." Office of the Secretary of Defense, 5 Aug. 2014.

Dolfini-Reed, Michelle, and Jennifer Jebo. *The Evolution of the Military Health Care System: Changes in Public Law and DoD Regulations.* Center for Naval Analysis, 2000.

Enloe, Cynthia. *Bananas, Beaches and Bases: Making Feminist Sense of International Politics.* Berkeley: University of California Press, 2014.

Enloe, Cynthia. *Does Khaki Become You?: The Militarisation of Women's Lives.* Boston, Mass: South End Press, 1983.

Enloe, Cynthia. *Maneuvers: The International Politics of Militarizing Women's Lives.* Berkeley: University of California Press, 2000.

"Family Types and Priorities." *Military Childcare Dot Com*, 2016, http://www.mccscp.com/wp-content/uploads/2016/11/Family-Types-and-Priorities-Handout.pdf. Accessed 15 Sep 2016.

Feinman, Ilene. *Citizenship Rites: Feminist Soldiers and Feminist Antimilitarists.* New York University Press, 2000.

Lamothe, Dan. "Army Ranger School Has a Groundbreaking New Graduate: Lisa Jaster, 37, Engineer and Mother." *The Washington Post*, 12 Oct. 2015, www.washingtonpost.com/news/checkpoint/wp/2015/10/12/army-ranger-school-has-a-groundbreaking-new-grad uate-lisa-jaster-37-engineer-and-mother/?utm_term=.983c230f6efb. Accessed 13 Jan. 2018.

Lieberman, Joseph. "S.4023 - 111th Congress (2009-2010): Don't Ask, Don't Tell Repeal Act of 2010." 13 Dec. 2010, https://www.congress. gov/bill/111th-congress/senate-bill/4023. Accessed 16 Sept. 2016.

Maury, Rosalinda, M.S., and Brice Stone. *Military Spouse Employment Report.* Syracuse University Institute for Veterans and Military Families, 2014.

Office of the Secretary of Defense. "Implementation Guidance for the Full Integration of Women in the Armed Forces." Memorandum. 3 Dec. 2015.

O'Reilly, Andrea. *Matricentric Feminism: Theory, Activism, and Practice.* Demeter Press, 2017.

Ryan, Missy. "Pentagon Extends Maternity and Paternity Leave for Military Families." *The Washington Post* 28 Jan. 2016, www. washingtonpost.com/news/checkpoint/wp/2016/01/28/pentagon-extends-maternity-and-paternity-leave-for-military-families/?utm_term=.d54552e37a6b. Accessed 13 Jan. 2018.

Schüssler Fiorenza, Elisabeth. *Wisdom Ways: Introducing Feminist Biblical Interpretation.* Orbis Books, 2001.

Spell, Krystel. "Military Family Stereotypes Debunked." *Baby Center Blog,* 11 Jun. 2011, https://blogs.babycenter.com/mom_stories/military-family-stereotypes-debunked/. Accessed 16 Sept. 2016.

State of Georgia. "2014 Georgia Code: Title 19–Domestic Relations, Chapter 9–Child Custody Proceedings, Article 1 - General Provisions." *Justia Law,* 2014, https://law.justia.com/codes/georgia/2014/title-19/chapter-9/. Accessed 19 Sept. 2016.

Sue, Derald Wing. *Microaggressions in Everyday Life: Race, Gender, and Sexual Orientation.* Wiley, 2010.

Supreme Court of Nevada. "Presumptive Maximum Amounts of Child Support." Memorandum. 26 Jan. 2016.

Training Circular 26-6. "Commander's Equal Opportunity Handbook." Department of the Army, 2008.

United States Congress. "Servicemembers Civil Relief Act." 50 U.S.C. App. §§501-597b. 2003 (1940), https://www.justice.gov/sites/default/files/crt/legacy/2011/03/23/scratext.pdf. Accessed 19 Sept. 2016.

Weinstock, Marjorie. "Male Military Spouses: 'Invisible' Family Members?" Uniformed Services University, Center for Deployment Psychology, *Staff Perspective,* 3 Mar. 2016, http://deploymentpsych.org/blog/staff-perspective-male-military-spouses-%E2%80%9 Cinvisible% E2%80%9D-family-members. Accessed 19 Sept. 2016.

Ziobro, Melissa. "Historical Perspective: Pregnancy in the Military." *Yumpu,* 15 Jan. 2010, https://www.yumpu.com/en/document/view/37398382/historical-perspective-cecom-us-army. Accessed 16 Jan. 2016.

# Chapter Nine

# Understanding War as Revealed to Me by My Son: (A Trilogy)

Beth Osnes

## Part One

As a preschooler, Leo comes up to me to bid me farewell, "Off to battle, Mom." "I've got my helmet, and I've got my shield, and I've got my sword, and I've got my dagger, and I've got my gun so I'm off to war, Mom."

I say, "Couldn't you ask your enemy to come over, and I'll make cookies for everybody and you could all just be friends?"

He looks at me like I just don't get it, and he says, "But I want to *use* my shield and my sword and my dagger and my gun."

## Part Two

Once in kindergarten, Leo was in the backyard with Margarith from his class on a playdate. It was late September, so it was still warm even though the leaves were starting to fall. Margarith declared they should build a home in the backyard. She instructed Leo to go get the swimming pool. He dutifully dragged the small blue plastic wading pool under the apple tree where she was standing. Margarith began to fill it with leaves. She then ordered him to collect the lumber by the side of the house so they could make a ramp entering their house. Margarith then got a rope and tied one end around the apple tree and other around the handle of the rocking horse parked directly outside their wading pool domicile. They both climbed into the pool, covered their legs with leaves and

Margarith announced their house was done. Together they sat for a few moments of domestic bliss. Leo fidgeted, began to look bored, and then announced, "Well, I have to go to war now." He picked up a stick and began walking off, brushing the leaves from his legs.

## Part Three

When Leo was eight, we took a family trip to Southeast Asia for me to do some research. In Cambodia, we saw many land mine victims with missing legs, or arms or hands, most of them men who had been working in fields and triggered the sleeping mines. The kids were curious about this so we told the them that land mines are like little bombs that blow up when you move them and that they had been planted all over this country during times of war. A week later as we were touring the Angkor Wat temple complex, we walked down a stone walkway, and there, placed on the stone floor, leaning against the wall was a pretty teenaged Cambodian girl with no legs and small stubs for arms. Her eyes looked up at us and then at her plastic bowl. I put some money in her bowl and smiled at her. Someone must put her there in the morning and pick her up at night. She couldn't possibly move herself anywhere. I caught up to Leo who had kept on walking. I could see he was shaken. His eyes were wild with questions. His brows furrowed. I walked beside him and put my arm around his shoulder, he said, "Don't people know what war does? Don't people know?"

## Epilogue

My son, about whom this is written, is now in graduate school and is a man with a beard, a girlfriend, and size thirteen feet. I see him now as having been forged by these experiences in his life, just as my understanding of war was enhanced by his insights at such a young age. He doesn't want to use guns anymore. He doesn't want to go to war anymore when he gets bored. The allure has changed as it does for so many of our kids who liked to play at war when young. When he was in high school, I remember him and I waiting in a doctor's office. We sat in silence for a bit and then I randomly said, "In the Bible it says the meek shall inherit the Earth. What do you think about that?" He thought about it a second, let out a laugh and said, "That is just so not going to happen." He doesn't believe being meek will get you very far, nor does he any longer endorse the violence of war. He, along with many of us, is finding his way in the middle.

## Author's Note

I was asked by the editors of this collection to respond to one of the peer review critiques of this piece that stated "I am troubled by the ways in which [the piece] reproduce[s] an imperialist gaze where a disabled third world woman serves as an object lesson, not a subject in her own right. The sentimental language also reproduces power relations of Western hegemony, gender essentialism, ablebodiedness, and the primacy of a universalized Western mother/son bond."

There is something that happens inside when someone disagrees with me. My better self rouses to attention, soothes my pride, and says, "It may hurt a bit, but you're about to learn something." I'm grateful to my reviewer for making me think more deeply about this piece of writing. This comment, though a bit jarring upon first read, helped me understand my position writing this as an able-bodied white woman who descended from the people who were likely colonists. I wrote this piece twelve years ago. It is a story I had access to along my path given my positionality. Yet in making it public in this book, I have been prompted to confront my still-lingering essentialist view of gender, the single story, and the obliviousness to assumptions that can come with privilege. In this complicated discourse, I do not feel as though I have arrived at the answers, but I am more committed than ever to wrestling with the questions. For me, this story is about shifts in perception. As in all offerings, this may be useful to some and not so much for others. This son of mine, who is likewise the descendent of an imperialist people with all that that entails, is now a PhD student at UC Berkeley studying political science. He is also a feminist and a pacifist. He was challenged deeply by his travels. The consequences of certain worldviews he had inherited came into his view when he encountered that young Cambodian woman, and he had to decide in that moment how to reckon her lived reality with his heritage. I believe I witnessed a shift. I share this story because I believe shifts in our thinking are essential to evolution and healing.

# Notes on Contributors

**Abeerah Ali** (PhD, thesis submitted, University of Karachi) is serving as an assistant professor at Fatima Jinnah Degree College for Women, University of Gujrat, Pakistan. She has a background in Punjabi literature and works in the field of democratization in Pakistan.

**Morten Ender** is professor of sociology and diversity & inclusion studies at the United States Military Academy at West Point, New York, USA, and the recipient of multiple teaching awards. His most recent book is co-edited and titled *Inclusion in the American Military: A Force for Diversity* (Lexington Books, 2017).

**Sarah Cote Hampson** is an assistant professor of public law at the University of Washington Tacoma. Her book, *The Balance Gap: Working Mothers and the Limits of the Law* (Stanford 2017), focuses on working mothers' experiences with work-life balance policy in academe and the U.S. military.

**Gal Hermoni**, a PhD student in cinema and cultural Studies at Tel Aviv University, holds a second degree in arts and cultural studies (Tel Aviv University). He is a lecturer in sociology of popular music, sociology of tech-nology and gender-food-illness dynamics, at the Open University, Israel. His recent article is "Penetrating the 'Remembrance Day' Playlist: Bereavement and the Induction Mechanisms of Cultural Glocalization." *Nations and Nationalism*, vol. 19, no. 1, 2013, pp. 128-145, co-written with Udi Ledel.

**Elle Kowal** Elle Kowal is a writer, a mother of two, a systems engineer, and a military officer. She has served on active and reserve duty in missile operations, finance, and space systems acquisitions, and currently supports U.S. space programs as a senior systems engineer. She can be found at www.ellekowal.com.

**Udi Lebel** is an associate professor in the Department of Sociology and Anthropology at Ariel University, and is a senior researcher in the Begin-Sadat Center for Strategic Studies at Bar-Ilan University, Israel. He is the author of *Politics of Memory: The Israeli Underground's Struggle for Inclusion in the National Pantheon and Military Commemoralization* (Routledge 2013).

**Naomi Mercer** is a lieutenant colonel in the United States Army and an independent scholar. She earned her doctorate in literary studies from the University of Wisconsin-Madison in 2013. She specializes in feminist dystopian and utopian writing and is the author of *Toward Utopia*, which explores feminist science-fiction writers' responses to religious fundamentalism.

**Beth Osnes** is an associate professor of theatre and environmental studies at the University of Colorado. She is co-director of Inside the Greenhouse (www. insidethegreenhouse.net). Her books include *Theatre for Women's Participation in Sustainable Development* and *Performance for Resilience: Engaging Youth on Energy* and *Climate through Music, Movement, and Theatre.*

**Anwar Shaheen** is a professor, Pakistan Study Centre, University of Karachi, Pakistan. Her major fields of interests are gender, culture, social change, civil society, conflict, and motherhood. She has published two books, six chapters in refereed volumes, and over twenty articles in research journals.

**Patricia Sotirin** is a professor of communication in the Department of Humanities at Michigan Technological University. She is co-author of two books on communication and aunting and co-editor of a collection on feminist rhetorical resilience. She has published on a variety of women's workplace and family communication practices.

**Nancy Taber** is an associate professor in the Faculty of Education, Brock University. Her research explores the ways in which learning, gender, and militarism interact in daily life, popular culture, museums, academic institutions, and military organizations. Her publications include *Gendered Militarism in Canada: Learning Conformity and Resistance* (University of Alberta 2015).